Experiences of Women of Color in an Elite US Public School

Catherine Simpson Bueker

Experiences of Women of Color in an Elite US Public School

palgrave
macmillan

Catherine Simpson Bueker
Emmanuel College
Boston, MA, USA

ISBN 978-3-319-84448-0   ISBN 978-3-319-50633-3 (eBook)
DOI 10.1007/978-3-319-50633-3

© The Editor(s) (if applicable) and The Author(s) 2017
Softcover reprint of the hardcover 1st edition 2017
This work is subject to copyright. All rights are solely and exclusively licensed by the Publisher, whether the whole or part of the material is concerned, specifically the rights of translation, reprinting, reuse of illustrations, recitation, broadcasting, reproduction on microfilms or in any other physical way, and transmission or information storage and retrieval, electronic adaptation, computer software, or by similar or dissimilar methodology now known or hereafter developed.
The use of general descriptive names, registered names, trademarks, service marks, etc. in this publication does not imply, even in the absence of a specific statement, that such names are exempt from the relevant protective laws and regulations and therefore free for general use.
The publisher, the authors and the editors are safe to assume that the advice and information in this book are believed to be true and accurate at the date of publication. Neither the publisher nor the authors or the editors give a warranty, express or implied, with respect to the material contained herein or for any errors or omissions that may have been made. The publisher remains neutral with regard to jurisdictional claims in published maps and institutional affiliations.

Cover image © Thinkstock / Getty Images

Printed on acid-free paper

This Palgrave Macmillan imprint is published by Springer Nature
The registered company is Springer International Publishing AG
The registered company address is: Gewerbestrasse 11, 6330 Cham, Switzerland

This book is dedicated to my parents, Nancy and David Simpson, who taught us to engage in and question the world around us, and to work towards making it a more just place.
To my children, Sam, Michael, and Rachel, who challenge me constantly to be my better self.
And, to John, who gives me the space and support to pursue that which is essential to me.

Acknowledgments

This book would not be possible without the dozens of women who volunteered their time to sit and talk with me about their experiences as young people. Women recalled events both heartbreaking and heartwarming. I was, and continue to be, amazed by their strength and resiliency, and I thank them for entrusting me with their stories. I deeply hope I have done justice to them.

This project would also have been stopped before it even started without the help of numerous residents, teachers, and administrators in the town of Mayfair who met with me to discuss the possibility of it, critique it, and then extend themselves to introduce me to graduates. Many of the most heartening stories prominently feature many of you and your commitment to a more just and equal world. Thank you for your time, your healthy skepticism, and your trust.

My research assistants Marielle Peace and Laurie Boyd were the most wonderful students I could have asked for. They transcribed hours upon hours of interviews, tracked down articles, and generally did whatever I needed them to do for the project.

I would also like to thank the Spencer Foundation for thinking this project worthwhile and making it possible through their financial support. My gratitude also extends to Emmanuel College and the Office of Academic Affairs for their support, both financial and otherwise. I am so appreciative of Mary Waters and Mary Brinton, both of the Department of Sociology at Harvard University, for hosting me for the year and giving me some space to "get away." I could not have asked for a better officemate while at Harvard than Asad Asad, who, in addition to giving me periodic pep talks, also provided me with important feedback on portions of the project. My dear friend, Teal Rothschild, was invaluable. Our meetings during my year of writing served as critical motivation and her critiques of the manuscript translated into a vastly improved project. I would also like to thank the various anonymous reviewers who provided important feedback on portions of what has become this book. My thanks, also, to the folks at Palgrave Macmillan, particularly Mara Berkoff, for thinking this project worthy of publication.

And, then, there is, of course, my family. They recognized how important this project was to me and adjusted their lives accordingly. They accepted me disappearing for days on end to write. Without Susan Jess ("Jessie"), who has loved and supported my family for three generations, none of this would have been possible. To Sam, Michael, and Rachel, this project really is for you; I promise.

Thank you, all. And, of course, any mistakes or omissions are my own.

Contents

1 The World of Mayfair 1

2 Two-Ness and Liminality in Mayfair 31

3 The Making of Community 65

4 Athletes and Boundary Breakers 89

5 Bridge Builders and Cultural Guides 115

6 The Acquisition of Cultural Capital 149

7 Race, Place, and the Power of Interactions 177

Appendix A: Interview Protocol for Residents of Mayfair 199

Appendix B: Interview Protocol for Reach Students in Mayfair 201

Appendix C: Interview Protocol for Aspire
Participants in Mayfair   203

Appendix D: Survey   205

Index   209

LIST OF FIGURES

Fig. 1.1 Processes of marginalization and incorporation   25

LIST OF TABLES

Table 1.1 Mayfair by the numbers   11
Table 1.2 Descriptives of sample, $N=37$ 22

CHAPTER 1

The World of Mayfair

As the warm August days give way to the coolness of September, three young girls prepare for high school. A young Latina girl thinks about what she will wear on the first day, talking it over as she walks into town, past her local high school, with her friend and neighbor. Fifteen miles away, a young black girl of similar age has begun to set her alarm clock for 5:00 a.m. to get herself used to the early morning wake-ups. She will need to catch her school bus at 6:00 a.m. to commute the hour out of the city into the suburbs. And 200 miles away, another young girl of color begins to pack her suitcase as she prepares to leave home and go off to boarding school. As the school year begins, all three young women will find themselves walking the same corridors, eating in the same cafeteria, and attending the same classes at Mayfair High.[1]

To enter into the town of Mayfair is to arrive into a highly manicured suburb that sits approximately 15 miles outside of a major city, known as Urbana, in the Northeastern United States. It is a suburb described as "beautiful" and "idyllic" by those who know it. The cars tend to be of the late model luxury variety, the public buildings and spaces are striking, the main street is lined with high-end retailers, and the residents are overwhelmingly white. The town "style," expensive but understated preppy, is seen on men, women, and children. Without having seen any road sign or "Welcome," people often know they have crossed a border. An individual who was recently driving with me into town, someone unaffiliated with both the community and the research project, commented unwittingly on how one of the main roads leading into town changes when it crosses over the town line, becoming less commercial and more scenic.

These kinds of distinctions or markers appear throughout the community of Mayfair. It is striking in many ways. It is a world where young children still take etiquette lessons in large numbers, where summer concerts take place every week on the town green, and people in the community still use "summer" as a verb. It is a town largely of the 1%, with home prices hovering at $1 million, a country club, golf courses, and multiple private schools. The town has in recent years made such top ten lists as "the most expensive American towns in which to live" and "the most highly educated American towns," based upon the percentage of adults over 25 with graduate degrees. To stop at this description of the community is to do it a disservice, however. Although on the surface, the town could be viewed as a movie set or a caricature of how the 1% live, it is, like all communities, far more complex.

Mayfair is a town where civic organizations continue to thrive in ways rarely seen in twenty-first-century America (Putnam 2000). Just some of these organizations include Rotary, League of Women Voters, a newcomers Club, Junior League, a parenting organization with monthly lectures and socials, a gardening club, a service league, as well as extremely active Parent-Teacher Organizations that raise hundreds of thousands of dollars each year for the public schools, and a library foundation that runs annual fundraisers and has had as its guest speakers nationally recognized names. This level of civic engagement is likely made possible by the significant percentage of women with advanced degrees who have left the paid workforce (Putnam 2000). The public high school frequently ranks in the top ten in the state, and over 95% of the high school graduates attend four-year colleges, with many of these students going on to the most elite colleges and universities in the world.

The social and civic engagement is nothing new to Mayfair, but has been a part of its fabric since the town's founding in the nineteenth century. From food pantry drives among children to fundraising for the local hospital to more recent environmental programs, Mayfair has historically possessed a communitarian streak, along the lines of what Alexander de Tocqueville (1835/2006) described in his assessment of American society nearly 200 years ago. This trend of socially aware engagement is perhaps best manifested in the town's decades-old participation in two voluntary racial desegregation programs—one a commuter program known as "Reach Across Boarders" and one a boarding program known as "Aspire"[2]—that open up the school system to small numbers of black and Latino non-residents from a variety of urban areas. One cannot definitively state whether engagement in such programs results from the community's effort to work against a history of racial injustices, a sense of noblesse oblige, or an attempt to preserve Mayfair's autonomy in the face of federal court rulings around the racial integration of schools. In all likelihood, some combination of these factors has been at work. Regardless of the motivations, hundreds of students of color have graduated from Mayfair High via these initiatives over more than 40 years.

Yet, the commitment to such programs and students vary, particularly during periods of fiscal austerity and tightening school budgets. One participant from this study, while a child in the school system, was told by a white parent in the town, "I don't even know why you are here." Teachers wonder if such programs do more harm than good to the students they are supposed to be serving. At the same time, a strong commitment remains among both town residents and members of the school system. This commitment is to both the individual students who access the district from outside, and to the larger community of Mayfair who they feel need to better understand and embrace an increasingly diverse world; it is a commitment to decreasing racial isolation on all sides of the border. Upon walking into the public library, patrons are greeted by a poster with faces of every skin tone underneath the statement "We are Mayfair." Town residents, teachers, and administrators promote diversity programs throughout the year to facilitate conversations about diversity of many kinds, but most often race. Such programs have been in place for decades, but have grown in amount, type, and participation in recent years.

This book explores the experiences of black and Latina women who graduated from Mayfair over the past three decades, explicitly examining how point of access into the system impacted them. What is life like for someone who is not of this world, but living in it for a portion of each day? What is it like for young female boarding students who make Mayfair their temporary home? How do these experiences compare to those of the small number of town residents with similar racial and economic demographics? To what extent do these young women of color partake in the many riches and opportunities that seem to float in the air all around Mayfair? How does Mayfair, the community and the high school, really do in terms of extending access to resources, opening up networks, and delivering on its promises? What distinct barriers, or benefits, result from particular points of access? Are there other factors that mediate the experience?

The dominant themes that emerge in the interviews with women of color who graduated from the system can be best summarized with the four "Bs": barriers, bonds, bridges, and benefits. Women, again and again, recount feelings of marginalization and liminality, resulting from and leading to barriers or bridge failures. These barriers only sometimes take physical form, and the symbolic obstacles are far harder to overcome, particularly if one is a young woman of color and of more modest means. Largely in response to feelings of marginalization and exclusion, women often develop tight-knit, internal networks and bonds that serve as critical lifelines for each other. There is significant evidence of internal, bonding capital that develops among young women of color. At the same time, women recall access to resources, opportunities, and, in a few cases, social inclusion that result from bridge building, both bridge spans that originate on their end and those that are extended from white Mayfair. And, there are benefits to living or attending school in Mayfair. Women discuss the various forms of cultural capital that they gain through formal programming, informal relationships, and by virtue of general exposure, with such capital playing important roles later in life. Benefits also flow to the white community as a result of the participation of these young girls of color in the system, although such communal benefits are rarely recognized. Further, the benefits these young women accrue and contribute often come at a significant psychological cost.

Although these themes of barriers, bonds, bridges, and benefits exist among the women generally, there are factors that mediate the experience. One's point of access to the district, where one is from and where one resides, has both physical and symbolic meaning for the women and their lived experiences in Mayfair, influencing the extent of isolation and exclusion that they feel, the strength of the internal bonds that they develop, their experiences as sources and recipients of bridge building, and the benefits that accrue. Unsurprisingly, money, or the lack, also mediates the experiences. At times, money serves as yet another barrier, a means of further separating these women from white, elite Mayfair. At the same time, the shared lack of money can act as a source of bonding both internally, and with white students of limited financial means. Money can also help to bridge differences, with its ability to create a set of common experiences.

Prior Research

Schooling and Inequality

Charles Tilly (1999) argues that "*durable* inequalities, those that last from one social interaction to the next" (p.6) are based upon repeated social exclusions across environments and institutions. These bounded categories, particularly around race, class, and gender, are consistently reproduced and can severely limit access to resources across settings. According to Tilly, durable inequality results from a handful of causes, one of which is the formal or official differences in access to skills and learning that result from segregated schools. The educational realm, perhaps more than any other, reflects and reinforces the stratification that exists in larger society (Bourdieu and Passeron 2000).

Racial minorities and lower-income individuals have consistently experienced more limited educational opportunities vis-à-vis the white middle class in American society (Kozol 1995, 2005; Eaton 2007; Theoharis 2009). The unequal opportunities have resulted in unequal outcomes, with the "black-white" test score gap documented for many decades (Jencks and Phillips 1998). Although the United States has certainly moved beyond a "black-white" racial dichotomy, educational differences continue to appear by racial grouping (Snyder 2015). The National Center for Education Statistics reports significant differences in high school completion rates by race. In 2011–2012, Asian students had a 93% graduation rate, followed by whites at 85%, Latinos at 76%, and blacks at 68% (Stetser and Stillwell 2014). Legislation such as the initial *Elementary and Secondary Education Act* of 1965 (20 USC 6301, et seq.) and the *No Child Left Behind Act* of 2002 (No Child Left Behind [NCLB], 2002) was put into place as a reaction to centuries-old educational inequities and the documentation of various types of "achievement gaps."

These racial gaps in primary and secondary school continue on through post-secondary education. From 1990 through 2014, college degree attainment increased for all groups, but significant differences remained. Among whites ages 25–29, approximately 40% possess a college degree, as compared with roughly 20% of blacks for this same age group (Kena et al. 2015).

Educational segregation has long been understood as a key factor in educational inequity. Court systems throughout the country have historically been and continue to be the venues in which individuals have sought educational justice via school desegregation (MacDonald 1999; Eaton 2001, 2007; Kendrick and Kendrick 2004). The first fight for the desegregation of schools took place in Boston, Massachusetts, in the late 1840s in *Roberts v. City of Boston* (*Roberts v. City of Boston*. Supreme Court of Massachusetts, Suffolk. 59 Mass. 198. 1849) when a black father sued the city of Boston to allow his young daughter to attend the nearby elementary school (Kendrick and Kendrick 2004). This initial attempt failed and formal or "de jure" school segregation continued on for over 100 years longer. It did not officially end until 1954 under the *Brown v. Board of Education* (*Brown v. Board of Education*, 347. S. 438. 1954) decision, but as is well known today, the U.S. Supreme Court ruling in the case did little to rectify inequalities on the ground. The Court may have deemed "separate but equal" as unequal, but little actually changed in the following years. Fights over truly desegregating schools lasted for decades longer, with Federal Judge Arthur Garrity mandating busing within the district of Boston, Massachusetts, in 1974, lawsuits in Connecticut lasting into the 1990s (*Sheff v. O'Neill*, 238 Conn. 1, 678 A.2d 1267. 1996), and an ongoing public conversation on the topic.

Even with the courts often on the side of desegregationists, schools largely remain segregated and have become more so since the 1970s (Reardon and Owens 2014; Flippen 2016; *Race Matters*, Annie E. Casey Foundation 2006). Work conducted by Gary Orfield at the *Civil Rights Project* has found that 80% of Latino students and 74% of black students attend majority non-white schools (50–100% minority), and approximately 15% of students from these groups attend "apartheid" schools, with less than 1% of the students identifying as white. It should also be noted that white students similarly attend highly segregated systems where many have virtually no contact with non-white students (Orfield et al. 2012).

Much of this educational inequity arises from segregated residential patterns (Massey and Denton 1993; Clotfelter 2004). James Coleman (1992) states that the United States has "the most rigid system of assigning schools" (p.261) due to school catchments based upon physical location. In short, residential segregation translates into educational segregation. But, the effect is more than racial in nature. Lower property values and smaller tax bases often translate into less money for urban, predominantly minority schools (Kozol 1995, 2005). Racial segregation also translates into disadvantage for middle-class students of color whose families, by choice or circumstance, remain in communities of color. Regardless of a household's own economic conditions, the average black or Latino child attends school with roughly double the number of low-income children as does the average white or Asian child (Orfield et al. 2012). The consequence is the perpetuation of durable inequality, resulting from the tightly bound nature of race and class in American society, and the consistent location of lower-income people of color in bounded geographic areas and institutions with more limited resources (Tilly 1999). Such consistent reinforcement of categories translates into a steadily disadvantaged segment of American society (Wilson 1987).

Voluntary School Desegregation

In response to the history of segregation and growing concerns over educational inequity, a variety of mandated and voluntary school desegregation initiatives developed during the 1960s. These programs have generally focused on taking students of color out of their lower-income neighborhoods and placing them in whiter, more middle-class suburban public school districts, or in private day or boarding schools.

Reducing racial segregation tends to have a positive effect on a variety of academic measurements, from closing racial achievement gaps to increasing graduation rates for students of color (for an extensive review of academic outcomes, see Reardon and Owens 2014). In addition to students of color finding greater educational opportunities in these wealthier, whiter school districts, the host communities also have much to gain from desegregation efforts. Voluntary racial desegregation programs argue the mutual benefits of desegregation: the expansion of educational opportunities, but also the reduction of racial isolation for everyone. Given that segregation has been identified as having a direct effect on how individuals think of those in the "outgroup," affecting both attitudes and behaviors (Enos 2014; Enos and Celaya forthcoming; Stephens-Davidowitz 2014), such educational desegregation programs are critical for all involved.

The focus of all of such efforts, from the mandated court orders to the voluntary programs, has been on school *desegregation*, removing legal barriers and changing the demographic representation within institutions. What has received less attention and public effort is school *integration*, a process by which boundaries are truly crossed (Carter 2012, 2015). The focus on school desegregation, as opposed to integration, is likely the result of multiple factors: first and foremost the need to remove the formal, legal barriers that have historically been in place, the greater ease of measuring desegregation efforts, and the challenge of understanding what we mean by integrated schools and communities and what we can do to actually reach that goal. In the twenty-first-century understanding of integration, all groups benefit from crossing boundaries, both physical and symbolic (Lamont and Fournier 1992), as opposed to earlier interpretations of racial "integration" which appeared closer to a form of one-way assimilation to the white dominant class (Farmer 1965; Du Bois, 1904/1994).

Although desegregation programs provide greater access to resources and theoretically better educational opportunities, the experience is often mixed for students of color in predominantly white environments. Research exploring the experiences of students of color in voluntary desegregation programs in public school settings has repeatedly found these young people to feel isolated at school but also marginalized in their home communities (Eaton 2001; Carter 2007, 2012; Holland 2012). Desegregation may be taking place, albeit in small numbers, but integration is not. Sports teams and public spaces remain segregated by race (Carter 2012), and friendship circles and dating partners remain largely homogenous, particularly for young women of color (Holland 2012; Ispa-Landa 2013). Even with these challenges and limitations, most graduates feel, in retrospect, that the education was worth the social isolation and emotional sacrifices, particularly given the alternative educational options (Eaton 2001).

Research examining the experiences of students of color in elite boarding schools has identified similar trends—social isolation and feelings of liminality—but also significant benefits (Anson 1988; Cookson and Persell 1991; Khan 2011). A study of 38 individuals who attended boarding schools around the country through *A Better Chance*, a national racial desegregation program that places high achieving students of color in highly ranked schools, found two major benefits for its graduates: 1) comfort in elite, white, society and 2) networking skills (Zweigenhaft and Domhoff 1991, 2003). The findings from this study suggest the importance of non-academic benefits that accrue to individuals of color in elite white schools.

Unequal Resources Within Homes and Communities

Although the educational realm exists as a major manufacturer of stratification in society, it also exists as a mirror, reflecting and reinforcing differences that already exist outside of the school setting. Both theorists and empiricists have examined the relationship between various aspects of family, household, and community, and school success in its many forms (Coleman 1988; Phillips et al. 1998; Dufur et al. 2013).

The distinct orientations, practices, and skills emanating from middle- and upper-middle-class white households serve as critical forms of capital in the school setting, rewarded by educational gatekeepers (Coleman 1988; Bourdieu 1986; Lareau 2011, 2015; Calarco 2014). At the elementary school level, children of higher socioeconomic status score better on standardized assessments, likely as a result of the expanded language skills with which they enter into school (Hart and Risley 1995; Fryer and Levitt 2006, 2013). At the high school level, more elite habitus and greater amounts of cultural capital are associated with higher GPAs and more professional goals (Dumais 2002). Elite backgrounds and knowledge also have implications for feelings of belonging or, conversely, marginalization (Horvat and Antonio 1999). At the collegiate level, possessing elite cultural capital has been identified with academic and social success, or the lack (Jack 2016). Unsurprisingly, such initial differences and eventual academic outcomes have implications later in the life course, outside of the school setting (see William Julius Wilson's vast body of work on the formation and maintenance of a racial and economic underclass).

A long-standing explanation for the poorer academic outcomes among native-born black students in the United States has been the "oppositional culture" theory, positing that descendants of "involuntary migrants," that is, slaves, develop a distrustful attitude toward education, arising from the experiences of the family, the community, and the larger history of the group (Fordham and Ogbu 1986; Gibson and Ogbu 1991; Ogbu 1992). This "oppositional culture" theory has received fairly limited empirical support, however (Cook and Ludwig 1998; Theoharis 2009; Zweigenhaft and Domhoff 1991, 2003). In fact, what has been identified is the role that school organization and academic tracking play in the creation of internal racial divisions (Clotfelter 2004) and school success being equated with "whiteness" (Tyson 2011). It is not households and communities of color creating these responses, but formal institutions.

Alternatively, the tremendous educational success of lower-income immigrant children has also been explained using a "cultural" argument. Such successes have been attributed to the involvement of parents and the value placed on education by both the family and the immediate community (Gibson 1988; Bankston et al. 1997; Kasinitz et al. 2009; Almeida et al. 2011). Lee and Zhou (2015) have helped to "unpack" what is meant by such cultural arguments, identifying the mechanisms by which Asian immigrant families promote educational success. The scholars examine how these immigrants identify and use public resources, specifically public schools, to maximize their children's opportunities. The families also have the ability to provide both ethnic-specific resources and support and a dual reference frame for their children, one which provides another example from the dominant, white middle-class experience.

As is seen in Lee and Zhou's (2015) work, household resources in their various forms can translate into community resources, often by purchasing a very small house or renting an apartment in a higher-income community with a strong school system. Such strategies are employed by the native-born, as well. For example, the U.S. Department of Education reports in *The Condition of Education* (Planty et al. 2009) that in 2007, 27% of all public school parents surveyed reported that they had moved so that their child could attend a particular school. Unsurprisingly, the 27% of movers are not evenly distributed among the population, with 29% of white parents reporting such a move, as compared to 18% of black parents, and 25% of Latino parents. Further, a third of students in suburban locations had moved there for the purpose of school enrollment. This form of school "choice" is not a choice, however, for many families who lack resources. For black and Latino families who have the financial wherewithal to move, other considerations arise, such as being the only family of color in a community.

Project

The primary purpose of this study is to better understand the experiences of black and Latina women who accessed an elite, predominantly white, suburban public high school in the Northeastern United States through three distinct points of entry.

As one can see in Table 1.1, Mayfair remains racially homogenous in the twenty-first century. As of the 2010 U.S. Census, approximately 85% of the population identified as white, just under 10% identified as Asian, slightly more than 2% identified as black or African American, and just under 4% identified as Hispanic or Latino. The primary change in racial composition of the community since 1980 (when the oldest participants in this study attended school) is the decrease in the percentage of the population identifying as white and the increase in the population identifying as Asian, with the largest changes in these categories taking place since 1990 when over 90% of the population identified as white.

It is a community rich in multiple forms of capital. The median household income is approximately $160,000, significantly above the state-

Table 1.1 Mayfair by the numbers

Key demographics	Town	State-wide comparison
Population	~=30,000	
Socioeconomics		
Median household income	~=$160,000	~=$70,000
Median home value	~=$900,000	~=$330,000
Percent high school graduates	~=99%	~=90%
Percent college graduates	~=85%	~=40%
Percent below poverty	~=3%	~=11%
Race and ethnicity		
Percent white	~=85%	~=80%
Percent black	~=2%	~=7%
Percent Asian	~=10%	~=5%
Percent Latino	~=4%	~=10%
High school information		
Size	~=1,400	
Percent eligible for free/reduced price lunch	~=6%	~=44%
Graduation rate	~=97%	~=86%
College attendance rate—4-year college	~=95%	~=70%
Average SAT score	1238/1400	1040/1400

Sources: The population, socioeconomic, and race and ethnicity statistics come from the 2010 U.S. Census. The Mayfair High School information comes from Mayfair High 2014 statistics, Big Prep Blog, the Department of Elementary and Secondary Education 2014, Kidscount.org, and Propublica.org. Statistics have been given in approximations for the sake of protecting community identity.

wide median income of under $70,000. The median house price is over $900,000. Approximately 3.4% of the population lives below the poverty line, as compared to 11% statewide ("Quickfacts," Census.gov, retrieved on April 27, 2014). Over 85% of town residents above the age of 25 have at least a four-year college degree, and over 95% of the high school graduates go on to pursue a four-year degree.

Mayfair is a particularly interesting setting in which to examine the issue of school desegregation for a number of reasons. Past studies exploring the experiences of people of color in elite, predominantly white settings have often focused on private schools (Anson 1988; Cookson and Persell 1991; Khan 2011; Zweigenhaft and Domhoff 1991, 2003). Although these studies are valuable in that they shed light on the institutions in which the elite reproduce themselves, Mayfair provides the opportunity to examine what takes place within a public high school, a setting in which access and opportunities are theoretically more open to all students. At the same time, the high school and community are well resourced, providing many opportunities generally found only in private institutions. But, Mayfair is of particular interest for another reason—it is one of the few public high schools that I know of where access is *not* limited to town residents, in the way that public educational institutions frequently are in the United States. The high school provides access, albeit limited, to black and Latino non-residents through two voluntary racial desegregation programs—one in which urban residents from the nearby city of Urbana commute on a daily basis, and one in which urban residents from a range of more distant cities board during the school year. The commuter program is known as Reach and the boarding program is known as Aspire.

The residents of the town became involved in small-scale racial desegregation programs during the Civil Rights Era. Reach began in the mid-1960s, busing students each day from the city of Urbana approximately 15 miles away. Access to this program is based upon availability of seats within participating suburban districts. The application process consists of signing children up at an early age (some children are signed up as soon as they are born) and is not based on academic credentials or economic need. Students come from a range of economic circumstances, from solidly middle-class to lower-class and dependent upon government aid. There are currently about 150 students in this program at all levels of the town's school system and about 40 students in the high school in any given year. These students participate in after-school and supplemental support programs and have host families in the community.

The town has also participated, since the early 1970s, in Aspire, a smaller national program where high achieving girls of color come from distant cities, some more than 500 miles away. The young women live together as boarders in a house owned by the organization and attend the public high school. Access to this program is based on both past academic performance and a rigorous interview and application process. Economic circumstances are not a consideration, and as with the commuter students, these young women come from a range of economic positions. This program also incorporates a variety of supplemental social and academic programs for the young women both during the school year and over the summer. Each of the women has a host family in the community with whom they spend one weekend per month. This program has graduated approximately 70 participants since its founding and there are generally six to eight young women from this program in the high school at any time.

In addition, the town has a small percentage of black and Latina residents, comparable demographically to the students who participate in the voluntary desegregation programs. This population lives in both market-rate homes owned by their families and state-subsidized housing. The Mayfair Housing Authority oversees two affordable housing properties for families, with a total of 100 two- and three-bedroom units. The presence of these three distinct groups of young women of color within the high school allows for an examination of the role that point of access plays in integrating social networks and accessing social and cultural capital.

Many prior studies exploring issues of race and education have focused on academic outcomes, such as GPA, test scores, graduation rates, or college completion, among students of color (Reardon and Owens 2014; Bowen and Bok 1998; Fryer and Curto 2014; Fryer and Levitt 2006; Jencks and Phillips 1998). Although these are certainly valuable areas of focus, the mechanisms leading to outcomes deemed successes are not always clearly understood. Earning a high school diploma, attaining a high GPA, or scoring well on standardized tests is often the result of, or at least closely linked to, a range of supports and resources. Further, these academic outcomes, although certainly important for other types of educational, economic, and social successes, are not the sole predictors of how people do in life. We have long understood that access to social and cultural capital plays a significant role in achieving various forms of success over the life course (Bourdieu 1986; Coleman 1988; Lareau 2011, 2015; Putnam 2000; Zweigenhaft and Domhoff 1991, 2003), that the school setting can play an important role in expanding these forms of currency (Khan 2011; Carter 2012; Zweigenhaft and Domhoff 1991, 2003; Cookson and Persell 1991), and that family and community also matter in such pursuits (Coleman 1988; Bourdieu 1986; Lareau 2011; Wilson 1980, 1987, 2015). Studies on academic outcomes also do little to tell us about the extent to which integration, as opposed to numeric desegregation, is occurring.

This project is intended to more fully understand the extent to which black and Latina women were able as students to integrate into the school and community, access the various forms of non-economic capital in Mayfair, and whether the type and amount of capital varied for women based upon point of access. To what extent were women from each of the respective residential groups able to build bridges and tap into integrated social networks within the school and community? Does growing up in the community and attending the local public school make one more apt to develop bridges and form integrated social networks, providing access to local social capital? Alternatively, does school participation through an engineered pathway in the form of a formal desegregation program increase access to various school and community resources, making bridge building easier? What sorts of barriers or bridge failures did women experience and did they vary by point of access?

Methodology

In order to begin to answer these questions, I conducted in-depth interviews with 37 black and Latina women who graduated from Mayfair High as residents, commuters, or boarders. These interviews were conducted between November 2014 and January 2016. The majority of women graduated in the 1990s and 2000s, with a smaller number of women going as far back as the 1980s.

I rely upon this qualitative methodology as the best means by which women can tell me in their own words what their experiences were like. Such in-depth interviews tend to yield the deepest, richest data, as well as uncover the mechanisms that may be at play in their experiences. I supplement these in-depth interviews with observations at PTO meetings, program meetings, and special events in the community. Such events include programming around race and diversity, sporting events, and extracurricular activities held by school clubs. I also spoke informally with both black and white parents, teachers, administrators, and volunteers in the community.

My own demographics, a white upper-middle-class woman who is part of the academic establishment, provided me with both insider and outsider status in this project. I was initially granted access to potential participants through my connections with board members of the racial desegregation programs, a "perk" of my race and class privilege. At the same time, I interviewed women of color, many of whom were or are working and middle class. Some women questioned my interest in their lives and my ability to really understand what their experiences were like. To them and to my readers, I can only say that I recognize my limitations based upon my social location and have attempted to allow participants to tell their stories in their own words. I have tried my best to "get out of the way," while placing their stories and experiences within a larger social construct.

Instruments

All participants responded to a core set of 18 open-ended questions. The questions were divided into three sections: questions about where an individual grew up, questions about her school experiences, and questions about how her residential "setup" as a resident, commuter, or boarder interacted with her schooling. I began by asking a series of questions about where the respondent lived as a child. These questions included, "Can you begin by telling me a little bit about where you grew up?," "How would you describe your overall experience living in _____?," and, "Did you feel a part of the larger community of _____ while growing up?" I then moved on to asking about the school experience, including, "How would you describe your overall school experience?," "What was the most valuable thing you gained by going to school in Mayfair?," and, "What was the biggest challenge of going to school in Mayfair?" Finally, I asked questions about the connection between home and school, including, "Do you remember if your family ever participated in any school related events?," "Did you ever bring friends from school over to your house?," and, "Did you ever go over to friends' houses?"

Women who participated in the school system as commuters were asked an additional 7 questions about their particular program and experience, and women who participated in the school system as boarders were asked an additional 11 questions, again specific to their program and experience. The slight variation by subgroup and the additional questions asked of boarders and commuters arose from the need to understand their distinct experiences as people attending school outside of their home districts, much of the heart of this project. The interview protocols can be seen in Appendices A (residents), B (commuters), and C (boarders).

Following the open-ended questions, participants were asked to respond to a short series of closed-ended questions. Again, all participants were asked a core group of questions, including graduation year from Mayfair High, average grades while there, information on post-high school education and occupation, self-identified racial and ethnic identities, as well as questions about the overall experience, based upon a Likert scale. Women who had been commuters and boarders were asked two additional questions. The first additional question asked about what would have made the transition to Mayfair easier and the second question asked how she thought her involvement with the particular program that placed her at Mayfair High had impacted her overall life experience. The brief, closed-ended survey can be seen in Appendix D.

Interview Process

I personally interviewed all of the participants. I had gone into the project intending to begin the interview process and then "hand it over" to a graduate student. After conducting the first several interviews, it became apparent to me that I was touching upon issues that, at times, were very painful for the participants. Women were thinking back to a period and place that had been challenging, even overwhelmingly so, at times. I was concerned with sending a graduate student, likely one years younger than many of my participants, to ask about difficult experiences and memories. I felt I needed to take on the responsibility myself.

I met with the majority of participants, face-to-face, and, with their written permission, recorded the interviews for the sake of transcribing them verbatim. Face-to-face interviews were conducted at the location of the participant's choosing and included apartments, libraries, coffee shops, and offices. I conducted telephone interviews when participants lived a significant distance from where I am located (more than a three-hour drive). In two cases, I conducted phone interviews with participants in my geographic area, but who specifically requested we conduct the interview by phone. Although phone interviews are not equivalent to face-to-face interviews, given that one is unable to see facial expressions and body language and the rapport generally cannot develop to the same extent, the phone interviews tended to last approximately the same length of time as the face-to-face interviews and revealed many of the same trends. Thus, the consistency of findings suggests we can have relative confidence in the data collected over the phone.

The interviews lasted, on average, one hour. A few particularly reticent participants completed the interviews in less time; a few particularly open and talkative participants spoke with me for over three hours.

After the data were collected, they were transcribed verbatim by two research assistants. I analyzed the data using a grounded theory approach, as developed by Glaser and Strauss (1967). This approach assumes a continuous assessing and reassessing of the data, as more data are collected and analyzed using a clearly developed coding scheme. In a slight modification of Glaser and Strauss's grounded theory method, the codes I applied were both inductive and deductive in nature. The deductive codes came from prior theory, and the inductive codes arose from the data themselves. The inductive coding scheme resulted from my two research assistants and me independently coding sub-samples of the interviews and comparing our codes. When all three of us had identified a particular theme, that became a code we used throughout all of the interviews. In this way, I systematically examined the data for themes.

Sample

As already mentioned, this study is based upon interviews with 37 women who attended Mayfair High with the goal of exploring the extent to which women of color were able to build bridges and access diverse social networks, and social and cultural capital within an elite, predominantly white public high school. This study specifically has an eye toward the role of residential setup. Given the latter question, it was critical to interview individuals from each of the three sub-populations: residents, commuters, and boarders.

In many ways, the experience of identifying participants for the project has become as illuminating as the formal interview data. The data collection, itself, is a story of social networks and social capital, both mine and those generously extended to me by many of the women who participated in the study. It is also a story about limited and exclusive social networks.

This project initially grew out of an invitation, a literal invitation, which I received to a fundraiser for the national boarding program Aspire, which has a chapter in Mayfair. The invitation included the names of many well-known, wealthy community members as supporters of the program and sponsors of the fundraiser. I began to wonder what the experience was like for the young women of color who accessed elite districts through this national program, with the majority of these young women coming from single-parent, more economically modest households in urban areas hundreds of miles away. Do these young women have access to the resource-rich social networks in which the board members and financial backers of the program are embedded? Do they acquire any of the social or cultural capital held by those who play financial and administrative roles in the program? What are the challenges of being part of such a program?

Although the women in the boarding program are unique by virtue of being boarders, they share similar racial and economic characteristics with two other groups of students at the public high school: 1) a small group of residents of color, some of whom live in Section 8 housing and some of whom live in market-rate homes owned by their parents, and 2) those who commute to Mayfair on a daily basis from the city of Urbana, approximately 15 miles away.

The demographic comparability of these three groups of women begged the questions of how the intersectionality of race, class, and gender influenced their experiences within the school and the larger community, and the way in which point of access mediated the experiences. Although the decision to limit the study to females initially grew out of the fact that the boarding program is open only to girls, and for the sake of comparability, I chose to focus on female residents and commuters, this gendered focus is theoretically supported. The groundbreaking theoretical work of Kimberlee Crenshaw (1989, 1993) and Patricia Hill Collins (2000) on the intersection of multiple marginalized identities, and the empirical studies suggesting distinct experiences of young women of color in a range of settings from the educational (Horvat and Antonio 1999; Holland 2012; Ispa-Landa 2013) to the legal and workplace realms (Crenshaw 1989, 1993; Hill Collins 2000), has helped the worlds of both academia and public policy to recognize the role of intersectionality. While both critical race and gender theory have grown in the academic realm and anti-racist and feminist political movements have grown in the public domain, we often continue to envision black men and white women as the centerpieces of these respective movements. As Crenshaw argues in her body of work exploring settings ranging from the workplace to the courtroom, the experiences of women of color cannot be fully understand by looking solely at the traditional borders dominant society has drawn around gender and racial categories, respectively. On the negative side of the ledger, women of color experience unique forms of violence, harassment, and discrimination from both white women and men of color. At the same time, women of color may possess unique and important forms of social and cultural capital, albeit undervalued in white, dominant society.

This study explores the extent to which these young women who were distinct from the dominant class racially and often, economically, were able to diversify social networks, access new forms of social and cultural capital, and the role that point of access seemed to play in the experience. How does intersectionality play out in this particular social context? Were these women able to build bridges and become part of integrated social networks and access social and cultural capital within the school and the town? How did point of access seem to influence the experience?

Given my connections to those involved with the boarding program, I approached a handful of board members and expressed my interest in learning more about the experiences of women who had gone through the program in Mayfair. Although I was at first met with skepticism by some board members, others were more open to the idea. One member of the board spoke with a handful of graduates with whom she had kept in touch and asked them if they would be willing to speak with me. Of the initial four that she approached, two agreed immediately and one agreed after having a phone conversation with me. I traveled to interview these first three women in November 2014 and at the end of each interview, I asked them if they knew of anyone else who might be willing to speak with me—thus creating a snowball sample. I was also granted permission to post information about my study on an alumni social network site. Three women contacted me via this avenue.

I similarly knew a number of board members involved in the commuter program, as well as parents who had served as host families, and teachers and administrators who had worked in the program. Interestingly, these many connections proved fruitless. I finally began to use various search engines to find people, searching for the name of the community and the name of the commuter program. This yielded my first participant from the commuter program, who then led me to another woman who had participated. Additionally, a contact within the community who had gone through a similar program in another town suggested that I begin by going through old high school yearbooks and, from there, searching out names on the web and specifically on social network sites. This strategy proved highly useful. After going through more than a decade of yearbooks, I identified several dozen women who had graduated from Mayfair via the commuter program. My research assistant and I looked up their names on the internet and when I was fairly confident it was the same individual, I would send an email to a social network account, if she had one. Several women responded affirmatively, and I again used the snowball technique to grow the sample. In addition, graduates of the commuter program at Mayfair High have their own closed social network site. I received permission to post my information on it, and a number of women contacted me about participating in the study. I also received additional names of graduates who were part of the commuter program from women who had been part of the boarder program, an early indication of what these women's social networks looked like while they were at Mayfair High.

The sample of women who had accessed the district as residents, living in either market rate homes owned by their families or Section 8 housing, proved the most challenging. This is largely because of the very small numbers of residents of color within Mayfair. I received the names of several former residents through a former participant of the commuter program, still more insight into what the social networks had looked like for many of these women during their time in Mayfair. I contacted these initial leads, with two responding affirmatively. Again, these former residents provided me with names of other former residents. A number of the women I reached out to in these iterations did not respond to my multiple requests to participate.

I also reached out to town officials who currently work at the Mayfair Housing Authority. They provided me with the name of the current president of the renter's association, who spoke with friends and neighbors. The president also invited me to attend and speak at a tenant's association meeting in the Section 8 complex, which I did. The town officials also allowed me to post flyers about my research project. In this way, I slowly reached a sample of residents and former residents who had graduated from Mayfair High.

I experienced two types of challenges in growing the sample of residents, particularly those who grew up in Section 8 housing, with these challenges being somewhat dichotomous in nature. The first challenge was simply finding women who had grown up in Section 8 housing in the community. I did not have access to town or state records on who had lived in Section 8 housing, and it is not clear that such records exist. Further, there was no clear point of contact, program, or social network that I could try and access in the way that I did with the commuters or boarders. There was a clear lack of group identity in any formal sense.

The second, somewhat dichotomous challenge was getting women to speak to me when I did track them down. If the first challenge spoke to the lack of social networks tying former residents together, the second challenge spoke to the ongoing existence of social networks. My sense from speaking with residents who did participate in this project was a fear of friends, family, and neighbors, past or present, taking offense to what they had to say, a fear of "word getting back." Even though I assured everyone complete confidentiality, this did not appear to put everyone at ease.

In addition to these challenges around identifying participants, there are some additional limitations that should be taken into account. Asking questions retrospectively could result in recall bias. Many of us forget exactly what happened even a few weeks ago. In some cases, I was speaking with women who had graduated 30 years prior. Participants may have forgotten particular events, the order or events, or the details. I attempted to mitigate these issues through questions that included prompts such as, "Did you ever participate in after-school activities, such as yearbook, dance, or softball?" and through the use of non-leading prompts, such as,

"Do you remember if that happened during your first or second year in high school?" A related issue is my intentional inclusion of women from across a broad time period. I did this so as to compare experiences over time. What I cannot account for are possible changes in the community, school, or programs. Having said that, the findings appear quite consistent over time, and variability appears to be the result of other factors, most often point of entry.

The final sample includes 37 women who attended Mayfair High over the past 35 years.

I only interviewed women who had already graduated from high school because I wanted to speak with women who had some perspective on their experiences, as well as some post-high school trajectory. As can be seen in Table 1.2, the participants are varied in terms of age, academic, and professional outcome, as well as means of access to Mayfair High.

Among town residents, six of the ten grew up in subsidized housing and/or received other forms of government support. Half of the town residents lived with only one parent, two lived with a mother and stepfather, and three lived in a nuclear household with two biological parents. The latter three came from the most affluent backgrounds, with college-educated parents who owned their own homes. Among the commuter students, nine of the fifteen women were raised by their mothers, in some cases with the assistance of grandparents. Three commuters grew up in two-parent households, and three grew up in households where parents had been married, but divorced while these women were living at home. The women from the commuter program describe their backgrounds ranging from "very low income" to "middle-class," with seven women growing up in homes owned by their families. The other eight commuters describe living in "the projects," other forms of government subsidized housing, and rental apartments as children. Among the boarding students, eight of the twelve women were raised by their mothers, often with the assistance of extended family, two were raised in two-parent households, and two grew up in households where the parents had been married, but divorced while the participants were living at home. About half of the boarding students describe lower-middle to middle-class households, living in private homes or apartments. The other half describe more lower-income households, living in government housing, rent-controlled, or rental apartments.

About half of all of the participants grew up in what would generally be viewed by larger American society as lower-middle to middle-class households, with one or even two parents working as civil servants or in pink-collar professions. Relative to the community of Mayfair, however, these

Table 1.2 Descriptives of sample, N=37

Id number	Pseudonym	Residential status	Year of HS graduation	Average grades	Overall experience, scale of 1–4	Graduated college	Current occupation
101	Alexandra	Resident	2005	Cs	Pretty good	No	Nanny
102	Jade	Resident	2009	Cs	Pretty good	No	Administrative assistant
103	Hannah	Resident	2011	Bs and Cs	Pretty good	Yes	Athletic coach
104	Gabriella	Resident	2006	Bs	Pretty good	Yes	Medical technician
105	Brianna	Resident	2013	Bs	Pretty good	In college	Full-time student
106	Flore	Resident	2007	Bs	Ok	No	Nanny
107	Faith	Resident	2014	Bs	Pretty good	In college	Full-time student
108	Veronica	Resident	1999	As and Bs	Ok	Yes	Graphic designer
109	Elisabeth	Resident	2006	As and Bs	Best	No	Flight attendant
110	Sara	Resident	2015	Bs	Pretty good	In college	Full-time student
201	Lorraine	Commuter	1985	As and Bs	Pretty good	Yes	Real estate broker
202	Edith	Commuter	1989	Bs and Cs	Best	Yes	Community organizer
203	Michelle	Commuter	1991	Bs and Cs	Pretty good	Yes	Accountant
204	Serena	Commuter	1994	As and Bs	Pretty bad	In college	Accountant
205	Joslin	Commuter	1993	Bs and Cs	Pretty bad	No	Medical technician
206	Deana	Commuter	2005	Cs and Ds	Ok	Yes	Guidance counselor
207	Noel	Commuter	2006	As and Bs	Pretty good	Yes	Teacher
208	May	Commuter	2007	As and Bs	Pretty good	Yes	Non-profit program assistant
209	Yolanda	Commuter	1998	Bs and Cs	Ok	Yes	Development director
210	Patricia	Commuter	2008	Bs	Pretty good	No	Maintenance worker
211	Coretta	Commuter	2005	Bs and Cs	Pretty good	No	Accountant
212	Sasha	Commuter	2000	Bs and Cs	Ok	Yes	Human resource director
213	Chantel	Commuter	2010	As and Bs	Pretty bad	Yes	Non-profit program assistant

	Name	Type	Year	Grades	Health	Family supportive	Occupation
214	Andrea	Commuter	1999	As and Bs	Best	Yes	Accountant
215	Monique	Commuter	1988	Bs	Pretty good	Yes	Travel agent
301	Christina	Boarder	2009	As and Bs	Pretty good	Yes	Medical technician
302	Elise	Boarder	2001	As and Bs	Pretty good	Yes	Business development
303	Priscilla	Boarder	1995	As and Bs	Ok	Yes	Writer
304	Isabel	Boarder	2010	As and Bs	Pretty bad	Yes	Medical researcher
305	Karenna	Boarder	2007	As and Bs	Pretty good	Yes	Non-profit program assistant
306	Tasha	Boarder	2004	As and Bs	Pretty good	Yes	Full-time graduate student
307	Jaqui	Boarder	2002	As and Bs	Pretty good	Yes	Teacher
308	Kelsey	Boarder	1997	As and Bs	Ok	Yes	Stay at home mother
309	Marian	Boarder	2013	As and Bs	Best	In college	Full-time student
310	Malia	Boarder	2011	As and Bs	Ok	In college	Full-time student
311	Alana	Boarder	1982	As and Bs	Pretty good	Yes	Social worker
312	Tamara	Boarder	2012	As and Bs	Ok	In college	Full-time student

young women tend to be of more modest economic means. By including both middle- and lower-income women of color in the study, we can begin to see the extent to which money mediates the experience in Mayfair.

Selectivity of Subjects

It is important to note that the women participating in this study are a selective group. First of all, many of the women of color who accessed this high school did so through one of two voluntary desegregation programs. In short, they opted in. By participating in these programs initially, these young women already possessed a certain amount of social capital, having been provided information about and encouragement and support to apply to these programs. Further, all of the women who participated in this project graduated from high school, so they, in many ways, are already success stories with significant amounts of resources. This is a selective group of women who make up this study.

The selectivity of the subjects is intentional. The women who participated in the project are success stories as they stand—women of color who hold a high school diploma from one of the most elite public high schools in the country.[3] Many studies and program evaluations might stop there—degree received, success attained! Their success as high school graduates does not answer all of our questions, however. In fact, such success begs a variety of new questions: Was there success beyond the classroom? Were these women able to develop relationships with the dominant, white population? Were they able to access the many forms of cultural and social capital seemingly flowing through the high school corridors and streets of this community?

The processes identified through these interviews, and which will be examined in detail throughout the next five chapters, are illustrated in Fig. 1.1. Although these processes and themes exist across all three groups of women, there is variation in each theme by point of access. Chapter 2, "Two-Ness and Liminality in Mayfair," examines the common experience of marginality cited by many of the women in the study and the various barriers to inclusion. The theories of Du Bois (1904/1994) and Turner (1969) find support here, with women straddling two worlds, yet really living between worlds. In Chapter 3, "The Making of Community," I examine the tight intra-racial relationships women develop with each other, largely in response to their feelings of marginality in both worlds and a sense of liminality over all. This theme again echoes the theories

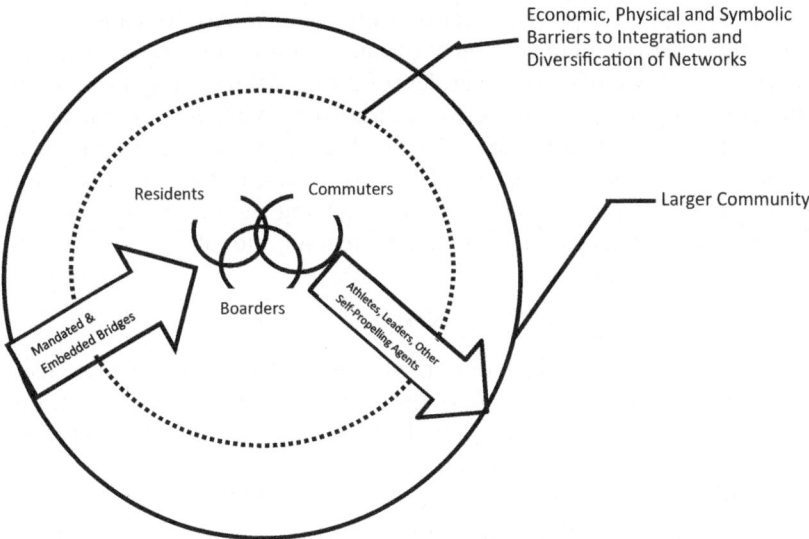

Fig. 1.1 Processes of marginalization and incorporation

of Du Bois and Turner. Chapter 4, "Athletes and Boundary Breakers," explores the way a small number of women are able to successfully build bridges into the white dominant community, diversifying their peer networks and integrating into the community. They do so primarily through athletic participation, and to a lesser extent through other extracurricular activities. I also examine the barriers—economic, logistical, and symbolic—that kept many young women from building such bridges through extracurricular participation and "breaking" in through this avenue. In Chapter 5, "Bridge Builders and Cultural Guides," I explore the embedded and mandated adult bridges in the community who develop relationships with these young women and provide them with both social support and social leverage (Briggs 1997; Dominguez 2011). These adult bridges, many of whom act as "cultural guides" (Lareau 2015), play critical roles in the lives of many of these women. In Chapter 6, "The Acquisition of Cultural Capital," I explore the other forms of capital gained, be it in embodied, institutionalized, or objectified form (Bourdieu 1986), and how these various forms of capital have impacted their lives. As in prior chapters, I also explore the ongoing barriers that exist that limit the acquisition of cultural capital. Finally, in Chapter 7, "Race, Place, and the Power of Interactions," I explore the various ways women make valuable contributions to the community, largely through transmuting stereotypes that remain for women of color, regardless of the residential group from which they come. The interactions between these women of color and the dominant population can potentially change "local knowledge," and ideally at some point alter societal scripts. These 37 voices, in their discussions of isolation and marginalization, of bridge building and bridge failures, may lead us from desegregation to genuine integration for all.

Notes

1. All formal names, including towns, programs, and individuals, have been changed. In the case of the study participants, some additional information may have been changed to protect identity, where it would not alter the substance of their story. For example, an individual identified as having graduated in 1989 may actually have graduated in 1993. An individual who works as a nurse may be identified as working as a teacher.
2. The commuter program, "Reach Across Boarders," is referred to as simply "Reach" for the sake of simplicity. Throughout the book, I use the terms "commuters" and "Reach" students interchangeably, as I do "boarders" and "Aspire" students.
3. One woman who participated in the boarding program did not graduate from Mayfair, but returned to her home for her final year of high school. This did not become clear until we were well into the interview. I decided to include her data, as her experiences very much follow the patterns of other women in the study.

Bibliography

Almeida, J., R.M. Johnson, M. McNamara, and J. Gupta. 2011. Peer Violence Perpetration Among Urban Adolescents: Dispelling the Myth of the Violent Immigrant. *Journal of Interpersonal Violence* 26(13): 2658–2680.
Annie E. Casey Foundation (2006). *Race Matters: Unequal Opportunities in Education*. November 25. http://www.aecf.org/m/resourcedoc/aecf-racemattersEDUCATION-2006.pdf. Accessed 14 March 2016.
Anson, R. 1988. *Best Intentions*. New York: First Vintage Books.
Bankston, C., S. Caldas, and M. Zhou. 1997. The Academic Achievement of Vietnamese American Students: Ethnicity as Social Capital. *Social Focus 30*: 1–16.

Bourdieu, P. 1986. The forms of capital. In *Handbook of Theory and Research for the Sociology of Education*, ed. J. Richardson, 241–258. New York: Greenwood Press.
Bourdieu, P., and J. Passeron. 2000. *Reproduction in Education, Society and Culture*. London: Sage.
Bowen, W.G., and D.C. Bok. 1998. *The Shape of the River: Long-term Consequences of Considering Race in College and University Admissions*. Princeton, NJ: Princeton University Press.
Briggs, D. 1997. Social Capital and the Cities: Advice to Change Agents. *National Civic Review* 86(2): 111–117.
Brown v. Board of Education, 347. S. 438 (1954).
Calarco, J. 2014. Coached for the Classroom: Parents' Cultural Transmission and Children's Reproduction of Educational Inequalities. *American Sociological Review* 79(5): 1015–1037.
Carter, P. 2015. Educational Equity Demands Empathy. *Contexts*, Fall 76–78.
———. 2012. *Stubborn Roots*. Oxford: Oxford University Press.
———. 2007. Why the Black Kids Sit Together at The Stairs: The Role of Identity-Affirming Counter-Spaces in a Predominantly White High School. *Journal of Negro Education* 76(4): 542–554.
Clotfelter, C. 2004. *After "Brown": The Rise and Retreat of School Desegregation*. Princeton: Princeton University Press.
Coleman, J. 1988. Social Capital in the Creation of Human Capital. *The American Journal of Sociology* 94: S95–S120.
———. 1992. Some Points on Choice in Education. *Sociology of Education* 65(4): 260–262.
Collins, P. 2000. *Black Feminist Thought: Knowledge, Consciousness, & the Politics of Empowerment*. New York: Routledge.
Cook, P., and J. Ludwig. 1998. The Burden of 'Acting White': Do Black Adolescents Disparage Academic Achievements? In *The Black-White Test Score Gap*, ed. C. Jencks and M. Phillips, 375–400. Washington, D.C.: Brookings Institution Press.
Cookson, P., and C. Persell. 1991. Race and Class in America's Elite Boarding Schools: African Americans as the "Outsiders Within". *The Journal of Negro Education* 60: 219–228.
Crenshaw, K. 1989. Demarginalizing the Intersection of Race and Sex: A Black Feminist Critique of Antidiscrimination Doctrine, Feminist Theory, and Antiracist Politics. *University of Chicago Legal Forum*, Issue 1.
———. 1993. Mapping the Margins: Intersectionality, Identity Politics, and Violence Against Women of Color. *Stanford Law Review* 43(6): 1241–1299.
Dominguez, S. 2011. *Getting Ahead: Social Mobility, Public Housing, and Immigrant Networks*. New York: New York University Press.
Du Bois, W. 1994. *The Souls of Black Folks*. New York: Dover Publications.

Dufur, M., T. Parcel, and K. Troutman. 2013. Does Capital at Home Matter More Than Capital at School? Social Capital Effects on Academic Achievement. *Research in Social stratification and Mobility 31*: 1–21.
Dumais, S.A. 2002. Cultural Capital, Gender, and School Success: The Role of Habitus. *Sociology of Education* 75(1): 44–68. Retrieved from http://search.proquest.com.ezp-prod1.hul.harvard.edu/docview/60079357?accountid=11311
Eaton, S. 2001. *The Other Boston Busing Story*. New Haven: Yale University Press.
———. 2007. *The Children in Room E4*. Chapel Hill: Algonquin Books.
Enos, R. 2014. The Causal Effect of Intergroup Contact on Exclusionary Attitudes. *Proceedings of the National Academy of Sciences of the United States of America* 111(10): 3699–3704.
Enos, R. & C. Celaya. (forthcoming). The Effect of Segregation on Intergroup Relations.
Farmer, J. 1965/2007. *Freedom—When?* New York: Random House.
Flippen, C. 2016. The More Things Change the More they Stay the Same: The Future of Residential Segregation in America. *City & Community* 15(1): 14–17.
Fordham, S., and J. Ogbu. 1986. Black students' school success: Coping with the "burden of 'acting white'". *The Urban Review* 18(3): 176–206.
Fryer, R., and S. Levitt. 2006. The Black-White Test Score Gap Through Third Grade. *American Law and Economics Review* 8(2): 249–281.
———. 2013. Testing for Racial Differences in the Mental Ability of Young Children. *American Economic Review* 103(2): 981–1005.
Fryer, R. & V. Curto. 2014. The Potential of Urban Boarding Schools for the Poor: Evidence from SEED. *Journal of Labor Economics* 32(1): 65–93.
Gibson, M. 1988. *Accommodation without Assimilation: Sikh Immigrants in an American High School*. Ithaca, NY: Cornell University Press.
Gibson, M., and J. Ogbu. 1991. *Minority status and schooling: A comparative study of immigrant vs. involuntary minorities*. New York: Garland.
Glaser, B., and A. Strauss. 1967. *The Discovery of Grounded Theory: Strategies for Qualitative Research*. Chicago: Aldine Publishing Company.
Hart & Risley. 1995. *Meaningful Differences in the Everyday Experience of Young American Children*. Baltimore, MD: Paul H. Brookes Publishing Co..
Holland, M. 2012. Only Here for the Day: The Social Integration of Minority Students at a Majority White High School. *Sociology of Education* 85(2): 101–120.
Horvat, E., and A. Antonio. 1999. "Hey, Those Shoes Are Out of Uniform": African American Girls in an Elite High School and the Importance of Habitus. *Anthropology & Education Quarterly* 30(3): 317–342.
Ispa-Landa, S. 2013. Gender, Race, and Justifications for Group Exclusion: Urban Black Students Bussed to Affluent Suburban Schools. *Sociology of Education* 86(3): 218–233.

Jack, A. 2016. (No)Harm in Asking: Class, Acquired Cultural Capital, and Academic Engagement at an Elite University. *Sociology of Education* 89(1): 1–19.

Khan, S. 2011. *Privilege: The Making of an Adolescent Elite at St. Paul's School*. Princeton and Oxford: Princeton University Press.

Jencks, C., and M. Phillips. 1998. *The Black-White Test Score Gap*. Washington, D.C.: Brookings Institution Press.

Kasinitz, P., J. Mollenkopf, M. Waters, and J. Holdaway. 2009. *Inheriting the City: The Children of Immigrants Come of Age*. Cambridge, MA: Russell Sage.

Kena, G., L. Musu-Gillette, J. Robinson, X. Wang, A. Rathbun, J. Zhang, S. Wilkinson-Flicker, A. Barmer, and E. Dunlop Velez. 2015. *The Condition of Education 2015* (NCES 2015-144). U.S. Department of Education, National Center for Education Statistics. Washington, DC. Retrieved from http://nces.ed.gov/pubsearch.

Kendrick, S., and P. Kendrick. 2004. *Sarah's Long Walk*. Boston: Beacon Press.

Kozol, J. 1995. *Amazing Grace*. New York: Crown Publishers.

———. 2005. *The Shame of the Nation*. New York: Crown Publishers.

Lamont, M., and M. Fournier. 1992. *Cultivating Differences: Symbolic Boundaries and the Making of Inequality*. Chicago: University of Chicago Press.

Lareau, A. 2011. *Unequal Childhoods*. Berkeley: University of California Press.

———. 2015. Cultural Knowledge and Social Inequality. *The American Sociological Review* 80(1): 1–27.

Lee, J., and M. Zhou. 2015. *The Asian American achievement paradox*. New York: Russell Sage Foundation.

MacDonald, M. 1999. *All Souls*. Boston: Beacon Press.

Massey, D., and N. Denton. 1993. *American Apartheid: Segregation and the Making of the Underclass*. Cambridge: Harvard University Press.

Ogbu, J. 1992. Adaptation to Minority Status and Impact on School Success. *Theory into Practice* XXXI(4): 287–295.

Orfield, G., J. Kuscera, and G. Siegel-Hawley. 2012. *E Pluribus ... Separation: Deeping Double Segregation for More Students*. Los Angeles: UCLA, The Civil Rights Project.

Phillips, M., J. Brooks-Gunn, G. Duncan, P. Klebanov, and J. Crane. 1998. Family Background, Parenting Practices, and the Black-White Test Score Gap. In *The Black-White Test Score Gap*, ed. C. Jencks and M. Phillips, 103–148. Washington, D.C.: Brookings Institution Press.

Planty, M., Hussar, W., Snyder, T., Kena, G., Kewal Ramani, A., Kemp, J., Bianco, K., Dinkes, R. 2009. *The Condition of Education 2009* (NCES 2009-081). National Center for Education Statistics, Institute of Education Sciences, U.S. Department of Education. Washington, DC.

Putnam, R. 2000. *Bowling Alone*. New York: Simon & Schuster.

"Quickfacts". Census.gov. Accessed on April 27th, 2014.

Reardon, S., and A. Owens. 2014. 60 Years after *Brown*: Trends and Consequences of School Segregation. *Annual Review of Sociology* 40: 199–218.

Roberts v. City of Boston. Supreme Court of Massachusetts, Suffolk. 59 Mass. 198. 1849.
Sheff v. O'Neill, 238 Conn. 1, 678 A.2d 1267. 1996.
Snyder, T. 2015. *Digest of Education Statistics 2013. U.S. Department of Education.* Washington, DC: National Center for Education Statistics.
Stephens-Davidowitz, S. 2014. The Cost of Racial Animus on a Black Candidate. *The Journal of Public Economics* 118(26): 15.
Stetser, M., and R. Stillwell. 2014. *Public High School Four-Year On-Time Graduation Rates and Event Dropout Rates: School Years 2010–11 and 2011–12. First Look (NCES 2014-391). U.S. Department of Education.* Washington, DC: National Center for Education Statistics http://nces.ed.gov/pubsearch.
Theoharis, Jeanne. 2009. I Hate it when People treat me like a FXXX-Up. In *Our Schools Suck*, ed. G. Alonso, N. Anderson, C. Su, and J. Theoharis, 69–112. New York: New York University Press.
Tilly, C. 1999. *Durable Inequality.* Berkeley: University of California Press.
Tocqueville, A.D., J.P. Mayer, and G. Lawrence. 2006. *Democracy in America.* New York: Harper Perennial Modern Classics.
Turner, V. 1969. *The Ritual Process.* New York: Transaction Publishers.
Tyson, K. 2011. *Integration Interrupted: Tracking, Black Students, and Acting White after Brown.* New York: Oxford University Press.
U.S. Department of Education. (2002). No Child Left Behind Act of 2001.
———. 1965. Elementary and Secondary Education Act of 1965.
Wilson, W. 1980. *The Declining Significance of Race.* Chicago: University of Chicago Press.
———. 1987. *The Truly Disadvantaged.* Chicago: University of Chicago Press.
———. 2015. William Julius Wilson says his Arguments on Race and Class Still Apply. *Footnotes* 43(6).
Zweigenhaft, R., and G. Domhoff. 1991. *Blacks in the White Establishment: A Study of Race and Class in America.* New Haven: Yale University Press.
———. 2003. *Blacks in the White Elite: Will the Progress Continue?* Lanham, MD: Rowman & Littlefield.

CHAPTER 2

Two-Ness and Liminality in Mayfair

Alexandra's Story

Alexandra is a former town resident who graduated in the mid-2000s. She grew up in Section 8 housing in Mayfair from the time that she was 10 years old until she graduated from high school. Now in her late twenties, she lives in Urbana, approximately 15 miles away from her hometown and works in childcare. We meet in an upscale cupcake bakery near Mayfair to talk, a location she has chosen. In the bakery case, the fancy cupcakes are decorated with a variety of local high school colors and motifs. She proudly points out to me the Mayfair cupcake. We sit down to talk and she tells me what growing up in a town like Mayfair was like for a lower-income girl of color—the benefits, the challenges. She discusses the high-quality education she received, the safety of the community, the opportunities she had, like learning how to ski. But, she also tells me about the sense of marginalization, of an assumption of otherness. Her teachers assumed that she lived in the city of Urbana and excused her tardiness, assuming it was due to traffic. People complimented her mother for driving her "all the way here." As she says, "I was in my own category—a black girl that was in Mayfair."

Two-ness and Liminality

If the problem of the twentieth century was the problem of the color line (Du Bois, 1903/1994), the problem of the twenty-first century is a bit more nuanced, but certainly not devoid of color (Wilson 1980, 1987,

1996, 2015). Racial and ethnic categorization, along with gender and class, has remained "durable" in American society (Tilly 1999), continuing to serve as the organizing and stratifying principles for individuals, groups, and institutions. These categories are so powerful that they influence everything from our sense of self to our daily social interactions to our physical and social placement in society (West and Zimmerman 1987; Omi and Winant 1994). These categorical pairings become entrenched in our minds and institutionalized in our systems, only further reinforcing individual opportunities and expectations which, in turn, fortify larger social groupings and structures, thus producing durable inequalities (Tilly 1999).

W.E.B. Du Bois examines the impact of identity, particularly racial identity, within the United States in the early twentieth century. He argues that the role and impact of identity varies based upon setting. In using his own life as an example, he compares his experiences as a black man in the United States to those of being a black man in Europe. Although his skin tone certainly does not change from place to place, his reception certainly does. At the same time, Du Bois argues the unyielding nature of structural barriers, the institutional components in a society that maintain racial, as well as class and gender, hierarchies. In short, the role and impact of identity is variable based upon setting, but the structure of any particular setting severely limits individual agency and one's ability to override it.

Race, although considered first and foremost an ascribed characteristic and a principal form of identity, is so embedded in American society that it also exists as an institution that has historically served as *the* line of demarcation in the United States. Du Bois (1903/1994) argues that a veil hangs between the races, separating white and black. It alters both the way whites see people of color and the way that people of color see themselves, embedding in the group a sense of marginalization. According to Du Bois, this marginalization and sense of otherness provide people with unique insights about the world around them, an ability to see with "second-sight." At the same time, black Americans may be left feeling a perpetual inability to merge being both black and American, resulting in feelings of fragmentation. Alexandra, the town resident who begins this chapter, relates a sense of division: "I was in my own category—a black girl in Mayfair." But, Alexandra also suggests the possession of insight. When asked what was valuable about growing up and attending school in the community, she states, "Honestly, it's just the whole fact that I can understand [white] people's way of thinking sometimes." She is illustrating, more than 100 years later, much of what Du Bois experienced and theorized around race in American society.

Decades after Du Bois, the cultural anthropologist Victor Turner (1969) coined the term "liminality" to describe what he calls being "betwixt and between" recognized cultural spaces. If Du Bois argues that certain individuals and groups occupy two worlds, Turner argues an existence between worlds, a dislocation from both.

Individuals and groups who occupy this space are expected to take on a certain humility, obeying their superiors without question as they go through *rites de passage*. As individuals go through the process of being remade, they lose a clear placement in the social structure, while not yet being given a new position, one that Turner argues is a "superior" and more revered form. Du Bois' theory of "two-ness" (1903/1994) suggests a permanent state, while Turner's theory of liminality (1969) suggests a temporary state, one that individuals and groups move through on their way to superior positions. Turner views this liminal state as a waiting room, while Du Bois views it as a way of life.

Even with these theoretical distinctions, Du Bois' and Turner's respective theories share certain similarities—a sense of marginalization and otherness. Further, the feeling of marginalization that comes from either existing in two worlds, or existing in neither, grows out of both physical and symbolic boundaries (Lamont and Fournier 1992). During Du Bois' time, the boundaries may have been physical—legally separate schools, bathrooms, and places on public transportation. Although legally sanctioned physical divisions are gone, housing segregation and other forms of distinct physical spaces still exist (Massey and Denton 1998; Small 2004).

Just as powerful are the symbolic boundaries. These are the many ways in which group membership and location are signaled to one another and the larger world (Turner 1969). It is also the many ways that divisions are created and reinforced (Tilly 1999; Lamont and Fournier 1992). Within Mayfair, it is the tracking of students into advanced placement or honors classes; it is the discussion of where one spent a spring vacation; it is the school-wide announcement that "Urbana kids, your bus is here" and it is time for you to leave. In each case, insider status is reinforced and outsider status is, too. And, in this way, categorical inequalities remain as the small-scale, individual interactions are matched up with societal stereotypes (Tilly 1999).

Marginalization and Liminality in Mayfair

Both Du Bois' theory of two-ness, a general and permanent state of "in-betweenness" for people of color, and Turner's theory of liminality find support throughout the data. Under virtually any circumstances, these young women would likely experience the fragmentation discussed by Du Bois by virtue of being an American of color, even in the late twentieth and early twenty-first centuries.

By virtue of living or attending school in Mayfair, however, these women experience something else—a sense of liminality. The expectation for Reach students, who come from Urbana, and the Aspire boarding students, who come from a range of cities, is that they will have greater educational and social opportunities than they would have in their home communities, resulting in an elevated status in society. They have opted in for theoretically better opportunities. Turner's theory of liminality (1969) suggests this is a passing phase, the price one must pay for moving up. But, Turner's theory neglects the gendered and racialized nature of society, and most certainly does not take intersectionality into account. A liminal phase on the way to higher elevation may be a temporary one for those who trod a widely accepted path, but what of those who fight against the widely accepted social structure? These women find themselves in an elite, predominantly white world, a world which does not fully accept them. At the same time, their partial incorporation in Mayfair places them outside of the worlds from which many originally came.

The unique location of these women arguably provides them with even more than double consciousness (Du Bois 1903/1994). They clearly see themselves as Americans of color and understand what that means; they understand how white America sees them; *and* because of their placement in this liminal space, they have added insight into how the larger social structure operates. They operate not simply between an America of color and a white America, but on a daily basis live in elite white America. Beyond simply seeing beyond the veil (Du Bois, 1903/1994), they see behind the curtain that hides the reproduction of inequality in American society.

The women of color who graduated from Mayfair High discuss many of the trends of marginalization and liminality identified in prior research on race, class, and educational desegregation (Cookson and Persell 1991; Khan 2011; Eaton 2001; Holland 2012; Carter 2006, 2007, 2012). This study also adds to the small body of work that has helped us to better understand the unique experiences of women of color in elite high school settings, and finds many similar trends (Holland 2012; Ispa-Landa 2013; Horvat and Antonio 1999).

The unique contribution that this study makes is the focus on point of access into a district and how it influences the processes of marginalization and liminality. This is particularly important as many racial desegregation programs are premised upon moving students of color across geographic borders. The findings here suggest that point of access impacts the experiences of the women, with each group experiencing marginalization and liminality in distinct ways. The boarding students, by virtue of how they accessed the school, are viewed in many ways as the exceptional cases, the deserving girls of color. Commuters, who are larger in number, all from the same city, and varied in academic performance, are viewed as the stereotypical urban underclass. The residents are viewed as outsiders, and could not possibly be from the town.

Boarders

The women who access Mayfair High School as boarding students are a small, but highly selective group from a variety of states in the Northeast and Midwest. All 12 of the women interviewed come from urban areas, per the mandate of Aspire, the national racial desegregation program of which they are a part, and their home communities tend to be racially and economically homogenous, in keeping with the state of housing segregation in the United States.

Because these women not only attend school in Mayfair, but also live there throughout the school year, the experience of transitioning from one state of being or status to another is in many ways harder for them than for the Reach students and residents who do not have to completely cut ties. As Aspire boarding student, Jaqui, says of the Reach students, "They got to go home at night." The boarders have no such reprieve. Turner (1969) would likely argue that their complete immersion into white Mayfair and physical separation from their homes and families is part of the transformation process. Be that as it may, the process is an exacting one.

A theme of liminality comes across strongly in conversations with seven of the boarders—Priscilla, Isabel, Jaqui, Kelsey, Marian, Karenna, and Alana. Although a woman might have felt that leaving home was her best (and, in some cases, her only) option, arriving in Mayfair presented a different set of challenges and an awareness of not quite belonging anywhere. These women describe feelings of isolation and marginalization in both their home environments and in their new setting, the place in which they will be "remade." They find themselves in situations for which they do not have the proper "cultural tool kit" (Swidler 1986), leaving them feeling like outsiders.

Priscilla, a graduate from the early 1990s who has gone on to become a successful Latina writer and attended a prestigious university in her home city, explained her sense of liminality in this way. When discussing her feelings about Mayfair, she states unequivocally, "I didn't feel like I fit in. I never, at any point, did I feel like I fit in." She retells a story of virulent racism that took place within her first few days of moving to Mayfair and which still holds power, decades after it took place. She describes walking home from school with another girl of color. A car passed by, slowed down, and the passenger rolled down the window. She continues, "And someone threw a lit cigarette at me and said, 'N—go home.' And I remember his face it's like red with rage…and that just damaged me, damaged me for a long time."

She longed for home, but attending school in Mayfair largely blocked out the possibility of ever going "home" in any real sense. Priscilla recalls a particular incident that took place during a visit home while in her first year at Mayfair. Priscilla says, "I remember hanging out with my friends and saying, 'Oh, that's awesome! I'm so psyched!' And they were like, 'Awesome? Psyched? What are you a white girl now, Priscilla? You sold out?' So I was rejected by them—that was tough." She experiences barriers in Mayfair as a person of color, but her socialization into that community works to construct barriers in her home community. Her language has changed, signifying to her friends from home that she has crossed a boundary and she is no longer one of them.

Kelsey, who graduated in the mid-1990s, and Jaqui, who graduated ten years later in the mid-2000s, both felt isolated and thought the boarding students were placed in their "own category" in Mayfair. Kelsey, for example, says, "I think I always felt like people looked at us as a group of, you know [boarding] kids as opposed to, you know just Mayfair students." Jaqui discusses having experiences in her home community similar to Priscilla's:

> I guess the hardest part is missing out on things and then often times when you come home and try to reconnect with your friends. Or some friends, not my closest friends but some people would be like, 'Now you're talking white,' but what does that even mean? People think you're better than them I guess.

These feelings of not quite belonging in either world are present for other boarders. Isabel, a woman from an immigrant family who went on to graduate from a highly prestigious college in the Northeast, says, "And it's sad because even when I go back now I realize that I could never see myself living there. Every time I look back I'm just reminded of—I feel like I could stay around [here] and pretend that I'm not from this very impoverished area." At the same time, she felt highly marginalized while in Mayfair and continues to struggle with feelings of isolation and low self-esteem, which she largely attributes to having gone to Mayfair. Even though she graduated from Mayfair in the twenty-first century, more than 100 years after Du Bois' writing, the veil (Du Bois, 1903/1994) remains firmly in place for her, as she discusses her constant concerns of being too big, too loud, and too scary, seeing herself as she feels whites see her.

Marian, a young woman who is still in college in the Northeast, and who largely integrated into Mayfair, still discusses feelings of liminality. Even though she was viewed by many in the community as a great integration "success," she struggled with feelings of being caught between two worlds. She talks about this sense of liminality: "I guess one [thing] that comes to my head immediately is just coming back home and people saying you act different, talk different. So kind of dealing with that. And kind of from people back home feeling a sense of abandonment. So I guess I was in those two different, because literally, two different lives."

This balancing act was also experienced by a predecessor of hers, a woman from the Midwest who had gone through the program decades before. Alana says about some of the challenges she faced, "I would say maybe coming home from some of the breaks, you know people think that you've changed a little bit. You're different, and it's probably because we had been at an all-white environment." At the same time, she states, "I never felt part of the Mayfair community at all." Again and again, these women cross some boundaries into the elite world of Mayfair, but never completely. And, their breaking through barriers in Mayfair places them outside of the communities from which they came.

Although the marginalization in Mayfair may at times result from the sort of virulent racism that Priscilla experienced during her first few weeks in town, it is often less extreme, but still damaging and isolating. Karenna, a boarding student from the mid-2000s, talks about her experiences in the community, specifically as an employee in a local retailer. She says, "I worked at Buttons and Bows my senior year and that was horrible. That was so bad, there were so many times that the lone black person walks into the store and they're like, 'Could you watch?' You know, there was a lot of that." This sort of experience illustrates the double consciousness that arises from living in and being part of (but only in part) this elite white community. She is clearly and explicitly told how people of color are viewed by white America and she is put in the unenviable position of standing at the crux.

The boarders are also distinct as high-performing girls of color, as that is how they gained access to the school district of Mayfair. As such, these women talk of white Mayfair having certain expectations of them. Alana recalls that when one teacher realized that she was part of the boarding program, rather than the less prestigious commuting program, the teacher's attitude completely changed toward her. The teacher apologized for not knowing that Alana was part of the boarding program and then offered her both academic assistance and emotional support. Elise remembers that she was immediately assumed to be part of the boarding program when she was running for class president, because that is what the women in this program are assumed to do. Elise asks why no one assumed that she was a resident or a commuter. Veronica, a town resident, who was very strong academically, was assumed to be a part of the boarding program. These women seem to be viewed as the "deserving" segment of the underclass (Jencks and Peterson 1991), or to use the older language of Du Bois, they are the "talented tenth" (Du Bois 1903/1994), stereotypes that only further marginalize them in Mayfair.

Commuters

Many of those who arrive by bus from Urbana to Mayfair on a daily basis also go through a transition, moving further away psychologically from where they spend their evenings and weekends. Ten women—Lorraine, Michelle, Serena, May, Yolanda, Patricia, Coretta, Sasha, Chantel, and Monique—explicitly discuss feelings of liminality. They felt disconnected from their home communities, as they did not attend school with neighborhood children, who often referred to the Reach students as "Oreos." At the same time, these women felt a lack of connection with the town and school community. If the Aspire students are viewed as the "deserving" charity cases by the wider community, the Reach students are viewed as the stereotypical inner city kids, assumed to be from violent, drug-riddled ghettos. Yolanda is asked if she lives in the projects and knows drug dealers. She says, "We're not living in a ghetto." Sasha is told by a white classmate, "I'd be so scared to live where you live."

Lorraine, a graduate from the mid-1980s, when asked if she felt a part of the school community, said simply, "Not at all." At the same time, she put it this way about her relationships at home:

> You know, the kids in my neighborhood, there was only one other girl on my block who was in Reach and she went to Latcomb. Most of the kids all went to the city schools. And I got teased by them, cause they used to call me white girl because I went to school with all white kids. I'm very light and I have long hair. And so I got teased a lot, and they said, they used to say, you know, 'Oh, she thinks she's better than us' or, 'She goes to school out there with all those rich white folk.' Yeah, so I got teased a lot.

Yolanda, who entered Mayfair in middle school and graduated in the late 1990s, says she felt a part of her home community until she started school in the suburbs. Her sense of wholeness became fractured (Du Bois, 1903/1994) upon her fuller introduction into elite, white society. At the same time, she says she never connected with the Mayfair students who grew up in town. She tells a story of trying to bring her two worlds together by bringing a white friend from Mayfair to her home for a sleepover:

> I got into this big argument with this girl in my neighborhood because she just saw any white person as a racist and I was also ostracized for bringing a white person into my community, and it was like, 'Oh, you're changed, you're different, you talk white.' And I didn't relate to them because I also had very different experiences from them that they just couldn't understand. So I think it made me feel like I didn't fit anywhere.

In ways large and small, Yolanda describes symbolic barriers throughout her experience. She recalls two sets of prom pictures taken—one of the students of color and one of the white students. She retells of showing up for school during her senior year, only to see all the town residents wearing tie dye shirts as part of a planned senior day—something about which the Reach students had not been informed. In one of the most extreme expressions of marginalization among all of the women interviewed, she describes her inability to form real friendships with the white students in Mayfair: "Because you see me as this circus animal or something, that you got to dissect me and ask me all these questions." With her double consciousness (Du Bois 1903/1994), Yolanda explains how she feels white Mayfair views her.

Another woman, Michelle, who graduated from Mayfair in the early 1990s and recently graduated from a public university while working for a state agency, describes an unexceptional experience. However, when asked if she would send children to such a program, she states without particular anger or emotion, "Maybe. I mean I don't see—I don't see anything wrong with it ... kids can, you know, go to a different country for a semester, or go abroad for school so I don't think there's a problem with participating in it." She, too, appears to feel a state of separation between herself and the world of Mayfair, a place 15 miles from her home that she likens to another country.

Sasha, a graduate of the late 1990s, also talks of feeling marginalized in both worlds: "I felt some middle—like in the middle somewhere, like I'm not part of Mayfair, I'm not part of Urbana, cause both groups make us feel different and separate." She goes further:

> Because like I said, if people felt separate from the Mayfair community, some did, some didn't, and you still somewhat felt separate from the city public school students, and a little ostracized from like—you're like almost a snob. And you're almost a little bit villainized for having opportunities, depending on that personal situation.

Coretta, a graduate of the mid-2000s, says, "And sometimes, you know, you did have to juggle. Like you had to juggle with, you know, being at home, Urbana is home, but at the same time you're in a new environment that's not where you came from. So you had to juggle and just make the best of it." Serena, a graduate from a decade earlier, matter-a-factly explains her double life:

> It was like, you know, you kind of had to split your life where you had friends in Urbana that kind of looked at you like you thought you were better than them because you weren't going to school in Urbana, and then you spend most of your days out in Mayfair, where you kind of felt like you didn't fit in.

Monique says simply, "It was like catching it from both sides."

The situation for May, a graduate from the mid-2000s who attended an elite college in the Northeast, is even more challenging as a light-skinned Latina from an immigrant family. As for her feelings about her school, she states, "Even if it's your school community, it's not." She goes on to say, "I didn't feel like I was a, you know, a part of the urban community... And even though I made Mayfair what it was for myself, I was aware that that wasn't entirely my community. And that I was living in these two very distinct worlds."

May felt the triple sting of marginalization: not being fully a part of her home community, school community, or program. She describes a distinct form of marginalization, a distinct veil resulting from her ethnicity:

> ...it just added another layer. So it's like you're white and wealthy in Mayfair, you know, you may be a person of color and wealthy, you may be a person of color and not wealthy, then you're in [the program], and there was literally like 5-7 Latino students and everyone else was black, and the one Asian young woman.

She goes on to explain her marginality in greater detail:

> Because I was an outsider in some ways and like I was white in some ways, or I was made to feel that way even if I didn't identify that way because I've always had like a very strong affinity to being Honduran and being Latina and speaking Spanish and doing those things that really mattered to me a lot, and carrying my identity with me but I did feel that way a lot because of having to prove myself, and proving my not whiteness.

She recalls going shopping with white friends after school one day, an experience that was unexceptional. Later in the day she went out with friends of color and had an entirely different experience, followed by store employees. Her light skin tone provides her with unique insight and the ability to exist on both sides of the veil (Du Bois, 1903/1994). Although May has the racial option or flexibility (Waters 1990), it is an option that she finds burdensome and one which places her even further apart from others.

Chantel, a graduate of the mid-2000s, discusses feelings of liminality in a less extreme way, with even a suggestion of being part of both worlds, as opposed to being a part of neither.

> Because I don't feel like I am solely of Urbana—I definitely don't feel like I could ever identify as a Mayfairian, but I think it's—yeah—it's hard to separate the two, because I am of both. I think there always is this—as a young person interacting with other young Urbana residents, there was always a 'That's a Reach student and that's a public school student' differentiation.

There is a suggestion in her response that being of these two worlds provides benefits or insights. She seems to feel some attachment to both worlds, rather than feeling doubly rejected.

The Residents

Ironically, town residents, those who should theoretically feel the most connected to the school and community, discussed their feelings of marginalization and liminality in great detail. Eight of the ten residents of Mayfair—Alexandra, Jade, Hannah, Gabriella, Flore, Faith, Elisabeth, and Veronica—discussed ways in which they did not feel a part of their own community, leaving them in some ways without any real home.

White residents, teachers, and administrators frequently assumed they were either a part of Reach, the commuter program, or Aspire, the boarding program. Through this geographic misplacement, residents were stripped time and again of their sense of belonging in their own town. Oftentimes, this confusion came out as parents and teachers thought they were being helpful. They would offer rides to these women as students, assuming they were walking from the train station. Teachers would allow these women to skip detention or after-school assistance for fear that they would miss their buses "back home." They would excuse tardiness, assuming it was from all of the traffic and compliment mothers who drove their daughters to school "all the way from home." These women, who lived no more than a few miles from Mayfair High, soon caught onto the benefits of these assumptions—tardiness was acceptable and detentions could be avoided.

As Alexandra, the woman who began the chapter, says:

> Even in high school, if I was to miss the school bus, driving from my home to school probably takes less than 10 minutes. Less than 10 minutes—I will come in a little late, I'm like 'Ah I missed the bus, so my mom had to drive me.' They'd be like, 'Oh, that's very nice of your mother to drive you all the way here.' They're like, 'Yeah, don't worry about it' and I'm like, 'If only you knew I live 10 minutes away from here but I'm gonna let you believe that she drove me from the city to here.'

Jade describes a similar reaction from teachers: "If like something happened—like, 'Oh, Jade, you have detention,' and then they'll be like, 'Oh, the Reach bus doesn't have late bus today, so you can go home.' They'll assume because I'm black—they'll assume because I'm black I [don't live here]."

In describing an interaction with a white parent in town, Jade retells another story of geographic misplacement:

> ...In high school, I broke my foot. And my friend was pushing me—cause she parked her car—cause they had like senior parking, but you had to pay

for that, so she didn't want to pay for it, so she parked near the grocery store and she would push me on a wheel chair to school. And then one of the parents was like, 'If you ever need a ride from the train station, I'll be more than happy to bring you to school' and it was like, 'Oh, that was nice of her to say that.' Clearly she was assuming that we were coming from the city.

It is not clear from Jade's tone whether she really thinks it is nice of the woman to offer a ride, as good intentioned as it is, or whether Jade is stating it in a sarcastic sense, given that it assumes an otherness, placing her outside of her own community yet again.

Another woman, Hannah, discusses her interactions with Mayfair families in Riggens, the local shop where she worked during high school:

I think a lot of the time people think that I'm just a random girl at Riggens, but they don't realize that I live here, I grew up here...and literally I've been here since I was 2 years old. And I think people don't realize that. My dad always says the same thing, he works at Surefire in Fredericksburg, and he'll be like people will come in and talk about Mayfair, and he'll be like, 'Oh, yeah' and then he'll be like, 'I live in Mayfair too' and he's like they completely change...So I think that people probably think that, they think differently of me until they realize [pause]. I don't know, I talk about this with my mom all the time. It's just so weird.

Faith, a lifelong resident of Mayfair, who lives at home and commutes to a prestigious art academy, tells her own story of first recognizing racial difference and isolation. She says:

So my first memory of living in Mayfair, I just thought I was like everyone else, same skin color, everything. And then at school, we were playing house, and one girl was like, 'Oh, you can't be the sister, you can be the friend because you're a different race' and that's when the race talk happened. And so then I was kind of aware so there's different races.

She describes feeling "heartbroken" about this occurrence. This racial "ah ha!" moment is similar to one Du Bois retells 100 years prior in *The Soul of Black Folks* (1903/1994):

In a wee wooden schoolhouse, something put it into the boys' and girls' heads to buy gorgeous visiting-cards—ten cents a package—and exchange. The exchange was merry, till one girl, a tall newcomer, refused my card— refused it peremptorily, with a glance. Then it dawned upon me with a certain suddenness that I was different from the others; or like, mayhap, in heart and life and longing, but shut out from their world by a vast veil. (p.2)

The differences of gender, time, and place seem to melt away when hearing two stories that are virtually indistinguishable. The sense of otherness and the presence of the veil continue to exist.

Later in elementary school, Faith experienced the geographic misplacement described by other residents, but in a more extreme way when she was mistakenly put on the Reach bus, and taken into Urbana, the nearby city from which the commuter students came. She tells her story, "And on my first day of school, I got put on the bus to Urbana with the Reach kids, and that was a huge thing because it was like we got all the way there before they realized that I was not one of the Reach students, so that was also kind of a wake-up call, and so ever since then I've been very sensitive to race." The teacher who placed her on the bus made a public apology the next day, but Faith describes that as only making her more uncomfortable. She just wanted to be out of the spotlight. Faith explains it as ignorance, rather than malice, but the sting of presumed otherness has never completely lifted.

Another resident of color, Sara, tells of her "ah ha!" moment in sixth grade—the moment at which she realized that she was different, and that such difference was a problem. The child of a highly educated and successful North African immigrant, she brought a hijab to school to show her classmates. They began asking her questions as to whether her father was a terrorist and if she knew those involved with the 9/11 attacks. She was devastated.

Sara's light complexion led to both unique insight and significant challenges. Like May, the Latina commuter student who discusses her experiences on both sides of the veil (Du Bois, 1903/1994) because of her skin tone, Sara finds life both easier and harder than her darker skinned peers. Of feeling connected and a part of the school and community, she says, "I would definitely attribute that to that fact that I'm also white, though...." At the same time, she says about white classmates, "And I think that's the thing that was really annoying for me because they would almost think that I was on their team or on their side or like I wouldn't have an issue with racist comments that they would make" because she was light skinned.

Veronica, a former town resident, also speaks explicitly to the role of race. During high school, she dated a white boy from a prestigious family. She thinks her connection to him gave her a "pass" and helped her to be more accepted socially. Even with this connection, she still encountered barriers and stereotypes as a woman of color. She describes it this way:

> I'd say multiple teachers would say, 'Oh, you're doing so well in my class, you know, all of my Aspire students do so well.' I'm like, 'Oh, wow, I'm glad I'm doing well, but I live here.' And that was another thing, if you were doing well, you were lumped in with the Aspire students. If you had issues or there was some sort of problem, usually they would lump you in with the Reach students.

She is describing the white community's categorization of the boarding students as the deserving and gifted, and the commuting students as the low-performing troublemakers. Veronica encountered other barriers and assumptions, as well. She and her high school boyfriend married after college and returned to live in Mayfair. They decided to move out after she was presumed to be their child's nanny one too many times. Local residents interpreted her skin tone as a marker of foreignness, negating the possibility that she could be their neighbor.

Elisabeth, a woman who lived and attended school in Mayfair for only her senior year during the mid-2000s, similarly felt marginalized. She says, "I felt I was outside of both groups," both the group of students of color who largely came from outside of Mayfair and the group of white students who hailed from the town.

This sense of liminality and marginalization of the residents of color is not lost on the Reach and Aspire girls. Commuters and boarders were clear on the perception of race and belonging in the community. Yolanda, a commuter, told a similar story to Faith's about a friend of hers who had grown up in town and was placed on the bus to go "home." She says, "Like my friend Jamal, he grew up in Mayfair. He's black though, and one day they put him on the Urbana bus. They didn't even know he lived in Mayfair ... he lived in Mayfair but I think the community assumed that all black kids were from Urbana." Karenna, a boarder, tells the same story. It is not clear whether it is the same town resident to whom Yolanda referred.

The speech patterns and vocabulary that mark the Reach and Aspire girls as too foreign in their home environments are not enough to override the skin color that presumes foreignness of residents in the town of Mayfair. Race continues to matter in late twentieth—and early twenty-first-century Mayfair, although the role that it plays varies by group. For the Aspire students, they are the standouts and exceptions, those deserving of the town's largess. For the Reach students, they are the stereotypical urban, underclass. For the residents, they are the "other."

"Sexlessness" and the Completion of Liminality

Turner (1969) argues that another common characteristic of the liminal experience is a sense of "sexlessness and anonymity." This particular aspect of marginalization, of living between two worlds, must be understood as both a racialized and gendered experience. More precisely, the intersectionality of race and gender (Collins 2000; Crenshaw 1989, 1993) is more than just additive, but translates into a distinct experience for women of color. Du Bois (1903/1994) clearly grasps the unique space in which women of color live, discussing in his essay the *Damnation of Women*, the less desirable status they hold, vis-à-vis their white peers.

This sense of being unattractive, undesirable, and even invisible to the opposite sex is a theme that appears in the data, even though no explicit questions were asked about dating, sex, or romantic relationships, unless the participant first raised the topic. Interestingly, this sense of romantic marginalization appears to vary by residential setup, with commuters and boarders raising the issue more frequently and with greater feeling than did residents, even though the latter suggested very high levels of existing in a liminal space, generally.

Commuters

Seven commuters, ranging in age from those who graduated in the 1980s to those who graduated in the 2000s, discussed the experience of romantic marginality, suggesting the durability of the racialized and gendered hierarchy in American society and echoing findings from Ispa-Landa's (2013) work on the gendered experiences of students of color in a racial desegregation program in New England.

Lorraine, who graduated in the 1980s, recalls discussing her boyfriends with her own teenage daughter.

> You know I was telling my daughter, you know because she was asking me, you know, who were my boyfriends when I was growing up, and I never dated anybody from high school cause there was, I mean there was, in our grade, it was me, Angela, Damita, Sharon, and Yvonne. So throughout elementary school and middle school and the beginning of high school, there

were 5 girls. And then the boys were Jackie, Greg, Bobby, and Darnell. There was only four boys. So the pickings were kind of slim, and I didn't really like any of them.

When I ask her about dating white boys, she responds by saying, "Uh, yeah, that never even, that never even entered my mind as a kid to date somebody outside my race."

Although in this case, the lack of interest appears to be more mutual, in other cases, the women give a sense of feeling actively rejected and stigmatized. Serena, a graduate of the mid-1990s, delves into a discussion of what romantic relationships looked like in high school in trying to explain her feelings of isolation:

> Especially more into high school, when you're supposed to have that experience where you get a crush on the football player—especially being on the cheer leading squad, like the football player's supposed to have a crush on, or, you know, like a football player likes you, I knew off the bat that that was never going to happen out there. And as far as the dances, I never wanted to go to any of the dances because that would mean I'd have to ask somebody outside of the school to come in...I would never have that experience with somebody in my school asking me to a dance because at the time, we got to high school, all the boys—the [commuter] boys had been kicked out and it just, you know, we just were never going to have that experience, and then they stopped allowing outside students to come in, so I would never have a date to a dance.

When I follow up this statement with the question about dating white boys, Serena responds by saying, "But no, none of the Mayfair boys would never, ever have dated a black girl, no. It didn't happen." Serena's comments also speak to how marginalization in one arena lead to other forms of marginalization; by not having a date, she did not go to dances. Joslin, a Reach participant who graduated in the mid-1990s, echoes these sentiments: "In Mayfair, the black girls are taboo. The black boys don't like us and the white guys are like, 'Uh, no. I wouldn't even be caught dead looking at her.'" These women are speaking to the notion of stigma, whereby they are deemed as off limits and unacceptable by virtue of their skin tone, what Erving Goffman would refer to as "tribal" stigma or the stigma of group identity (1986).

Yolanda, a Reach graduate of the late 1990s, discusses how she dated boys of color from Urbana, the city from which she commuted, with one particular boyfriend having done jail time. She says, "And my mother hated him...He wasn't allowed in the house. But I was attracted to that because the white boys didn't like me." She later found out that a white boy in her school did have a crush on her. She retells the story about confronting him: "So then I found out that he liked me. And he was like, 'Well, you know, it's not like we can really go out, the whole white black thing. I was like 'What?' But I was shocked A. that he liked me and then B. his reasoning was because he didn't want to be ostracized, right, for dating a black girl."

Two Reach graduates also explicitly discuss feeling unattractive within the climate of Mayfair. A graduate from the mid-2000s, Deana states, "...You go through your own struggle of beauty, what's supposed to be acceptable, how you're supposed to look—all of those things are a result of [attending school in Mayfair]." Sasha, a graduate from nearly ten years earlier, states, "We never dated in Mayfair." She goes on to discuss why she and her female classmates of color who commuted to Mayfair dated boys from their home communities, rather than their classmates.

> ...It's almost like this is how I felt in high school: I felt like because the boys—my brothers—and maybe even the other male Reach students—because they're in that environment, that is the standard of beauty. Do you know what I'm saying? I just felt it. I feel like, when I—cause you hear Urbana guys talking a lot and who they look at and they were describing me. The guys in the neighborhood were describing me. That's their ideal of beauty. And so that's how I felt. I'm going to go where I'm wanted. And so it was just a different vibe.

These comments reinforce the findings of earlier research (Ispa-Landa 2013) in which girls of color are described as being too loud and aggressive within the elite, predominantly white high school context. They fail to measure up to the white, middle-class norms of beauty and femininity.

There are a few instances of interracial dating among the commuters, examples of women being able to move out of this romantically marginalized state, but they are few. For example, Noel states:

> That's where I learned to have an open pallet for dating. So even to this day, I don't—I don't have a preference. My family always says they never know. I don't have a preference. I dated some of the [commuter] boys, I dated some of the white boys, I dated different kinds of white boys. I just remember that that was where I learned that life could be bigger than what some people may see it to be.

Boarders

Four Aspire boarding students—Elise, Isabel, Karenna, and Alana—also discuss feelings of marginalization on the dating front. Elise says in an eloquent, but painful way:

> I also felt a void in terms of relationships because I think in high school that's when you have boyfriends and girlfriends, and I didn't really have those experiences. It's almost as if I felt invisible because in Ridgeford, even when I was in middle school I had a boyfriend. You have relationships and, you get the cutesy cat calls—not that I was asking for them, but you feel acknowledged. And going through the town of Mayfair, it's like, 'Am I not part of this…am I not a part of this hunt?' so to speak.

Elise goes on to say that other Aspire girls with whom she lived had similar experiences.

Isabel, one of the most successful graduates in terms of academic outcomes, but one who remains scarred in many ways by her time in the community, also discusses the differing standards of beauty: "I just wasn't part of that standard of beauty in high school. I always felt different from them. I just never felt that anybody could be attached to me because of how I looked." This comment echoes the sentiments of Deana and Sasha, but sadly, Isabel seems to have internalized these feelings to a greater extent.

And, Alana, a boarder from 30 years prior, speaks of the practical consequences of these feelings and patterns of behavior, stating, "That's probably why we didn't go to cotillion, why some people didn't go to prom. I mean, if you didn't have a date, why would you go?" These practical implications echo Serena's comments, a commuter student from a decade later, who discusses not going to dances because she did not have a date.

The Aspire girls were also rendered "off limits" by the rules of the program, which highly discouraged any form of dating. Isabel talks about a roommate who was sanctioned by the board for having a boyfriend. Karenna talks about board members of the program "flipping out" because she was dating someone at the high school. In this way, the young women of color are made "sexless" and placed "off limits" through another channel, one that is structural.

Among the boarders, there is one mention of dating a town resident. Christina, a boarder who graduated in the mid-2000s, did have a white boyfriend. She says, "I was dating this guy who was white. He joined the

Step Team and it was really cool." Christina discusses spending a lot of time with his family and even staying over at his house, but this example is clearly the exception to the rule, just as Noel seems to be the exception among commuting students.

Residents

Interestingly, the town residents who discussed high levels of marginality within the community, being identified as outsiders and, in one case, even placed on a bus and sent to Urbana with the Reach commuters, are less likely to discuss this form of romantic or sexual marginalization. Of the residents interviewed, only two discuss marginalization in this sphere. Gabriella, a former town resident from the mid-2000s who has been a frequent participant in beauty pageants, says, "I don't think the Mayfair men found us too attractive." She talks of having wanted "blue eyes and blonde hair," suggesting an internalization of the white American standard of beauty. Another woman also discusses the cultural standard of beauty within the community, although not by name. Hannah, in discussing her sister who went on to become a model, states, "I think my sister might have said like, 'Oh, I wish I had white girl hair' or like something, like my sister definitely used to say that." These comments are similar to those made by Deana and Sasha, both commuters, in regard to the racialized nature of beauty standards.

The town residents actually show more evidence of interracial dating than do commuters and boarders, with three of them discussing having had white boyfriends. Hannah, who discusses her sister wishing for "white girl hair," also talks about her own experiences dating. She says, "I had a boyfriend in high school that probably never would have dated a black girl, and then he met me." Flore, a socially integrated town resident from an immigrant family, states:

> I had white boyfriends. I dated really affluent people from really affluent families and it's—there are certain things—like I said, it didn't matter to some people because they just—as long as you're, you know, well-rounded and things like that, it's—it doesn't matter. You know, it doesn't matter—it shouldn't matter.

Another woman, Veronica, married her white high school boyfriend, illustrating the highest degree of integration one can reach.

Variation Across Groups

Although in many ways the town residents are in the most precarious position, having no clear psychological home to which to return, they do illustrate somewhat higher levels of romantic integration, not necessarily possessing the same degree of "sexlessness" as their commuter or boarder peers. And, while both the commuters and the boarders illustrate this theme of "sexlessness," the implications vary based upon point of access.

In multiple instances, commuters discuss dating boys from their neighborhood. As Sasha says, "The guys in the neighborhood were describing me. That's their ideal of beauty. And so that's how I felt. I'm going to go where I'm wanted." Although Yolanda's mother may have had a problem with some of her choices of high school boyfriends, Yolanda *had* choices. Other commuters, such as Lorraine, Edith, and Serena, echo this sentiment, discussing going to dances and proms with boys from home or, in a few cases, boys of color from the commuter program.[1]

The commuter students may feel significant amounts of liminality growing out of their constant shuttling back and forth between two worlds, but that daily shuttling does permit the maintenance of two sets of social networks. These women are able to retain some sense of self and confidence in their attractiveness, as their dual frames of reference provide them with ongoing contact with both worlds. This is not an option available to the boarders who are living hundreds of miles from home. They do not have the dating options afforded to the female commuters, who may complain that the "pickings are slim" as Lorraine says, but there are "pickings," nonetheless.

The Gendered Nature of Romantic Marginalization

So, is this romantic marginalization and "sexlessness" characteristic of those living in liminal spaces, generally, or is there a gendered component to it? Although I only interviewed women for this project, five of the women with whom I spoke—Lorraine, Joslin, Yolanda, Sasha, and Elise—suggest a clear intersection between race and gender. They discuss brothers, friends, and other men of color who they viewed as having significantly greater romantic options.

This concept of intersectionality has a long history in the literature, with women of color experiencing unique challenges from both men of color and white women (Du Bois, 1903/1994; Hill Collins 2000; Crenshaw

1989, 1993). For example, research finds that young men of color, even in the same social context, have greater social and romantic options, vis-à-vis their female counterparts who fail to meet the white, middle-class definition of beauty and femininity (Holland 2012; Ispa-Landa 2013).

Lorraine, one of the earliest graduates in the study from the mid-1980s, states, "What I find is that, and you know it's still true to this day, is that the guys, they would go after the white girls." Joslin, a graduate from the mid-1990s, also reflects on the larger societal responses to a black woman-white man relationship, just as Lorraine does, and comes to a similar conclusion:

> It is weird, and society is still kind of like that where black men are comfortable and the white girls are comfortable to date each other, whether your families have a problem with it or not, but white guys—like they can think black girls are hot and they're not going to come up to you. It's not going to happen. It just doesn't look good I guess. With Mayfair, you don't get someone saying, 'Oh, come to prom with me' or, 'Let's hangout' or whatever. Never.

Elise, a woman in the boarding program who graduated in the mid-2000s, notes a similar trend: "And the black men at our school, if you participate in a sport, you're very much, oh you know, make up a name 'Mike'—people fawn over you. Women fawn over you. Girls fawn over you, but if you're a black woman, you don't get that same attention."

And two women cite specific examples of this dating pattern. Yolanda talks about a male member of the commuter program. She says:

> A lot of people didn't, even though he was [a commuter], he didn't hang with us the way that he—he hung out more with the Mayfair residents. He'd stay the night out there a lot, and possibly because of him being an athlete, he had to be out there and he also dated white women because they were throwing themselves at him—

Sasha talks about her younger brother, also a graduate of Mayfair through the commuter program and now a college student, who has a white girlfriend from Mayfair. He continues to spend significant amounts of time at her home. These direct observations of male family and friends and broader notes about the state of the community suggest a climate that is uniquely challenging and marginalizing for women of color.

The Role of Physical Barriers in the Production of Difference

Up to this point, the sense of liminality and isolation has largely been discussed in terms of symbolic barriers—barriers around language and accent, opportunities and interests, preferences and ideas around belonging. Women in the study also discuss a series of physical factors that lead to and grow out of this sense of liminality and marginality.

The Commute and the School Bus

The commute plays a critical role in the Reach students' sense of liminality, of existing between two physically distinct spaces. Although Eaton (2001) in her book on a cross-district racial integration program in Massachusetts discusses the theme of the commute as a defining factor of her subjects' experiences, the discussion of the commute and, specifically, the school bus is limited. Early risings and trips to the bus stop are discussed among the commuters in Eaton's study, but Eaton does not explore the ways in which the commute creates and reinforces an outsider status. Thirteen of fifteen commuters interviewed discuss the role of the commute as a barrier to integration in the school community, furthering feelings of marginalization. These long commutes also limit time with friends in the home community, completing the sense of liminality.

Andrea, a graduate of the 2000s, says, "Going to school in Mayfair, it changed your day. So I didn't get home until 4:30. And then by the time you do homework, I had to be in by street lights, so I didn't do too much hanging out...." Patricia also connects the long commute with the inability to maintain friendships at home. Michelle says, "You know, you weren't in any one of your communities enough time to be a whole part of that community." She says she did not really see her city friends until the summer because her days in Mayfair were so long with the commute. The geographic distance between home and school serves as a physical barrier that encourages feelings of liminality.

Further, it is critical to note the role of the physical school bus, in addition to the commute, in the lives of these women. The bus serves as both a symbolic and physical barrier that marks groups. Coretta says, "Although you do make friends that already live in Mayfair, but they're not exactly your peers, you know, you feel like your peers are whoever I come to school on the bus with. That's my group." Sasha echoes this sentiment. Sara, a town resident, says that commuter students were often criticized for being "cliquey," sitting together in a group in the cafeteria in the morning before school started. Sara attributes this tendency to the bus. She says:

> People tended to think that kids in the commuter program isolated themselves, but I wouldn't say that's the case. I would say that other kids wouldn't make an effort to get to know them. I mean these kids are coming in on the bus system early in the morning from the time that they're in elementary school. They're going to talk to the kids around them—the friends that they're going to make—it completely makes sense.

Sara continues on:

> ...Cause they come to school at like 7 every day. So that's where they go early in the morning—an area in the cafeteria to hangout. They sit down before classes start—people usually sit in the cafeteria once they trickle in, before classes start. And I just think they're sitting as a group because they came in as a group and they're friends with each other.

The school bus is the literal vehicle by which the students move between two worlds, marking geographic or physical distance, but it also has other implications, drawing symbolic boundaries and barriers.

The end-of-day announcement of the commuter bus is another means by which commuter students feel difference. Deana talks about the many issues they had with the administration: "Down to how we're called by the intercom when the bus is here." She talks about the students being referred to as commuter students, with the commuter bus having arrived to take them home, making them feel further distanced from Mayfair. Noel makes a similar comment about how the commuter bus is identified at the end of the day. She says, "What I didn't like was a lot of the labeling. I didn't like, 'Urbana kids, your bus is here. Urbana kids, your bus is here.'" At a PTO meeting I attended over the course of data collection, a Mayfair teacher of color stated that he cringes anytime the commuter school bus arrives late and the announcement over the high school intercom states, "The Reach bus is late today." As he says, they do not make that announcement when the bus from the west side of town is late.

Yolanda discusses another way in which the commuters felt marginalized by the transportation situation.

And then there was another time where senior week, we didn't really get a chance to participate in a lot of things as Reach seniors because of the timing of things. And on our last—like towards the end of school, we decided to have a water fight right on the bus. So the bus driver didn't know. Of course it wasn't safe. But, everybody had like water balloons and super soakers, and as we left Mayfair, we just went into this all out water fight. And as punishment, they took the bus away from us. And so we had to take the subway in.

One woman, Sasha, recalls her mother's experience with school bussing and buses: "I'm surprised that she was so open to [the commuter program] because she did have some negative experiences like being on a bus and white kids throwing beer cans at you, you know? That type of stuff." Although in a different time and place, the physical school bus stands as a marker of difference and otherness.

The Cafeteria

Although the geographic distance and school bus are symbolic and physical markers specific to commuter students, the physical setup of the high school allows for separation and encourages feelings of difference among students of color, generally. The physical area most frequently cited by women in the study as allowing for racial separation is the cafeteria, in keeping with Beverly Tatum's (2003) aptly named book *Why Do All the Black Kids Sit Together in the Cafeteria?* Tatum argues that students of color, particularly as they reach middle and high school and attempt to come to terms with their place in a racially charged society, seek out periods of "downtime" and comfort from those going through similar experiences. Lunchtime is often one of the few times during the day when students of color can be alone together. Unlike the school bus, which serves as both a symbolic and physical barrier over which students of color have little control, the physical separation in the cafeteria is to some extent a choice, a setting in which these students can exert preferences. Carter (2007) similarly found that cafeteria self-segregation in a predominantly white high school provides students of color a positive, self-affirming space in an often hostile and isolating environment.

As Deana, a Reach commuter student, says in talking about the setup of the cafeteria and the segregation, "It was comfortable. And I was okay with the comfort because I felt like I was uncomfortable in many other places in the building." Malia, a boarder, makes a similar comment about the separation:

> It was always kind of a little bit segregated, but not because we didn't want to interact. It was more so going through the whole day of classes mostly being the only black person in class. Or you know, we had nothing to talk to some people about from the day, so it's like lunchtime or a free period we just want to have the opportunity to hang out with people who are like us.

More than half of the women interviewed in this study discuss the physical separation permitted by the structure of the cafeteria. Six of ten residents, six of fifteen commuters, and eight of twelve boarders discuss the "balc," a separate space within the cafeteria. Gabriella, a former resident, states, "I don't know if it's still there, and I hope it's not the same, but yes, the lunchrooms were segregated." Alexandra, a town resident who graduated approximately a decade ago, says, "We did segregate ourselves." Tasha, a boarder, also states that the high school cafeteria was "super segregated." Yolanda, a commuter, says, "We did not go in the cafeteria except to get our food, and we would eat upstairs with each other." Hannah, a resident and more recent graduate, says, "We'd call it Africa up there, and then we'd call it America down here, so the balc, where all the black kids sit. And it's been like that since—my dad went to Mayfair High School—it's been like that since he was there." Isabel, a boarder, also references the balc as "Africa," as does Sara, a town resident. The term "Africa" may have been started by the white students, but as with other group slurs, they are at times re-appropriated by the group being targeted.

A few women talk about how the physical separation at lunchtime led to what they felt was targeted monitoring and unequal treatment by the teachers, only furthering feelings of difference and a desire for greater separation. Noel, a commuter, says, "It really did feel like racial profiling. 'Like why are you up here? They're downstairs having a food fight and you're up here watching us.'" Noel and her friends learn to manipulate the veil in their own way. She says, "And sometimes, we would just whisper at lunch, just to see them move closer to hear what we were saying." Serena, a commuter from the early 1990s, similarly discusses unequal treatment by the faculty of the high school:

> And it was always like they'd come to us, 'Okay, you guys need to break it up and spread out a little bit.' And, we're like, 'Why? We're just, you know, kind of sitting here.' And then the football team could be, you know, all rowdy downstairs and no one is saying anything to them, but with us it's like, 'Break it up, break it up.'

But, "breaking it up" is not nearly as easy as all that, for while the faculty and administrators may have wanted to see greater racial integration in the lunch room, the students, both students of color and white students, guard the borders. Noel says about where she and her fellow classmates of color sat, "We didn't choose it. When we got there as freshman, you just followed the older kids, and that's where we sat." Christina, Tasha, and Marian, boarders from years apart, talk of beginning their high school experience sitting on the balc because that's where the older girls sat. As Tasha says, "I did what the older students did." They are simply following the unwritten rules of Mayfair High, rules written and reinforced by both white students and students of color.

When boundaries, both symbolic and physical, were breached by sitting in the "wrong" place, students sanctioned one another. Yolanda tells of a white friend of hers having lunch on the balc with her. Afterward, the friend told Yolanda, "You know, people were upset that I was up there sitting with you guys." Flore, a resident, who sat both upstairs with the students of color and downstairs with her white friends from sports teams, would be called names such as "Oreo" by her fellow students of color. She was accused of thinking she was better than them. Hannah, a very attractive, three-season athlete, was told by her friends of color, "You never sit up here." She did not take the comments seriously, but they were made nonetheless.

Women tell of being scared to break the accepted code. Gabriella still scolds herself for not going against the norm. Marian, who had the status, due in large part to her looks and her integration through sports, to break the structural boundaries, still experienced sanctions. She describes being scared to sit downstairs when she first arrived in Mayfair, fearful of breaking some unwritten rule. Her friends of color would say of her, "Marian's with the white people today" when she sat downstairs. Gabriella talks about the white students who were able to sit upstairs. Like Marian, they held a certain position within the student body that allowed them to break boundaries. They were "probably top of the class—the smart ones… they were respected anyway because of how highly, how well they did in their classes." They, like Marian, had the status to cross boundaries.

MONEY AS A BARRIER IN MAYFAIR

Race and gender are not the only factors that shape these women's experiences. As Wilson has long pointed out (Wilson 1980, 1987, 2015), race and class interact in important ways. Being a woman of color presents a set of barriers in American society, in general. The intersection of being a woman of color and of more modest means presents distinct challenges in a community such as Mayfair. Even those who are from more middle-class households find themselves in a world of wealth with which most are unfamiliar.

Boarders

Half of the boarders in Aspire explicitly talk about feeling like charity cases—people assumed that they could not afford various items, parents of white students offered them money, and they felt the need to defend their parents' ability to care for them. Whether or not money was tight at home, the assumption of being in need was widespread and marginalizing. As a small number of high-achieving, often lower-to-moderate income woman of color who boarded, they found themselves in a highly isolated position. The "noblesse oblige" attitude that multiple boarders experienced from white Mayfair residents left them, at times, feeling alone and defensive.

Although some boarding students do come from households solidly in the middle of the economic spectrum, others do come from stark economic conditions. Priscilla says, "I didn't really understand how poor we were until I went to Mayfair." She says, "Mom always had food for us," but this is in comparison to the extreme wealth Priscilla is first exposed to at age 13 in her new community. Jaqui, a graduate of the boarding program 15 years later, echoes these sentiments almost exactly, saying, "I didn't realize how poor I was until I went to Mayfair." She says, "Initially you were just shocked." Isabel, a more recent graduate, says, "Just looking around me it was just a reminder of how poor, and black I was." This point of comparison, one which Isabel never had before arriving in Mayfair, translates into feelings of self-loathing, "I never felt worse." Being a young woman of color and living in an elite, white environment is challenging to begin with, but the barriers are only made worse when class becomes a part of the equation. This environment, one which becomes the de facto home for the boarding students, is both physically and symbolically a new world, and one in which barriers abound.

Tasha, a full-time graduate student in an art program, came from a lower-middle-class family where she had "tons of toys" and did a slew of extracurricular activities. She talked about an eye-opening experience in Mayfair when she and her friends were turning 16. In trying to explain the barriers that existed and the sense of marginalization, she says, "For example, for my birthday I got my first cell phone. Another friend I had at Mayfair got a Range Rover...So I was like, 'Wow!'" Isabel also talks about students getting cars at age 16. Malia discusses the economic differences and its implications for the creation of barriers. She says everyone outside of the boarding and commuter programs were, "White and from Mayfair you know, were higher SES...They all had nice cars and they dressed nice and you know, they always wanted to go out and do stuff. I would say that they're pretty different from me."

Commuters

Money, or the lack, also impacts Reach commuter students, although it seems to play a less extreme role than for the boarding students. The Reach students may have had some exposure to this environment at an earlier age, and they additionally have their homes to return to nightly, suggesting the benefit of a dual reference frame (Lee and Zhou 2015). The social and cultural capital, emanating from the homes and communities with which they still have nightly contact, likely serve as important resources to these daily commuters, as has been identified in prior research on black students straddling multiple worlds (Carter 2003, 2006, 2012).

Yolanda talks about both racial and class differences acting as barriers in Mayfair: "We realized, 'Oh you're white, I'm black, you're rich, I'm middle-class,' and then things started to change." Coretta, a solidly middle-class woman from a two-parent household, talks about the extreme differences in wealth and thinks the transition might be easier for students of color if there was "not such a drastic change from going from the inner city to this crazy, rich town or anything like that." Andrea says, "So, if I was staying at a host parent's house or went to a friend's house, I mean, they have beautiful homes, they're driving luxury cars."

Yolanda, Coretta, and Sasha also talk about the role of cars in delineating difference, a topic raised by Aspire students Tasha, Isabel, and Malia. Yolanda says, "By the time we got to the driving age, seeing some of my friends driving Range Rovers and Porsches and Mercedes and, you know, I had a little Mitsubishi that my mom would let me drive sometimes." Coretta similarly compares her means of transportation to those of her peers in Mayfair: "I got to grow up in this town that was so, you know, so manicured and 16 year olds have Mercedes Benzes and I have a Chevy Cavalier. There was a huge difference." Sasha, a woman from a two-parent, middle-class household, compares her means of getting home, via a "bus pass," with that of her classmates, a BMW. Having access to a car at age 16 suggests a certain level of privilege in its own right, but when comparing a Chevy or Mitsubishi to a Range Rover or BMW, life begins to look very different and a sense of relative disadvantage ensues.

Residents

For those Mayfair residents who were lower-income, the intersection of race and class led to particular feelings of marginalization as they had no other point of comparison; there exists no dual frame of reference from which they could draw feelings of strength and self-worth. Mayfair, generally speaking, is the only world they knew. The barriers to overcome are multiple and, in many ways, magnified by living and going to school in this setting. Alexandra, responding to a question on her sense of belonging in Mayfair, had the following to say:

> I feel like I was in my own kind of class when it came to everything. I wasn't completely accepted by all the Mayfair people because I'm not rich like the rest of them and I don't have money like the rest of them and I'm black, and then when it came to the Reach kids, I wasn't one of them, because I live in Mayfair. I don't go into Urbana so they just assume I'm not street smart so I didn't fit in completely with them due to that. And so it's just like my own type of thing—I was in my own category—a black girl that was in Mayfair.

Flore, a woman who grew up in Section 8 housing, recalls feeling particularly left out as one of the few women of color who attended the school as a town resident. For Flore, the intersectionality of race and class placed her outside of her own community. In discussing her relationship with white students and families who lived in Mayfair, Flore says, "They assumed—and it's funny, even friends that, and even white people they assumed that I was from Mayfair and it's not until they would drop me off [in Section 8]—they're like, 'Oh!'" Flore is from Mayfair, but seems not to view herself in that way. Du Bois (1903/1994) would argue that the benefit of possessing "second sight" is seeing the world from multiple perspectives, but the danger is only seeing yourself through the eyes of the other.

Hannah, a woman with racially integrated social networks, struggled in her relationships because of her economic constraints. She says, "A lot of my friends would spend so much money and be like, 'Let's do this, let's do this' and I'd be like, 'I can't. My parents don't have money like that.'" For Hannah, the issue is more connected to class than to race. Brianna, a younger resident of Section 8 who is biracial, makes a similar comment:

> I come from a low-income family, so knowing a lot of my friends could like, had like money that they could just buy whatever they wanted and kind of do whatever they wanted. [It] was a little bit challenging for me because I couldn't always do the things that they could, which was a little straining...

As with the boarders and commuters, the issue of cars arises. Gabriella talks of getting her license and how this new phase highlighted differences. She says, "At 16, all my friends got brand new Beemers and Mercedes Benz and I had a friend who was flipping out because daddy got her a black one instead of whatever, hot red, and here I come in my '93 Honda Civic. Yeah, it was completely different. So yeah, some of them, you know, fell off, we didn't hangout."

The Reach students see the challenges faced by lower-income residents in Mayfair. Serena and Joslin, both graduates of the commuter program, say the wealthy, white students referred to the road on which the majority of Section 8 housing is found as "Urban Lane" or "Hidlington," the name of a less wealthy town next door. May, another commuter, discusses her observations: "How your teachers treated you and how they didn't, right, and when you look at race and residential ways, right, it's like some of them live in Section 8 and all of these things that just make them stand out in different ways." Yolanda also talks about the intersection of class and race and how it affected this particular subset. Referring to the residents of color, she says, "And then most of the Mayfair community were like, 'Oh, you're poor. You're one of them.' And so they definitely hung out more with the commuter students, but in particular, the commuter students that lived in subsidized housing as well." Monique similarly talks about the lower-income students in Mayfair, saying, "In Mayfair, you know, Mayfair had a lower-income area. And so it was like okay, the Mayfair kids, the commuter kids, and the Section 8 kids, so even amongst them, even though everybody has a Mayfair address, I recall that there was kind of segregation between those two groups." To be a lower-income girl of color is to face multiple barriers to inclusion.

Conclusion

Again and again, women tell stories of marginalization in multiple worlds. Those who came to Mayfair for greater educational and social opportunities encountered various barriers within the school and community. Barriers, which are both physical and symbolic, appear to be primarily race-based, but also have economic and gendered components. For many, symbolic boundaries exist around the formation of friendships, romantic relationships, and a general sense of belonging in Mayfair; physical barriers limit the amount of time women have to develop or maintain friendships in either world, and even where they can and should sit at lunchtime. The presence of these women of color in Mayfair suggests attempts at school desegregation, but their experiences suggest a lack of integration. Contemporaneously, they also begin to see and feel the construction of new boundaries in their old worlds, positioning them in a liminal space. This sense of liminality is present among both commuters and boarders, although the smaller numbers, lack of a nightly "touch point," and, in a few cases, extremely low-income homes translate into particularly strong feelings of both marginality and liminality for the latter group. While these young women, both commuters and boarders, may be receiving an education that they would be hard-pressed to get in their home communities, the findings here suggest that much more concern needs to be paid to their mental health and social well-being. Both the district and the specific programs should consider additional forms of support, perhaps in the form of a social worker or school psychologist, who could provide these young women of color with the tools and emotional backing that they need in this environment.

Those who live in Mayfair, many of whom have no other point of comparison, are frequently told in both word and deed that they do not fully belong there. These women, while experiencing some of the same racial and economic barriers to inclusion as their out-of-town counterparts, encounter distinct stereotypes and assumptions of otherness. They are assumed to be from elsewhere in a form of geographic misplacement. They appear to be somewhat more integrated in terms of romantic relationships, but remain on the margins in many ways.

In the absence of a physical or symbolic home in Mayfair, women create a new community, one that grows up in the liminal space in which they find themselves. The next chapter, "The Making of Community," examines the connection between feelings of liminality and the sense of community that develops among women of color in Mayfair.

Note

1. It should be noted that a few women discuss certain dances in which the school did not allow dates from outside of the community, a policy that would most likely impact the commuter students and, as a result, further marginalize them. It appears to be a policy only applied to certain events, however, and possibly during certain time periods.

Bibliography

Carter, P. 2012. *Stubborn Roots*. Oxford: Oxford University Press.
———. 2006. Straddling Boundaries: Identity, Culture, and School. *Sociology of Education* 79(4): 304–328.
———. 2007. Why the Black Kids Sit Together at The Stairs: The Role of Identity-Affirming Counter-Spaces in a Predominantly White High School. *Journal of Negro Education* 76(4): 542–554.
———. 2003. "Black" Cultural Capital, Status Positioning, and Schooling Conflicts for Low-Income African American Youth. *Social Problems* 50(1): 136–155.
Collins, P. 2000. *Black Feminist Thought: Knowledge, Consciousness, & the Politics of Empowerment*. New York: Routledge.
Cookson, P., and C. Persell. 1991. Race and Class in America's Elite Boarding Schools: African Americans as the "Outsiders Within". *The Journal of Negro Education* 60: 219–228.
Crenshaw, K. (1989). Demarginalizing the Intersection of Race and Sex: A Black Feminist Critique of Antidiscrimination Doctrine, Feminist Theory, and Antiracist Politics. *University of Chicago Legal Forum*, Issue 1.
———. 1993. Mapping the Margins: Intersectionality, Identity Politics, and Violence Against Women of Color. *Stanford Law Review* 43(6): 1241–1299.
Du Bois, W. 1994. *The Souls of Black Folks*. New York: Dover Publications.
Eaton, S. 2001. *The Other Boston Busing Story*. New Haven: Yale University Press.
Goffman, E. 1986. *Stigma: Notes on the Management of a Spoiled Identity*. New York: Simon and Schuster.
Holland, M. 2012. Only Here for the Day: The Social Integration of Minority Students at a Majority White High School. *Sociology of Education* 85(2): 101–120.
Horvat, E., and A. Antonio. 1999. "Hey, Those Shoes Are Out of Uniform": African American Girls in an Elite High School and the Importance of Habitus. *Anthropology & Education Quarterly* 30(3): 317–342.
Ispa-Landa, S. 2013. Gender, Race, and Justifications for Group Exclusion: Urban Black Students Bussed to Affluent Suburban Schools. *Sociology of Education* 86(3): 218–233.

Jencks, C., and P. Peterson. 1991. *The Urban Underclass*. Washington, DC: Brookings Institute.

Khan, S. 2011. *Privilege: The Making of an Adolescent Elite at St. Paul's School*. Princeton and Oxford: Princeton University Press.

Lamont, M., and M. Fournier. 1992. *Cultivating Differences: Symbolic Boundaries and the Making of Inequality*. Chicago: University of Chicago Press.

Lee, J., and M. Zhou. 2015. *The Asian American Achievement Paradox*. New York: Russell Sage Foundation.

Massey, D., and N. Denton. 1998. *American Apartheid: Segregation & the Making of the Underclass*. Cambridge: Harvard University Press.

Omi, M., and H. Winant. 1994. *Racial Formation in the United States: From the 1960s to the 1990s*. New York: Routledge.

Small, M. 2004. *Villa Victoria: The Transformation of Social Capital in a Boston Barrio*. Chicago: University of Chicago Press.

Swidler, A. 1986. Culture in Action: Symbols and Strategies. *American Sociological Review* 51(2): 273–286.

Tatum, B. 2003. *Why are all the Black Kids Sitting Together in the Cafeteria?* New York: Basic Books.

Tilly, C. 1999. *Durable Inequality*. Berkeley: University of California Press.

Turner, V. 1969. *The Ritual Process*. New York: Transaction Publishers.

Waters, M. 1990. *Ethnic Options*. Berkeley: University of California Press.

West, C., and D. Zimmerman. 1987. Doing Gender. *Gender & Society* 1(2): 125–151.

Wilson, W. 1980. *The Declining Significance of Race*. Chicago: University of Chicago Press.

———. 1987. *The Truly Disadvantaged*. Chicago: University of Chicago Press.

———. 1996. *When Work Disappears*. New York: Vintage Books.

———. 2015. William Julius Wilson Says His Arguments on Race and Class Still Apply. *Footnotes* 43(6).

CHAPTER 3

The Making of Community

Coretta's Story

Coretta, a Reach student from the nearby city of Urbana, graduated from Mayfair High in the mid-2000s. She grew up in a middle-class, two-parent household in a diverse neighborhood, with people from a range of races and ethnicities. She says she never "went without a thing" and even had her own car. She has stayed in the same geographic area and works as an accountant. She describes her overall high school experience as "pretty good" and views the town as a "good place to grow up." She says she made friends easily. Even with this middle-class upbringing, exposure to a racially and ethnically diverse home community, and an outgoing personality, her community in Mayfair was racially homogenous. When asked about her specific friendships and connections, she talks about other young women of color. She says, "We're a small group of African American kids...You know, we're that group, we stand out. And so you kind of feel like that's all you have is just the kids that come from the city with you." She says of her friendships with fellow commuting women, ten years after graduation, "There was a real love there that never really died."

BRIDGE BUILDING AND COMMUNITAS

If there is a silver lining to the feelings of isolation and liminality that many women in this study express, in keeping with prior research on school desegregation (Holland 2012; Eaton 2001; Carter 2006, 2007, 2012,

2015; Ispa-Landa 2013), it is what Victor Turner describes as the development of "communitas" and "comradeship" (1969).

Turner argues in his conception of liminality that social relationships tend to be based on structure and hierarchy. Individuals know where they stand in relation to one another within groups and institutions. However, social relationships change when individuals and groups enter or exist in liminal spaces. Although structures may not be completely gone nor hierarchies entirely absent, they are significantly less present.

Turner envisions the formation of a new community among members of the liminal group, the development of "comradeship" based upon their shared position. As individuals become detached and marginalized from their original, socially recognized group, but before they have reached their new, theoretically higher status in society, they move toward the formation of a new group comprised of others who have similarly been thrust out of one group, but not yet accepted into another. These unanchored souls look for common ground and company. In short, they seek out community.

In a more racially and US-specific discussion, Du Bois (1903/1994) talks decades before Turner about the sense of community that forms from marginality—two sides of the same coin. He writes, in *The Souls of Black Folk*:

> I have called my tiny community a world, and so its isolation made it; and yet there was among us but a half-awakened common consciousness, sprung from common joy and grief, at burial, birth, or wedding; from a common hardship in poverty, poor land, and low wages; and above all, from the sight of the Veil that hung between us and opportunity. All this caused us to think some thoughts together... (p.41)

Du Bois conceives of community as growing out of shared pain, suffering, and sometimes joy, but primarily from the persistent marginality experienced by people of color in early twentieth-century America. All people, at one time or another, experience "joy and grief," but this communal experience and connection is the result of the shared liminality of black Americans. If two-ness leads to double consciousness (Du Bois 1903/1994) and allows for greater insight into the soul of a society, it also leaves those individuals who possess this skill somewhat stateless. It is through this fractured state that new community takes root as everyone in this shared situation seeks out a sense of home.

Women of color may experience the development of community in distinct ways from either white women or men of color, growing out of the intersection of multiple marginalized identities (Crenshaw 1989, 1993). Although women of color may be uniquely challenged as a result of membership in multiple, overlapping categories that have historically been subjugated, these women may also be able to access particular social networks and distinct forms of capital resulting from their intersectionality (Robinson and Ward 1991; Carter 2007).

COMMUNITY IN MAYFAIR

The previous chapter lays out the sense of marginality and liminality experienced by the women, while they were students in Mayfair. They exist in places in-between, essentially in holes between formalized statuses, groups, and organizations; they exist in a liminal space. Even stronger and more common than the sense of marginality experienced by the women is the sense of community within and among groups of color. Although these women may not all equally experience "poverty, poor land, and low wages" (Du Bois 1903/1994), or their modern-day equivalents, there is to varying degrees a shared consciousness and sense of group identity that develops from the existence of the "veil." Women of color build internal bridges to one another, bridges which serve as sources of emotional support and other types of resources. Due to the varied points of access, these individuals also bring with them distinctive forms of capital that benefit those outside of their particular residential group, but inside the networks that they have formed in Mayfair.

Prior research has found that students tend to form same-race, same-gender friendships (Hallinan and Smith 1985; Hallinan and Williams 1987), but this trend may be particularly pronounced for women of color in this community. This tendency is found among women in all three groups represented in the study, although it appears to varying degrees and in different ways based on point of access into the system.

Commuters

The Reach graduates with whom I spoke clearly felt kinship with their fellow commuters, much more so than with the white student body. When asked if they felt a part of the community and school, whom they spent time with and befriended, and what those friends looked like demographically, ten women—Lorraine, Edith, Michelle, Joslin, Noel, May, Deana, Yolanda, Coretta, and Sasha—talk implicitly or explicitly about their close relationships with other commuters.

Multiple women talk about the more general Reach community in the city[1] and the friendships that developed. Michelle talks about the void she felt in her school and home communities—that persistent sense of liminality—and the important role her fellow commuters played in giving her a sense of place. She says, "I definitely felt I was part of the Reach community...Reach kids knew Reach kids. And I think I was part of that community, but not part of the overall city...community." Yolanda describes a similar scenario: "By the time I was in high school, you know, we would—we created like this kind of Reach social community of other Reach kids, and we would try to hang out with those guys." Sasha found these cross-district relationships to be of tremendous importance and felt they should have been cultivated to a much greater extent, given the common feelings of liminality among Reach students around the city of Urbana, regardless of the suburban school community to which they commuted. She discusses how even today when she meets someone else who has gone through a similar racial desegregation program, she feels a kinship with them.

Women also talk about their friendships specific to the Mayfair Reach population. For example, Lorraine and Edith discuss attending their prom with other Reach students. May says she primarily spent time with her commuter friends. Yolanda says, "Most of my friends were mostly Reach kids because they understood, right. They got that being in the middle—and that's what it felt like." Sasha comments on the nature of her relationship with both the Mayfair residents and the commuters: "And we got along—that's the thing. Like we didn't hate each other, we were friendly and all of that. Everybody knows my name, I know their names and all that. But it was just like, a mutual understanding that our worlds are different, you know?" Again and again, this theme of marginality and community runs through the interviews.

Coretta, who begins this chapter, makes a similar comment about her friendships with the Mayfair students. She says, in referring to her fellow Reach students, "Like if I stick to that group, I can extend friendship outside of that group, but still, I'm like in this group. Like I kind of feel like there's always a line." In this statement, Coretta touches on an important, and seemingly counterintuitive trend—the ability to reach out and make friends across racial groups because of her position within her

Reach group. It is as if this sense of home, this comfort zone, provides Coretta with the confidence and strength that she needs to stretch beyond comfortable boundaries. This finding of the importance of non-dominant forms of cultural capital and its role in cultural flexibility has been found in prior research (Carter 2003, 2006, 2012).

Coretta continues, "You know, we're that group, like we stand out. And so you kind of feel like that's all you have is just the kids that come from Urbana with you." She talks in more detail:

> Everybody has their own clique, if you will, and I think it was just because we all related to each other. We all wake up early, we all ride the bus together, we spend—those bus rides were quality time, you know, and I think even over all the different grades, even within that group of kids on the Reach bus, there were still subgroups. Like I had my little circle—it was me and 4 other girls, and then girls in another grade had, you know, their little group of friends and there, you know, there's a bunch of different groups, but I feel like there's still—you know, we're the Reach kids.

As Turner (1969) argues, hierarchy and structure is not completely gone in liminal states, but it is heavily reduced. We see that very combination with Coretta—hierarchy and grouping do exist in the form of "subgroups" and "little groups of friends," but there exists a significantly more level environment than what would be seen in most settings because at the end of the day, "We're the commuter kids."

Deana discusses how her friendships with her commuter friends got stronger at a certain point in time: "You fit into certain pockets." This idea that as they got older, they became more attached to their commuter friends appeared in Noel's interview, as well. She says, "I mean once—at the end of middle school, it was clear that I just prefer my black friends. I mean it wasn't that I didn't hang out with them [the white students], but it was just...." Again, it is not a full-on rejection of or by the white town residents but rather a growing sense that develops at adolescence that Mayfair is not their place. This concept of adolescence pushing students of color closer together has been identified previously (Tatum 2003).

Five women from the Reach program—Lorraine, Serena, Noel, Coretta, and Sasha—use the language of fictive kin (Stack 1974) to describe their community, talking about the commuter group as "family," "sisters," and "siblings." This vocabulary provides insight into the closeness of the relationships that formed. Serena says, "I think—it's funny because like now, the [commuter] kids, we look at each other more as a family, now, even though like maybe then you didn't get along with them." Another woman, Noel, says that it was, "Like a whole Reach family was on the school bus." Coretta states, "That's kind of what you turn into. It turns into a family." Sasha talks about her "siblings."

Boarders

The boarders also talk about each other as their primary and often closest friends. Over and over again, the women in this group emphasize the depth and importance of their relationships with one another, again using the terminology of family (Stack 1974). Ten of the 12 boarders interviewed use the vocabulary of "sisters," "sisterhood," "siblings," or "family." One gets the sense that the fellow boarders are almost lifelines for each other.

In talking about with whom she spent time, Christina says, "Yeah, my Aspire girls. We went out a lot together, you know. That was one of our sayings, when we go somewhere we're usually all together." She talks of the "sisterhood of the house." Isabel, who relied heavily on her fellow Aspire boarders, talks about her social life in relation to the "girls":

> And I had the community of girls. There were six of us to just help me if I ever felt like I needed someone. I needed someone to help me braid my hair, if I needed someone to give me makeup advice because I stabbed myself putting on mascara. I still think I might. Or just, you know if we had a dance party.

Multiple women talk about how fellow boarders were the only ones who could really understand what they are going through—again that sense of existing between worlds, failing to belong entirely in either. Priscilla says, "But that kind of companionship and understanding, the girls specifically could relate to." She talks about the experience being very "familial." Priscilla goes on to say "…it's really comforting to know that other people went through this experience with me. These are girls that I trust and feel very, very close with." Tasha makes a similar comment: "But the thing was I had my girls. I had my [boarding] girls, so it wasn't that I was alone…Like we became sisters in the house. They were my support system." Alana, who graduated decades before, makes a similar statement: "We were our own support. It was hard to make friends with the white students there. A lot of them at that time were not trying to meet up half way at that time." Kelsey likens them to a "family unit." Malia says the best thing that she got out of the program was "the relationships that I have with all my [boarding] sisters," and Tamara talks of the importance of the bonds that she developed with her fellow boarders.

Jaqui looks to the other students of color in Mayfair, mainly the commuters, to explain the bonds among the boarders: "It was very hard just trying to figure out where you fit in. And yeah it was [commuters] they got to go home at night. So I guess finding your place. What ends up happening is you just really get a really close connection with the people you live with...." She says, "After a while, you become sisters and you fight about everything and you have your little arguments, but that was the fun part." Jaqui continues:

> I mean it was definitely different where you're only six people in the school that board. So in that way it felt like this bonding moment, so we did everything together for the most part. At least my cohort we did everything together. Shopping together, eating together, homework together because we had study hours. But that was a really positive part of the experience.

Karenna, a graduate from the mid-2000s, talks about the importance of the relationships she developed with her fellow boarders, and the critical aspect of the shared experience:

> I also really value the friendships I had with the girls in the house…it's really comforting to know that other people went through this experience with me. These are girls that I trust and feel very, very close with. I mean I just saw one of them two weeks ago and I'm still very close with some of the girls from the house. I mean we went through hell together but came out such amazing people and went on to do really great things.

Four women—Malia, Karenna, Priscilla, and Alana—also discuss the duration of their relationships with their fellow boarders. It may not be surprising that Malia, a woman who graduated within the last five years, is still in touch with her roommates: "Because even today that same group will still talk every single day" on group "chats." Karenna, a graduate from nearly ten years ago, also talks about ongoing relationships, as well, and had seen one friend from the house just two weeks prior to the interview. But, some relationships have endured even longer. Priscilla, a graduate from the early

1990s, says, "I mean I just saw one of them two weeks ago and I'm still very close with some of the girls from the house." And, Alana, a graduate from the early 1980s, says:

> There was eight of us, but there became six of us now. So we just felt like we created our own sense of family in that house. We had each other to protect ourselves. We now call each other sisters for life. We have our own Facebook page that's private. We had the reunion two weeks ago. We are going to do it every year. Next year we're going on a cruise.

These reflections among the boarders suggest strong and enduring bonds, which often developed in response to being hundreds of miles from home, in an environment that was not always welcoming, and at a particularly crucial phase of adolescent development (Tatum 2003).

As Tatum (2003) discusses, adolescence is the point at which racial identity becomes particularly salient for children of color. Although race is a defining element of humanity, it plays a distinct role for adolescents of color who are trying to find their own sense of self in a society that is still plagued by high levels of racial segregation, inequality, and stereotyping. The particularly delicate age at which these women find themselves in Mayfair is likely playing a significant role in their close bonding and development of community, as pointed out by a few Reach students who discuss the changing nature of their social relationships as they move from elementary school into middle and high school. The boarders', as compared to the commuters', more frequent use of family terminology and discussion of ongoing friendships years after they have graduated is likely the result of similar issues of adolescent development, race, and identity, but with the added factor of being away from home.

Residents

The residents also tend to develop and maintain homogenous networks, largely based on their shared feelings of marginalization. But, again, the residents often find themselves in the most liminal placement of all. They are people of color in an overwhelmingly white town; they are often of more modest means in a place of great affluence. And, while this is their community, they are often mistaken for the "other," participants in the school district through one of the two voluntary racial desegregation programs. The commuters can return home at night to an environment that feels more comfortable, and the boarders know of such places, but the residents live here, in Mayfair. Some residents grew up entirely in town, having no point of comparison.

Alexandra talks about her best friend, who was a neighbor in Section 8 housing and a young woman of color. But because the residents of color are so few in number, they are the most likely to develop cross-group friendships with women of color who are Reach commuters and Aspire boarders. This trend of racially homogenous, but cross-group, friendships is cited again and again by town residents.

Veronica, an upper-middle-class graduate from the 1990s who went on to marry her white high school boyfriend after college, experienced more racially integrated social networks. Even with her higher socioeconomic status and her connections with white Mayfair, she talks frankly about the role of race in friendship formation:

> But I would say that in terms of Reach and Aspire students, we met because we were the same color or you know, you kind of somehow connect with each other because of that. There were so few of us that we kind of tried to, you know, connect with each other. Not to say that they were my best friends, but they were definitely my friends.

Sara, an upper-middle-class, recent graduate of Mayfair and a full-time college student, says she was "grateful" for the two programs in town. Although she is light skinned and could "pass," the majority of her friends are non-white and came from the Reach and Aspire programs.

Jade, a resident of Section 8 housing while growing up, talks about the relief of finding girls of color through the Reach program: "So it was kind of hard at first, and then once I went to school, everyone was nice and they introduced us to the Reach kids that came in, which made the school even more diverse, so I was more comfortable." She talks about the racial similarity of her friends, who "all lived in Urbana. Well, not all of them. Most of them lived in the, lived in Urbana. They were similar to me." Brianna, another resident of Section 8, says, "I made more friends going into high school through the Reach program and through Aspire as well." One of her closest friends is a young woman who started in Mayfair in ninth grade as an Aspire boarding student. Another woman, Faith, a recent graduate who grew up in a comfortable home in Mayfair and is now at a prestigious art institute, echoes the sentiment of Brianna when she discusses the larger social pool as she got older:

So going into high school, I liked that—well middle school, high school, because that meant all the elementary schools joined together and that made a lot more diversity. So that's when a lot of my friend groups were combined. That's when a lot of the—I became friends with a lot of the Reach kids, and then in high school was the Aspire girls. I'm still friends with them to this day, we still hangout. And that made it feel more like, okay, you can find your place within the system, the school system.

Faith talks about her best friends coming from the Aspire boarding program. These residents clearly view the women of color who access the district through non-traditional points of entry as critical to their social and emotional experiences.

Cross Group Relationships

Commuters and boarders also talk about cross-group relationships. Although seven boarders—Marian, Christina, Elise, Priscilla, Karenna, Tasha, and Alana— talk about tensions between the two groups which seem to grow out of perceived preferential status that the boarding girls receive vis-à-vis their female commuter counterparts, they also talk of the important relationships that formed across the groups. The positive cross-group friendships appear to outweigh any tensions and grow out of both mutual feelings of marginalization by the dominant group and shared kinship with each other. Both boarders and commuters discuss the value and strength of the cross-group relationships.

Marian, a boarder, says simply, "Cause the Aspire kids and the Reach kids bonded. We all hung out." She discusses the common backgrounds and interests that existed across the two groups, and how these commonalities helped women across groups to develop relationships: "So we started the Step Squad and I think it helped us bond. And the Aspire kids actually—I remember the two captains of the step squad were two girls from Clifton."

Isabel, a boarder who struggled with loneliness and homesickness, says that her best friend was from the commuter program. Karenna talks about "two really close guy friends" and two female friends who were commuters. Jaqui, another boarder, says, "All my really good friendships were with students from the Reach commuter program, my roommates obviously. Then I had one black friend who, her family, like her mom participated in Aspire, so I really got to know her and hang out with her." Marian says,

"There were not that many blacks, so a lot of times Reach and Aspire were friends most of the times." Malia says that with one exception, all of her friends were either fellow Aspire girls or commuters. Tasha also talks about having friends in the commuter program, as does Elise.

Although commuter students tend to have the largest social pool of students of color to pick from, vis-à-vis town residents and boarders, not all commuter students find a place for themselves within this population and cross-group friendships really matter to them. Chantel, a commuter, talks about her relationships with the boarding students as she felt she had more in common with them than with her fellow commuters: "I connected with [boarding] students, and really no one else. And I think that was mostly because I was isolated and then isolated myself as a high achieving [commuter] student."

Monique, a commuter, also talks about the relationships that developed between the boarders and commuters, citing the common urban background and learning about each others' home cities. Serena, another commuter, similarly discusses the shared urban background. She says the boarding students were the only ones who would ever come to the city to hang out, even though she invited the white, Mayfair residents, as well. The one white student who did come to visit Serena was picked up by her mother in the middle of the night because she was scared of the police sirens that she heard outside.

The Role of Place in the Creation of Bonds

Physical space plays a role in the formation of bonds and the development of community, just as it matters in the creation and maintenance of barriers discussed in the prior chapter on marginality and liminality. Again, the types of space that come into play in the bonding process vary somewhat by residential group.

The School Bus

The school bus plays a particularly important role in the experiences of the commuting students. As discussed in the preceding chapter, the bus encourages feelings of liminality, as students literally move between two distinct settings, failing to fully belong to either. But, the bus also encourages feelings of community and allows for group formation and internal bride building or bonding. Deana, Sasha, and Coretta talk about how the bus delineates their friends. The bus acts as a marker of both who is a close friend and who is an acquaintance. Deana says, "I hung out with the girls who I got on the bus with...." Coretta makes a similar comment in regard to the role of the bus as a marker: "Although you do make friends that already live in Mayfair, but they're not exactly your peers, you know, you feel like your peers are whoever I come to school on the bus with. That's my group." Sasha similarly refers to the bus as means of drawing lines: "We felt like there were the Urbana kids and the Mayfair kids. The Reach kids, they developed this incredible bond, because we're all on the same bus." In this way, the bus encourages both marginalization from the larger group of students and a sense of community among the commuter students.

The bus also becomes its own space—almost acting as a community center or friend's bedroom where tricks are played, disputes are hashed out, and relationships are strengthened. In the prior chapter, Yolanda talks about the school bus being taken away from commuter students as punishment for a water balloon fight that they had on the bus, but Yolanda also describes the event as a bonding experience for those commuters; it is an attempt to engage in some of the end of high school hijinks in which they had been left out of in the larger setting of Mayfair High. Recall Yolanda's testimony about the event:

> And then there was another time where senior week, we didn't really get a chance to participate in a lot of things as Reach seniors because of the timing of things. And on our last—like towards the end of school—we decided to have a water fight right on the bus. So, the bus driver didn't know. Of course it wasn't safe. But, everybody had water balloons and super soakers, and as we left Mayfair, we just went into this all out water fight.

Although the last sentences of her discussion about the bus incident retell punishment and retribution by the administration for the water fight (recall that the commuters lost their bus for the week), the bus allowed for this bonding event to take place. Another woman, Andrea, recalls the bus rides fondly:

> The bus rides were fun. Well, we had water fights on the bus. I think our bus monitors and drivers used to play pranks on each other cause they used to be—at first it was separated—an east bus and a west bus...So when it was east and west, we used to prank each other. And we'd put stink bombs on

each others' buses and—I was in elementary school, I just remember this stuff. We'd be waiting for the kids to come on and someone's stink bomb would go off—so we would do pranks like that. So that part was fun.

Sasha discusses the setting of the bus as a place to connect and form community: "It's almost like siblings and you have 30 of them. And it's like some of them are older, some are younger—you know? It's like a mini high school on that bus. The same dynamic, so the different grades and the different backgrounds and experiences...." Noel also talks about the physical space of the bus as a place to be together. She says, "The only time we saw each other as like a whole Reach family was on the school bus...."

This is not to suggest that the school bus was a place of fun and harmony for all. Yolanda, the woman who describes the water fight, states plainly, "I hated the bus rides. I hated them. So much stuff happened on the bus, too. The bus was just terrible. It was just terrible." Sasha talks about the fights that would break out during the commute in the context of a "mini high school" on the bus. What it is to suggest is that the school bus, in addition to being the literal means by which the students commute between the two worlds, also acts as a critical marker of liminality and, on the flip side, a setting for the development of "communitas" (Turner 1969).

The House

For young women in the Aspire boarding program, the physical space of the shared house plays a similar, but more extreme, role than the school bus plays for the commuters. These women truly find themselves in a liminal space: they are young women of color who are frequently in the most advanced academic classes; they are not from the town, but they live in it. Because they are living in the community without their parents, they are also subject to strict rules put into place by the program and have more limited freedom of movement. The house serves as a place of reprieve for the boarding students, as well as a setting for bonding.

Christina, Isabel, Priscilla, Tasha, and Karenna all talk about hosting dance parties or watching movies at their house. Karenna says:

> I mean you know we did a lot together. We just did a lot together and I know my first couple of years we used to host dance parties at the house where it was just us and Ms. Jones' kids. The ones I was telling you about

and kids from school. They would just come hang out because it was hard for us to go places because one, we had to have drivers. We had to have volunteer drivers, so that was transportation.

The development of their own small community is often the key to survival and success in Mayfair.

Two town residents and a commuter student also talk of spending time at the "house." Sara, an upper-middle-class resident whose parents live near the house where the boarding students live, says, "I would go to the house all the time. I'm still very close with the house parents." Faith, a middle-class resident whose parents lived about 2 miles from the house, says, "It felt like I lived there." She says, "And we'd like—we'd watch Youtube videos and learn new dances and stuff or do each other's hair—it was just like all types of fun stuff." Sasha, a commuter student, similarly says, "We were always at the house."

The Commuter Office

The commuter office is a physical space in the high school set aside for the commuter coordinator. It is also a place for the commuter students to meet and talk, both formally and informally. Yolanda talks about the space in this way:

> I hung out in the commuter office. I don't know how many towns have it, but we had our whole classroom, and like that's where we hung out if we weren't on the balc [in the cafeteria]. That's where I went when I had a free period. Because we had pictures of African Americans—famous African Americans up on the wall and black staff, so that's where I wanted to go.

Yolanda says it "served as the student center for the commuter kids." May relays a similar picture: "So we were just always in there, you know, between classes and sometimes it would even be where you made up from your fights with your friends because you would both end up there and you would both have to talk."

Although it is intended for the commuter students, it becomes an important physical space for students of color, more generally. Town resident Jade talks about spending time in there with the other students. Flore, a resident who did not get along with the commuter coordinator and did not spend time there, does talk about other students of color being able to go "hang out there." Boarding student, Christina, says of the Reach coordinator, "I would be at her office all of the time speaking with her." Similarly, Elise says, "So there was a dedicated room in the High school where we would all just hang out." This physical space becomes another setting for the development of bonds among students of color, within a larger, less friendly high school.

Money as a Source of Bonding in Mayfair

The prior chapter explored how gender and race, in connection with class, led to feelings of marginalization within the community of Mayfair. In extreme cases, women spoke of realizing the depths of their poverty back at home. In less extreme cases, middle-class commuting students compared their older, less expensive used cars with the shiny, brand new BMWs, Mercedes, and Range Rovers that the most elite town residents received upon turning 16.

Money, or the lack, also appears as a means by which students are able to bond with each other. In some cases, class position even seems to trump the role of race. These discussions are limited, but do appear in conversations with both residents and commuters.

Hannah, a town resident who lived in Section 8 and was highly integrated through her sports participation, talks about her white best friend and fellow athlete, Susan. She says, "My best friend, Susan, her parents are not the wealthiest people, so we would laugh about all of our friends that were extremely wealthy and spend like $1,700 at Swank and something crazy like that." Coretta, a commuter student, talks about her closest friend who was white. Coretta's best friend lived in another town and had access to the school because her father was an administrator. Coretta talks about the similarities she had with her friend, as a commuter student, but also as someone from a more middle-class background. She says of their family and household, "So it was very similar, very down to earth."

Five commuter students—Serena, Joslin, Deana, Yolanda, and Andrea—talk about the bonding that took place between the commuter students and residents, but very specifically Mayfair residents living in Section 8 housing. Serena, when asked if she had any friends from Mayfair, said only in the Section 8 neighborhood. She says, "But that was the only area really in Mayfair that I felt comfortable in because they could kind of understand, you know." Serena describes it as less "uppity" than the rest of the town. Joslin describes a similar scenario when asked the same question:

"But I'd say most of my friends were on the—I guess the poorer part of Mayfair...Yeah, I had a couple. I had a few that I hung out with." She tells me that they lived in Section 8 housing. Deana also talks about the few friends that she had from the community. They were white residents, but she explicitly tells me that they were residents of Section 8, saying, "So I think we connected on that level of not really feeling like we belonged there." Andrea also talks about connecting with the residents who lived in Section 8. She says, "I didn't grow up in a tough neighborhood, but I still resonated with that side a little bit more—but the people I hung out with were the people from Section 8 who were a little bit more—to say—listened to the rap music, wore the same type of clothes that we wore, the same style. So that's how we connected more."

Yolanda also discusses the connections between the commuter students and the Section 8 residents. She talks about her observations:

> ...Most of the [white] kids who grew up in Section 8 were—I mean I don't know if they were treated worse actually, than the commuter kids...There were definitely similarities, but I think that they weren't always accepted by certain commuter students because they were viewed as trying to be black. And then most of the Mayfair community were like, 'Oh, you're poor. You're one of them.'

She says many of the Section 8 students tried to connect with the students who came out from the city: "And so they definitely hung out more with the commuter students, but in particular, the commuter students that lived in subsidized housing as well." The Section 8 residents, black and white, would eat upstairs on the "balc." Their bonds grew from shared marginality.

The Benefits of Bonding

The bonds that form within and across groups translate into emotional support, shared resources and opportunities, all forms of what we have come to know as social capital. Social capital has been described in a variety of ways, often making it difficult to pin down precisely. Xavier de Souza Briggs (1997) defines social capital as "resources stored in human relationships, whether casual or close" (p. 2). Robert Putnam (1993, 2000) discusses social capital as the collective value of our connections, as well as the pressure individuals in the network feel to reciprocate for what they have gotten out of these connections. James Coleman (1988) argues that social capital is best understood by what it does—it allows outcomes to happen that could not otherwise. These individual or group outcomes are possible as a result of information flows, obligations and expectations, and social norms, all mechanisms that can only exist *within* relationships. One cannot share or gain access to external resources if one exists in isolation.

These relational-level resources exist, broadly speaking, to fulfill two types of individual needs: (1) emotional support and (2) instrumental assistance or social leverage that allows individuals to "get ahead" (Briggs 1997; Dominguez 2011). Both forms of social capital can exist within a group that is organized around some defining characteristic that gives a group a "collective consciousness" (Adler and Kwon 2002). This is known as bonding social capital—the emotional support and access to resources that arise from membership in a particular group. Unsurprisingly, the most common organizing principles or "fault lines" in society, specifically divisions around race, ethnicity, and class (Briggs 1997), often serve to circumscribe this form of social capital. The development of these bonds *across* the three groups provides access in Mayfair to a variety of resources that each respective group lacks in its own right. This is the very power of social capital—access to resources through one's social networks. These emotional resources include friendship, housing, familiarity, and numbers—all benefits that would not accrue to an individual existing in isolation. Social leverage includes job contacts, internship opportunities, and school information.

Emotional Support

The many examples of friendship and emotional support discussed earlier in the chapter are clear illustrations of bonding social capital. The marginalization which leads to community creates a cohesive group identity, be it the "kids on the bus," "the girls in the house," or the students of color within Mayfair, generally. The bounded nature of the group, while isolating at times, is community building in other instances (Du Bois 1903/1994; Turner 1969), providing support and affirmation (Carter 2007, 2012). It is critical to see that the unique social and physical locations of these young women, which on the surface may appear exclusively as deficits, are often sources of capital (Robinson and Ward 1991; Carter 2003, 2006, 2007). These women possess significant resources, which they share with those in their tight-knit group.

In addition to the theme of cross-group friendships found throughout the data, women talk about the practical or logistical benefits of being part of networks that included women with varied points of entry into the system. Although described as logistical in nature, these benefits translate into much more, including the ability to participate in after-school and weekend activities and thus feel more a part of the Mayfair school and community. Such resources may not materially alter an individual's position, but they do allow for a greater sense of belonging.

For example, the Reach students often struggle with being able to attend events in Mayfair that take place at night or on the weekends. Both the Aspire students and the residents are able to provide commuters with a place to stay so that they can more fully participate in the life of the school. Christina, a boarding student, says, "…sometimes the Reach girls would stay over if there was something we were all doing the next day and getting ready for." Boarding student Tasha also talks about having commuter students stay at the house so that they did not have to take the subway back home. Marian, a boarder from a later time period, similarly says, "Like people from Urbana a lot of times would try to come to the house because they lived all the way in Urbana." Sasha, a commuter, talks about being able to go to a party at the Aspire house in Mayfair and staying overnight there. A resident, Brianna, provides similar opportunities to her commuter friends: "Like a lot of my friends that were Reach did not want to go to a lot of the school events just because they didn't have anywhere to stay or the commute was too hard for them. So I would always have them stay over at my house…." Hannah, another resident, tells a similar story. She says, "Yeah, we were considered her host family. So she was always around us. And then, also another girl who was Reach who did sports, so they would always come over to our house. Say there was a Friday game or something or like anytime, they would come over." Again, the relationships across groups provide critical social support to these women and make the experience in Mayfair more accessible.

At the same time, being able to access the city nearby and stay over comes as a welcome reprieve for boarders who only get to return to their own city during school vacation. A commuter student, Chantel, says, "I did also have Aspire friends stay over, and that was also—it was like they were getting to come home almost." A boarding student, Jaqui, confirms that feeling: "It was fun. I mean, again like going from Mayfair to their house just reminded me of being at home." Access to the nearby city through the commuter students provides the boarding students with a touchstone, a place that feels familiar, welcoming, and safe.

Isabel, a boarding student, tells of the experience of going to stay with a commuter friend in the city. She says, "Her family was great. Living situation wise it was similar to mine but her mom was a lot more affectionate than my mom. And we would go shopping, as well, and I would sleepover. And we'd put together—they were Ecuadorian, so very different breakfast, lunch, and dinners. So yeah, it was nice." Isabel describes "loving" those times. Tasha also describes going to friends' homes in the city. She says, "I went to people's houses in [the city]. Mayfair, not so much." Alana, an earlier boarder from a significant distance, tells of staying at the home of a commuter student during spring vacation because she could not get all the way back to her own home. These are all clear illustrations of social and emotional support, a form of social capital resulting from this bounded community.

At the same time, the commuters provide critical mass, another form of emotional support. As Faith, a resident says, "having the commuting students there allowed you to feel like you could find your place in the system." She continues:

> I guess what I disliked about Mayfair? I don't know, sometimes, because there's not a lot of residents—African American residents that aren't in Aspire and aren't in Reach, sometimes I would feel, if there was a snow day, or the Aspire girls were having a special event, I would feel by myself and I would feel like I didn't have any friends because I would be the only person that was able to come to school still because I'm down the street instead of in Urbana...

Similarly, Jade says that when she first moved to Mayfair, she felt isolated because there were so few children of color. She became more comfortable when she met the commuter students. She says:

> I was used to being around people that looked like me and I was comfortable around them, and then you go to a neighborhood and people don't look like you and you just feel different. You just don't feel like you fit in. And even if it's not like—even if they're not racist or anything you just don't—you just stay acting like what you would normally act like. So it was kind of hard at first, and then once I went to school, everyone was nice and they introduced us to the [commuter] kids that came in, which made the school even more diverse, so I was more comfortable.

Sara, a lifelong resident of the community, similarly appreciated the boarding and commuting programs for this reason. Marian, a boarding student, also cites the small number of students of color at Mayfair and the importance of the commuter students in that regard.

Finally, the students of color, regardless of their point of access into the school system, benefit from the administrative support in place for the commuter students. Because the commuting program has the largest number of students and is, in part, publicly funded, there is a commuter coordinator and an office. Having an administrator of color who has a "place at the table" of administrators benefits students of color, regardless of point of access. Residents and boarders, as well as commuters, talk of feeling they had a person they could go to and receive support from in the form of the commuter coordinator. In this way, the social capital initially possessed by one group becomes expanded to serve as social capital for young women of color, more generally.

Social Leverage

The women also discuss numerous instances of social leverage resulting from this internal or bonding social capital. For example, Edith, a commuter, describes how the specific commuter community was helpful to her in her job search, while the more generalized school community was not. She says:

> If I don't know where to start, then I need a guide—it's—and if you don't know my culture, or me, or what will sell in my neighborhood, then it just— I didn't get help from them, no. But I did get help from higher classmates [in the commuter program]. But that was my same culture though, you know. And, I got a job at Finney Way at Best Bakery.

Job information appears to flow through the commuter networks in a variety of instances. Two women talk specifically about gaining access to a particularly helpful employment opportunity in the city, one which not only provided a steady paycheck but mentorship from adults of color who worked in the organization. The commuter network and this organization appeared to have significant overlap. Noel says, "Actually, two other people in [the commuting program] were working at Rise Up and so they let us know. And I got hired. And so I worked at Rise Up from 14 until I was 18, and then when I was in college, I sat on the board as a youth representative." Another woman, Deana, talks about learning about this organization through her Mayfair commuter contacts. May also talks about accessing a job through the Mayfair commuter network. Although this was a retail job, and not one with the larger support system and opportunities found at Rise Up, it was still the result of the commuter network.

These instances of job information and access resulting from the commuter network speak to two distinct and important processes. Firstly, this flow of job information illustrates how commuters, unlike boarders, were able to maintain their home networks. Though home and school may have, at times, felt like years and worlds apart, the physical proximity allowed for the ongoing maintenance (to greater or lesser degrees) of "local" friendships, ties, and access. This also suggests why the commuter community, while close knit, does not show in these data the same level of emotional dependency that appears in the boarder data. The commuters have and are able to maintain dual networks.

Secondly, the spread of job information through these networks also speaks to the role of "weak" ties (Granovetter 1973). The women who speak of getting jobs through the commuter network do not suggest the information was coming from best friends, but rather from "one of the girls" as May says. This social leverage is still the result of internal or bonding social capital (Briggs 1997).

Conclusion

The sense of isolation that the women of color experience often translates into a sense of community, both within and across groups, in keeping with the theories of Du Bois (1903/1994) and Turner (1969). This race-specific friendship formation is particularly critical to young people of color as they enter into adolescence in white-dominated social contexts and attempt to make sense of themselves and their social worlds (Tatum 2003; McFarland et al. 2014). This search for homophily is not unusual, nor is race an unusual characteristic upon which to sort oneself. Race as a sorting factor has not only been found as a predictive factor in initial friendship formation but as a strong determinant of friendships over time (McFarland et al. 2014). And, as school size and racial heterogeneity increase, so too does racial segregation in friendship networks.

Although Mayfair is considered a mid-size rather than large high school (approximately 400 students per graduating class), it is large enough to give all students significant social options. Race further becomes a salient sorting factor for young women of color in this setting, largely because they access the school system in such distinct ways, creating a clear sense of otherness through a variety of physical and symbolic boundaries (Lamont and Fournier 1992). These boundaries, clearly delineating who is of Mayfair and who is not, lay the groundwork for the two-ness and liminality experienced by so many and, consequently, the search for connection and community among those who share this location of living in two worlds, but not fully living in either.

The role of physical space matters in the formation of relationships and the building of bonds. For the commuter students, the bus plays a critical role. The house plays a comparable role for the boarding students, although it is one that also comes to be a setting for bonding *across* groups. The same is true for the commuter coordinator's office which becomes a de facto lounge for students of color.

In addition to the relationships and sense of community providing critical emotional support and friendships (seemingly to the greatest degree for the boarding students), the networks also provide access to additional resources. The social capital that flows through these networks is context specific, as, to some extent, all resources are. In this case, however, certain resources are particularly useful to the women because of their physical location. For example, one who lives in Mayfair does not need housing in Mayfair, but one who lives in the city does sometimes need housing in the town. Similarly, job information is useful, but only to the extent that it is about jobs that are in an accessible location. So, commuter-to-commuter job information flows may be very helpful, but commuter-to-boarder job information is less so.

This chapter has identified the sense of community that grows out of the boundaries established around these young women of color. The bonding social capital that exists within this community is important and powerful. For individuals and groups to "get head," however, more than just internal resources are necessary. The next chapters will explore the extent to which women were able to move beyond desegregation to actual integration, accessing external resources through the development of bridges women built out into the white community and through the bridges that the white community built in.

NOTE

1. This statewide commuter program places students of color from a number of different urban areas in dozens of suburban communities around the state. Placement is generally based upon availability of seats, with some preference given to siblings. As a result, two children on the same neighborhood block who are both participating in this voluntary desegregation program may attend two different suburban districts.

Bibliography

Adler, P., and S. Kwon. 2002. Social Capital: Prospects for a New Concept. *The Academy of Management Review* 27(1): 17–40. http://www.jstor.org/stable/4134367

Briggs, D. 1997. Social Capital and the Cities: Advice to Change Agents. *National Civic Review* 86(2): 111–117.

Carter, P. (2015). Educational Equity Demands Empathy. *Contexts*, Fall, 76–78.

———. 2012. *Stubborn Roots*. Oxford: Oxford University Press.

———. 2007. Why the Black Kids Sit Together at The Stairs: The Role of Identity-Affirming Counter-Spaces in a Predominantly White High School. *Journal of Negro Education* 76(4): 542–554.

———. 2006. Straddling Boundaries: Identity, Culture, and School. *Sociology of Education* 79(4): 304–328.

———. 2003. "Black" Cultural Capital, Status Positioning, and Schooling Conflicts for Low-Income African American Youth. *Social Problems* 50(1): 136–155.

Coleman, J. 1988. Social Capital in the Creation of Human Capital. *The American Journal of Sociology* 94: S95–S120.

Crenshaw, K. (1989). Demarginalizing the Intersection of Race and Sex: A Black Feminist Critique of Antidiscrimination Doctrine, Feminist Theory, and Antiracist Politics. *University of Chicago Legal Forum*, Issue 1.

———. 1993. Mapping the Margins: Intersectionality, Identity Politics, and Violence Against Women of Color. *Stanford Law Review* 43(6): 1241–1299.

Dominguez, S. 2011. *Getting Ahead: Social Mobility, Public Housing, and Immigrant Networks*. New York: New York University Press.

Du Bois, W. 1994. *The Souls of Black Folks*. New York: Dover Publications.

Eaton, S. 2001. *The Other Boston Busing Story*. New Haven: Yale University Press.

Granovetter, M. 1973. The Strength of Weak Ties. *American Journal of Sociology* 78(6): 1360–1380. doi:10.1086/225469.

Hallinan, M., and S. Smith. 1985. *The Effects of Classroom Racial Composition on Students' Interracial Friendliness*. Madison, WI: Wisconsin Center for Education Research.

Hallinan, M., and R. Williams. 1987. The Stability of Students' Interracial Friendships. *American Sociological Review* 52(5): 653–664.

Holland, M. 2012. Only Here for the Day: The Social Integration of Minority Students at a Majority White High School. *Sociology of Education* 85(2): 101–120.

Ispa-Landa, S. 2013. Gender, Race, and Justifications for Group Exclusion: Urban Black Students Bussed to Affluent Suburban Schools. *Sociology of Education* 86(3): 218–233.

Lamont, M., and M. Fournier. 1992. *Cultivating Differences: Symbolic Boundaries and the Making of Inequality*. Chicago: University of Chicago Press.

McFarland, D., J. Moody, D. Diehl, J. Smith, and R. Thomas. 2014. Network Ecology & Adolescent Social Structure. *American Sociological Review* 79(6): 1088–1121. doi:10.1177/0003122414554001.

Putnam, R. (1993). The Prosperous Community. *The American Prospect*, Spring.

———. 2000. *Bowling Alone*. New York: Simon & Schuster.

Robinson, T., and J. Ward. 1991. A Belief in Self Far Greater than Anyone's Disbelief: Cultivating Healthy Resistance Among African American Female Adolescents. In *Women, Girls, and Psychotherapy: Reframing Resistance*, ed. C. Gilligan, A. Rogers, and D. Tolman, 87–103. Binghamton, NY: Harrington Park Press.

Stack, C.B. 1974. *All our Kin: Strategies for Survival in a Black Community*. New York: Harper & Row.

Tatum, B. 2003. *Why Are All the Black Kids Sitting Together in the Cafeteria?* New York: Basic Books.

Turner, V. 1969. *The Ritual Process*. New York: Transaction Publishers.

CHAPTER 4

Athletes and Boundary Breakers

Marian's Story

Marian graduated from Mayfair High as part of the boarding program. She came from a city approximately 200 miles away, where she lived with her mother (a civil servant), her grandmother, and younger brother. She now attends a prestigious university in the Northeast. She is outgoing in personality and striking in appearance, winning the title of "Most Magnetic Senior" during her time in Mayfair. Even with these qualities, she found her early days in Mayfair to be a "culture shock." As she says, racially "I went from being a majority to being a minority." Marian had come from a solidly middle-class household, experiencing travel and other opportunities, but she says, "Everything was different. I have never seen kids with such wealth." The marginality she felt due to race and class distinctions led her to develop close ties with other women of color in the boarding and commuting programs. Marian broke out from and diversified her close-knit, racially homogenous network during her junior year, when her two closest friends from the boarding program graduated. She says, "It was basically like when they leave what are you going to do by yourself? Don't get me wrong, people in Mayfair were extremely friendly. People reached out to me all the time. I think I wasn't ready to reach out to them because it was such a different culture." But, Marian feels like the situation really changed when she began to play field hockey at the end of her sophomore year. She quickly moved through the ranks and was captain of the team in her senior year. In thinking back on her four years in Mayfair, Marian says, "But just to see, remember, how I was from freshman year to senior year

© The Author(s) 2017
C. Simpson Bueker, *Experiences of Women of Color in an Elite US Public School*, DOI 10.1007/978-3-319-50633-3_4

I was so comfortable in the town. People thought I lived there all my life. It almost made me forget how in the beginning it was so different until I got that letter."

Diversifying Social Networks

The "letter" to which Marian is referring is her varsity letter, and her story speaks to sports as one path to the diversification of networks and genuine social integration. Much has been written about the importance of diverse social networks in influencing an individual's opportunities and outcomes, as well as significantly shaping his or her worldview. As Susan Eaton points out in *The Other Boston Busing Story* (2001), the desire for school integration was and is about more than just equalizing educational resources. It has been about breaking down racial barriers and putting children from different backgrounds in contact with one another on a regular basis for the purposes of lessening stereotypes on all sides and broadening worldviews. It is also about the spread of information, access, and other forms of resources that play a critical role in an individual or group "getting ahead" (Granovetter 1973; Briggs 1997, 1998; Dominguez 2011). Even the addition of one employed adult or one white adult in the social network of a person of color translates into improved job information (Briggs 1998). As has been discussed in prior chapters, however, much of what we see in Mayfair is a story of desegregation, but not integration, in keeping with prior research (Carter 2012, 2015; Holland 2012; Cookson and Persell 1985, 1991).

The last chapter illustrated the power and importance of the internal social networks or bonds that developed within a community largely bounded by race, class, and gender, and the bonding social capital that provided emotional support, job information, access to housing, and other resources. Although the "internal" flow of such resources is certainly helpful, bonding social capital is often redundant, as members of the group tend to have similar sources and sorts of information. Social capital that flows into a group from an external source—bridging social capital— is often most helpful in providing new forms of resources (Briggs 2002).

But, what actually happens when children of different races and ethnicities are brought together? Prior research has found that younger students are more likely to have more racially diverse networks, but students of color tend to seek out same race friends as they enter into middle and high school and try to make greater sense of their racial identity in a racially charged society (Tatum 2003). In programs that bus students of color into predominantly white districts, those students tend to maintain racially homogenous social networks (Eaton 2001; Holland 2012). In boarding situations where students of color are even fewer in number, these students tend to feel significant isolation and marginalization (Cookson and Persell 1985, 1991; Khan 2011). The diversity of social networks that does take place is largely the result of limited social options, given the dearth of students of color in these environments. The overall experience tends to be one of two worlds existing side by side, but not really engaging with each other in any significant way (Carter 2012, 2015). In short, few bridges exist, at least among peers.

Although the previous chapters suggest a scenario that is far from integrated, with women feeling marginalized and forming bonds of sisterhood, that is not the whole story. A handful of instances exist illustrating significant racial integration and the building of bridges out into the white community. These illustrations are far beyond simply making acquaintances with students from the dominant class; they suggest deep, meaningful, and long-standing friendships. Such stories also suggest movement from desegregation to genuine integration (Carter 2012, 2015). So, when does placing students in the same school system translate into the diversification of social networks and real integration? Under what circumstances do these women form friendships of substance, rather than perfunctory relationships, with individuals largely remaining isolated by race, ethnicity, and class? And, if paths toward integration have been effectively forged by some women of color, why do we not see more women taking this route?

Sports in Society

Sports, like many other institutions in American society, is a forum in which barriers are created and maintained (Messner 2002, 2007, as well as Michael Messner's vast body of other work on the topic). Some individuals and groups are encouraged to participate, while others are not, through the use of a variety of deeply intertwined structural and cultural barriers (Lamont and Fournier 1992). Individuals gain access, or at least the possibility of access, to certain sports based upon their social and geographic location in society. Race, gender, class, and geography all play critical roles in the opportunity to learn about and participate in certain athletics. Looked at structurally, basketball courts are found in urban, predominantly lower-income communities of color, whereas soccer fields are found in the predominantly white, higher-income outlying suburbs. Although the geographic placement of one type of sports facility versus another may have to do with the physical space available, there are more long-reaching implications. Limited physical access to certain sports translates into a limited cultural toolkit (Swidler 1986) around such sports.

In addition to the physical barriers in place that separate sports by social group are the cultural barriers—the symbolic boundaries that are created and maintained to include some and exclude others. These symbolic barriers are powerful across many levels—from the way an individual views herself to whether and how individuals interact with each other to how groups are socially and politically organized and maintained in society (Lamont and Fournier 1992; Lamont and Molnar 2002). And while some sports, such as polo or squash, may be extreme examples of both the physical and symbolic boundaries that exist, such barriers are also present in more mainstream sports.

On the flip side, however, sports can be used as a means of integration, given that it is an institution that theoretically prizes physical prowess and winning above all else. Although one can easily recall instances where racial or gender segregation have been placed above the goal of winning—the refusal of the Boston Red Sox to give Jackie Robinson a contract and barely a tryout (Borer 2008)—athletic abilities can go a long way toward integration. If one can score a point and help bring a team closer to victory, that significantly increases the likelihood that he or she will be granted access. And, while Jackie Robinson's historic integration of baseball exists at the macro-level as a sort of "look how far we've come" mantra, the role of sports in diversifying groups should not be dismissed. At smaller levels, sports can also be used as an effective tool to integrate groups (McFarland et al. 2014), and unsurprisingly, schools that successfully integrate extracurricular activities are more successful in integrating friendship networks (Moody 2001).

Sports in Mayfair

Sports matter in Mayfair, as they do in most twenty-first-century elite suburbs across the United States (Lareau 2011). Soccer clinics abound and teams are stratified by skill level while children are still in elementary school. In recent years, an elementary school team won a national championship, leading to the placement of signs declaring the team the national winner at various points of entry into the community. One is literally and symbolically entering into an environment where sports and winning are highly valued.

The importance of sports to the community likely explains why athletics can work as a tool of integration in Mayfair. And, as discussed in the opening of the chapter, sports do act as one of the most effective means of social integration in the town, leading to the significant diversification of social networks, the formation of relationships with white students that women of color feel are deep and meaningful, and the removal of some structural barriers. This is not to suggest that this form of integration through sports happens often, but when it does happen, it is powerful.

Residents

Five residents talk about their involvement with sports and the role that it played in helping them to develop cross-racial friendships, although it is most pronounced for two women—Hannah and Flore. Hannah, a woman in her mid-20s who grew up in Section 8 housing, played sports in college and now works in the field of athletics. She discusses the difference between her experience in Mayfair and that of her sister's:

> I played sports throughout my whole life, and so I think that's why my experience was a lot better than her experience because I played soccer from kindergarten throughout my senior year of high school, I played basketball, and I ran track. And so I made most of my friends through sports. So going into middle school, I already knew people from other schools in Mayfair because of soccer. And I was on like the A traveling team, so we spent a lot of time together. And so that was great.

In explaining why her sister's networks were predominantly black, Hannah says, "We've always talked about that and my sister said that most of her friends are black, and most of them are Reach students and it's because she didn't really do sports." Alternatively, Hannah was heavily involved in sports each season, with her closest friends coming from those sports teams. She talks of her best friend, Susan, a white woman who grew up in a middle-class household in Mayfair, and explains their relationship as growing from their mutual sports participation. Hannah would even sit with teammates and eat downstairs in the cafeteria where the white students ate. And, she talks about feeling badly that she lost touch with some of her friends from her immediate neighborhood—fellow young women of color who grew up in Section 8 housing—because of their lack of involvement in sports. She has crossed a symbolic boundary into sports, an institution viewed as "off limits" by many of her racial and economic counterparts. This boundary breaking on the field leads to boundary breaking off of the field.

Flore, another woman who grew up in Section 8 housing and was an athlete throughout her childhood in Mayfair, says, "Yeah, I played soccer, played tennis for a little while and then—let's see—soccer, cross country, I did it all." In discussing how and why she felt a part of the larger community, but marginalized in her immediate neighborhood, Flore says, "We were that family where—a lot of people in Section 8— they didn't play sports, they didn't do any of those things. I did those things." She talks about how her closest friends were those from her sports teams—both school teams and more regional teams of which she was a part. These were the women with whom she spent weekdays and weekends practicing, competing, and socializing. She discusses attending parties in Mayfair and neighboring towns with her teammates. Flore would also sit in the downstairs portion of the cafeteria with white teammates. And, as discussed in a prior chapter, she told of how white, Mayfair residents "assumed that I was from Mayfair" because of her incorporation into the community, largely as a result of sports participation. Participation in certain sports translates into a sense of community membership.

Brianna, a recent graduate who grew up in Section 8 housing, had this to say when asked if she felt a part of the school community: "I believe so, since the relationship that I had with my teachers was really good and when I played sports [softball] for the first two years of high school, like that was good for me, too." Faith, a young art student who grew up in a middle-class neighborhood in a home owned by her parents, talks about playing volleyball for two years. Although it did not appear to be a memorable experience for her ("Wow. Oh, I totally forgot about that..."), it was still another means of contact and extended networks.

Interestingly, Gabriella, a woman in her mid-20s who primarily grew up in a rental apartment in Mayfair and identifies as Latina, found Latin dancing to be a means of integration. She talks about how she developed diverse networks through the dance classes she taught and the dance team of which she was a part in high school. She says:

> I used to teach Salsa, Merengue—I opened it to the teachers, as well. It got to the point where parents were like, 'Hey, can you come? I'll pay you'... The dance team loved it—they picked it up and I choreographed the team,

so we performed in their show, they had like two or three or four shows, and it was cool, so we got to perform each night. And then in my group—my dance group, I had like freshmen and sophomore boys, they were black, white, Haitian and [commuters and residents]. It was a mix. It was a great group of people I had.

While Latin dance could have been a marginalizing experience, it seemed to work as an effective means of integration for this woman. Instead of her dance participation being boundary making, marking her as different, it appears to have helped attract students, teachers, and parents from a range of backgrounds.

Although Hannah and Flore are "poster women" for the role of sports in integration, and Brianna, Faith, and Gabriella's comments suggest that sports can help to cross racial boundaries and lead to greater diversification of networks, their comments about relatives, neighbors, and friends begin to suggest the divisions around race, class, and sports participation in Mayfair.

Commuters

While five of ten residents discussed participating in sports to various degrees and, in some cases, seeing their networks and friendships diversify significantly because of their sports participation, only four of fifteen Reach graduates—Noel, Yolanda, Patricia, and Monique—discuss this trend. These four women hail from a wide range of time periods—the late 1980s, the late 1990s, and the mid-2000s. These participants discuss the role that sports played in integrating them into the community, but none so completely as is seen with Hannah and Flore.

Noel, a highly successful woman who graduated in the mid-2000s, says of sports, "It helped I did cheer leading, I did soccer, I did acting...I interacted with different groups of kids." She goes on to link her sports participation with other forms of integration: "...Because I did soccer I would stay after at different people's houses and that was the norm." In this regard, her sports participation begins to break down other barriers—socializing at the homes of white students in the community. Integration through sports appears to beget other forms of integration.

Yolanda, a graduate from the late 1990s, when asked if she felt a part of the school community, had this to say:

Only when I was a cheer leader. My freshman year, I was a cheer leader for the football season. And I did feel that way because I was obviously at all the games and practice, and went to Jane Smith's house. We had, you know, cheer leading breakfasts, we'd go to the games, that kind of thing, sleepovers. But after that, I very much just clung more to the Reach experience.

She goes on to discuss the power and role of sports: "Cause I do think that athletics provided a place where it was like, 'We're equal.' It was either you could play or you can't, right." In this way, sports can further exclude certain individuals and groups, but it can also include.

Yolanda, when discussing some of the benefits of having gone to school in Mayfair, makes another prescient comment about sports and their ability to stratify. She says, "I liked that I had never heard the term lacrosse, right, which was funny because some of my friends played lacrosse and field hockey, and I was like, 'What is this?' Tennis, basketball, you know, track, those, you know." Yolanda provides perhaps the clearest example of the symbolic boundaries that exist around sports—what sports are made familiar to individuals and groups, based upon their location in the social structure, and what sports remain unfamiliar. Like Noel, she also illustrates how contact on the athletic field leads to contact in other settings—at the homes of white students for team breakfasts and sleepovers. Although sports do not appear to break down barriers in the way that they did for Hannah and Flore, they help Yolanda to make inroads and diversify networks.

One active member of the commuter community, Monique, who graduated in the late 1980s, makes an observation similar to Yolanda's about the barriers around sports, specifically lacrosse. She says of her own sports participation:

> And then, you know, having white friends—and I had a lot of—I mean, again, I'm just—I'm friendly with who's friendly toward me. And I did play sports, you know, while I was there, but I didn't do the typical sports. I didn't run track, I didn't play basketball, you know, I played soccer. You know, I played lacrosse.

In this way, Monique is also highlighting the racialization of sports, with some sports, such as track and basketball being the "typical" sports for students of color. She goes on to play the sport that one of her successors, Yolanda, ten years later had never heard of. Monique, in explaining her participation in soccer, lacrosse, and also field hockey, says, "And I just wanted to try different, different things." She is strategically engaging in particular sports to get the most that she can out of the Mayfair experience, in a sort of intentional diversification. Monique, a woman who seems to have been highly prescient as a teenage girl, was aware that these opportunities were uncommon for young women of color from urban areas and she had the confidence, courage, ability, and family support to take advantage of them.

Boarders

Among the Aspire boarding graduates, five of twelve women—Christina, Elise, Priscilla, Isabel, and Marian—discuss their participation in sports and the extent to which it increased their sense of inclusion, and the diversification of their social networks, including the expansion of cross-racial friendships. Of these five women, three not only participated but went on to captain their respective teams during their senior year. As highlighted in the opening of the chapter, Marian, a graduate of the 2000s, clearly had the most changed experience in the community as a result of her sport's participation. She, like Hannah and Flore, views her athletic engagement as a formative experience. She says:

> Yeah, I think [sports] is also what helped too. I ran track freshman and sophomore year but I always wanted to play field hockey. When I ran track it was with one of the girls from the house. That's when I realized everything I did was with the girls from the house with activities. So I was like, 'Let me be on my own.' So I tried out for field hockey and that helped too because that was my first year playing and I made the lowest level team… Then I asked my mom if she could send me to field hockey camp and then she actually sent me, so she paid for the thing so I could play all year round. It helped me improve so then I made varsity and that really just took over. Those girls were literally my family, so then that's kind of who I hung out with. They were the people from the town, so that also helped. They literally became my best friends. Then we would hang out all weekend. Then after that, I became captain so then I met even more people. That really also changed my world.

This passage illustrates a number of critical aspects of sports. On the one hand, Marian is highlighting sports as a path to inclusion and the development of a larger and more diverse set of friends. As with her resident and boarder counterparts who engaged in sports, the contact on the field breaks down barriers off the field. Marian goes on to say, "People thought I lived there [in Mayfair] all my life. It almost made me forget how like in the beginning it was so different until I got that [varsity] letter. I totally forgot how much of a struggle it was until my sophomore year." Marian clearly gains emotional and social benefits from her bridges built through athletics, including a sense of membership and belonging in the community.

Marian's consideration of her own sports participation also raises other issues, including the ongoing racialization of sports. She, like Monique, sees some sports, due to the racial composition of the teams, as providing either redundant or new opportunities and experiences. Marian is participating in the same sort of intentional diversification, choosing sports because of the experiences and contacts they will provide.

Marian's analysis of the racial composition of certain sports is similar to that of a predecessor of hers, Christina. Their decisions, based on that racial analysis, differ, however. Instead of resisting segregation by sport, Christina found comfort in it: "That was like another bonding thing, my track team. That was a small community also because a few other girls in the house did it so we all ran track practice then we'd go home together." Although Christina developed very diverse social networks through a variety of channels, she still cited track and football as teams from which she found black friends. She says, "I was closer to the ones who were on the track team and the ones who played football."

Sports participation is also discussed by Elise, a highly successful woman who graduated in the early 2000s. Her sports participation suggests a sense of fuller membership in her program and in the community, as is verbalized by Marian and Flore about their own sports participation. She says, "I was the golden child when it comes to the boarding program. So I did a lot. I was the captain of the gymnastics team when Mayfair High School was just starting it back up. They never had a gymnastics team." She not only participates in this newly formed sports team but ends up successfully captaining it.

Two women—Priscilla and Isabel—who graduated almost two decades apart but had comparably challenging and painful experiences in Mayfair, had similar comments to make in regard to sports participation. Priscilla, a Latina woman who graduated in the early 1990s and who described her overall experience as "hard" and "horrible," had this to say when asked if she ever felt part of the school community, "Sometimes. Like when I was playing—I played softball." Isabel, a woman who graduated nearly twenty years later and felt isolated throughout her four years in town, said:

> I met a lot of friends through the Honors Club and through archery. I was one of the co-captains my senior year so that got me really involved, and I was pretty good at the farther distances. I was state ranked so I had a lot of support from people in the High School because of that they would always come and would be really excited and always wanted to watch me...I felt a lot of love from my classmates in that respect I—but that was it. Just an athletic sports capacity.

For Isabel and Priscilla, as well as other women, sports participation helps to alter boundaries, but does not remove them entirely.

The Implications of (Non) Participation

Sports also surface in conversations around both feelings of personal marginalization and the theoretical connection sports can provide. As Jade, a town resident who grew up in Section 8 housing, says about sports:

> I think when you play sports, you connect more with people and you get to know more people and you're more comfortable. You're more of a family when you do sports. People have team dinners and you just know each other more [and] better when you do sports. I didn't do too many sports, so I just knew who I knew.

When Jade is asked if she felt a part of the school community, she replies, "I would say the no part [to being part of the school] because I didn't play sports." She recognizes sports as a possible means of integration and a bridge to important resources—social contacts and emotional support—but she is unable to capitalize on this insight.

Similarly, Alexandra, another resident from Section 8 housing who did not participate in sports, talks about encouraging her cousins to participate in sports in Mayfair, clearly understanding the expansive role that it can play. On giving advice to cousins who live in the community, and to one cousin in particular, she says:

> I think I helped them out a lot to tell them to definitely to stay into sports and to definitely be social. Because like I said, it's really good to know people, and especially in that area because even though sometimes there are the ignorant ones but, the ignorant ones, they would still help you out and make sure you do well cause it's always good and if you ever need references and stuff it's just always good to know people. Just try to get that—embed

that in his head and he's been doing pretty well with it, but it's just, keep good relationships with people and stuff like that.

Alexandra views sports as a critical means of developing and maintaining relationships and networks that may be useful in the future. Although Alexandra may not have read social capital theory, she recognizes its importance in life, particularly in terms of job opportunities, an observation that is supported in the literature (Granovetter 1973; Briggs 1998). Gabriella also talks about encouraging her younger cousin who lives in another community to participate in gymnastics.

Kelsey, a relatively recent graduate of the boarding program, cites her lack of sports involvement as an isolating factor.

> You know, if I had had the ability to place myself into their sports culture, that wouldn't have made it lonely. I would have a richer experience in terms of friendships…I do know that I did not have that common link that gave us a reason to, you know, associate with one another. They talk about team spirit. They would come to class every week with some kind of face paint on, wearing different colors or crazy tutus for the different teams. I mean it was fun for them. It was something that you could clearly identify who was part of what team and what clique, and you know I think that would have made a difference. If I could have been a part of that, but you know I just—I never took a sport and I couldn't even be part of the summer program. I wouldn't have anywhere to stay and I don't think I would have wanted to stay.

From a practical standpoint, Kelsey felt shut off from sports participation as a result of both a lack of experience and a lack of summer housing. These barriers to sports participation translated into feelings of marginalization and an inability to connect with town residents. From a symbolic standpoint, the way in which teams engage off of the field—wearing a common outfit on game day, for example—illustrates the way in which symbolic boundaries are formed and used to create a sense of group inclusion or exclusion.

Sasha, a Reach graduate from the late 1990s, discusses feeling like sports were not an option for her. She, like Yolanda, Patricia, and Marian, taps into the racialized component of particularly popular Mayfair sports, underlying the concept of symbolic boundaries that exist within the institution of sports—be those boundaries based upon an individual's notion of a sport, a group's broader exposure to a sport, or some other means of marking a sport accessible to one segment of society but inaccessible to another. Sasha says:

> I felt like sports were a Mayfair thing. I didn't feel like I would be able to join and feel included in the soccer team or the lacrosse team or anything like that. I felt like—maybe because I didn't see anyone that looked like me on those teams, you know, and so I didn't feel like it was something that I could join and be a part of...

The feeling of exclusion not only limits Sasha's access to soccer or lacrosse but also to a variety of resources that may flow through these racially and economically distinct networks.

The Gendered Nature of Sports (Non) Participation

Although this is a project focused on women of color, a number of the participants discussed their own experiences vis-à-vis their male counterparts, be they siblings, friends, or acquaintances. May, a Reach graduate, directly discusses sports as a gendered experience, without being asked. She says:

> ...when you're physically there, you still know that you're different and you still know that you're serving a purpose and you have to—you just get it and you see it in a different way. Especially I think as women. It makes a huge difference because a lot of us, I would argue, were not athletic, in my [commuter] program. I don't know about now, but when we were there, those four years, we weren't on the basketball team, we weren't on the soccer team, we weren't involved in those things.

Some women look directly at the experiences closer to home. For example, Jade says this of her brother's sports participation and the barriers it has helped to break down: "So basically he plays sports, he's more around his friends than he is our family. He's always going to the [vacation homes of friends], like all over the place. So his experience was definitely different than mine." Again, crossing boundaries in the sport's arena translates into traversing other barriers in place and creating more racially integrated friendships and social networks that produce emotional support and opportunity.

Sasha, whose two younger brothers attended Mayfair, in comparing her experience to theirs, says, "…They have the most diverse—one of them has a really diverse group of friends. And my youngest brother has mainly white friends—a handful of black friends." She attributes their diversified networks and the interracial romantic relationship that one of her brothers is in in Mayfair to the fact that "they were both big on the football scene in Mayfair." This is not to suggest that their participation was always smooth or free of racial tension. In fact, she talks about some negative racial experiences one of her brothers had on the team, but she still views their participation as critical to their development of a more diverse group of friends.

Christina, a boarder, talks about her cousin in another state who also attended a predominantly white school system. She explains him this way: "…he ended up going to Jones College. He played lacrosse and everything." His lacrosse career grew out of the predominantly white school of which he had been a part prior to college.

Other women talk about what they observed with males in their commuter program. Noel, an athlete during her time at Mayfair, says the following:

> I think for the black boys, they play sports, and you know, sports kind of helps make ties for you. I did play sports—I played town soccer and I played soccer for the school for seven years, so I think that helped in some ways, but I mean I also did cheer leading, like it helped but it didn't matter. Like I still was with the black girls.

For Noel, sports participation helps to make barriers more porous, but it does not entirely dissolve them for girls as she feels it did for boys. Another commuter, Yolanda, talks about a male student of color with whom she graduated and says:

> He was different because I think he grew up in Somerset Park, and he quickly started playing sports. He played on the football team, which was predominantly white…So Bradley, a lot of people didn't, even though he was [a commuter], he didn't hang with us the way that he—he hung out more with the Mayfair residents. He'd stay the night out there a lot, and possibly because of him being an athlete, he had to be out there and he also dated white women because they were throwing themselves at him…

As is the case with some of the female athletes, sports integration facilitates social integration. And, as with Elise and Marian, sports participation grants a certain status in the community, the status of being a "golden child," the status of being thought of as a town resident.

Somehow, these young men seem to have overcome the numerous barriers that appear for the women in this study, resulting in more integrated social networks for the men. This may reflect larger-scale trends around the gendered nature of sports in American society (Messner 2002, 2007). Given that male athletes tend to possess higher status than their female counterparts and that male sports events are better attended and are off greater focus in high school (Eder and Parker 1987), it may be that parents in Mayfair are more willing to drive male student athletes of color to their home communities after practice or have them stay over in Mayfair. It may also be that the parents of boys place a higher premium on their sons' sports participation, vis-à-vis their daughters, thus making early sports socialization more common and, later, making them more likely to find ways around the challenges encountered in Mayfair.

Sitting on the Sidelines in Mayfair

If sports participation seemed like a good idea to many of the women interviewed, and clearly worked as a means for greater diversification of networks and the development of close, cross-racial friendships for a small subset of women, then why didn't more young women follow the path?

Certainly sports are not for everyone—some simply have no interest, others have no ability. Lorraine, a Reach graduate from the 1980s, says, "I'm not an athlete at all." Coretta, a Reach graduate from the mid-2000s whose family exposed her to a wide range of sports including soccer and gymnastics at an early age, says simply, "I had no interest in sports." Veronica, a resident from the 1990s, say she was simply more interested in art and music.

But, a dearth of interest and ability do not appear to be the primary culprits for this lack of involvement. And, although someone like Coretta had broad sports exposure, there are other instances when one wonders the extent to which preferences and abilities were shaped by the barriers connected to race, class, gender, geography, or some other aspect of socialization. Unfortunately, we can only hazard guesses about the underlying social causes behind disinterest or inability. What the data do explicitly reveal are a series of barriers women discuss to explain their lack of involvement in sports.

The Commute

A common structural barrier that emerges, specifically among the Reach students, is the commute. The commuters have to add on approximately one hour each way to their daily routines, making the prospect of staying late for practices daunting. Edith talks about the commute as generally limiting her involvement in extracurricular activities. Seven women from the commuter program—Lorraine, Serena, Deana, Patricia, Sasha, Andrea, and Monique—explicitly discuss the impact of the commute on their total lack of involvement in or their discontinuation of sports. As Serena discusses, the transportation aspect was challenging:

> We lost our after school late bus, so if you wanted to participate in any kind of sport, it was up to you to take the train home or find, you know, ways home and it was just hard to have that—that experience that most kids have where, you know, you get the letterman's jacket, you get to do varsity, you get to do all this stuff. But we knew that if we did any kind of sport, we'd have to find our way home. The train—at that time, the train didn't run. It ran like maybe every hour or sometimes every two hours. So you could get out of your sport at like 6 o'clock and the train isn't in until 8 o'clock. You're not getting home until 9, and then you still have schoolwork, you know. So, it just, that part of it made it really hard to participate and do anything that you really may have wanted to do.

Another commuter, Andrea, makes a similar comment. She would have liked to try sports, but it just seemed like too much of a challenge with the long commutes each day. She says, "I wanted to play sports more when I was going to school, but I did not like the time it took because when you play the after school sports, I wouldn't be home until 8 something. So I had to get up at 5 o'clock in the morning to catch my school bus to go to school. So that's the only thing that I didn't like about it."

Patricia, who discussed her participation on a dance team, also viewed the transportation as challenging: "And it was fun [the dance group]. And we had a late bus so it was easier to do, but if you missed that, you had to take the train, which was a pain in the neck."

Sasha, the woman from the late 1990s who felt like sports were not an option for her and more of a Mayfair thing, goes into more detail. She says:

> And then also it was a challenge because of just resources. There weren't, you know, you kind of had to be tricky about is there an after school bus, and what

time does it leave, and practices are late and games are on the weekends and it's like there's only so much you can do in Mayfair, you know?

Sasha goes on to say, "You know, it's a very long day…It's no wonder we don't do after school sports and, you know, all those things because it's like then I'm not getting home till 6.…" She goes on to discuss the challenges her younger brother, an athlete in Mayfair, faced in regard to transportation:

> …When they cut resources from the Reach program, they cut the late bus, the after school bus, and it's not fair to the Reach students. For example, my youngest brother was in football at the high school, and I—we had to like alternate picking up. They slashed the budget. We had to drive. We couldn't cut him out of sports, that's devastating. So we had to just drive out there all the way to Mayfair, and after work all day…

Deana talks about why she stopped participating in sports: "It's grueling. Like you have long days, high expectations of you, it's hard to balance everything between like—that's why I think I stopped playing tennis. It would just be too much on the high school level to play, school, late bus, home, get up at 5:30 in the morning." Monique, a commuter who participated in soccer, lacrosse, and field hockey when she first started at Mayfair High, says:

> And then I didn't play sports all throughout, but, you know, I did play probably a year or two. And I just wanted to try different—you know, different things. You know, but the commitment, that was a piece of it, cause it was a commitment and you were after school for, you know, several hours afterward and then you have games and, you know, my mom would come and, you know, pick me up, and it just became a lot. So I kind of moved away from, you know, the sports piece of it.

Gotta Pay to Play in Mayfair: The Costs of Participation

Sports participation (or the lack) is not simply racialized, gendered, or geographically influenced; it is also heavily mediated by economic factors. In addition to the structural barrier of transportation, or the lack, women also identify monetary barriers to sports participation. The direct cost of sports participation, in the form of school fees and equipment, limits engagement.

Three women—a resident, a commuter, and a boarder—talk of the prohibitive cost of town sports. Hannah, the former college athlete, says:

> So I think like just because of the money situations—like for sports it's gone up, it's like $275 now I think. And it's like I play three sports so it's like every single season my mom had to pay that. But she, when me and my sister were there, Ms. Smith would make it like $75 because she knew my parents and my uncles and my grandmother and she knew our situation, and it was two of us, so she made it cheaper, but then I think since my sister left, my mom had to pay the full thing. So I think that was a little bit ridiculous, just financially their expectations that the school has for everybody.

Edith, a commuter from the early 1980s, says, "You know I want to do this but just like hockey sticks, or equipment, or baseball equipment, or basketball, you know what I mean? I was, my family, financially, I wasn't able to partake in any of those things." A boarder from the same time period, Alana, tells a story of one of her roommates, a young woman who briefly participated in cheerleading: "And after they told her how much things were going to cost, the uniform, the things for the games, the crafts, she didn't have the money."

Lost Opportunity Costs

Women also discuss the need to make money, and thus discontinue sports participation. Residents Jade and Gabriella both talk about the need to work. Jade says, "But I didn't do too many sports in high school cause I preferred to work, make money." This is not a choice many of the wealthier residents in town need to make. Gabriella says:

> I couldn't wait for Saturday. But even on Saturday, having to wake up to go to basketball was like I don't even want to go. Or go to practice or—I'm so tired, so then you start to think, what's my priority? Do I stay in this basketball thing or do I get rest so I can continue working and get more money? So that's what I'm going to do. So then your interests change and you start doing different things, and you start drifting apart.

Two commuters and a boarder talk about this same conflict. Joslin says, "When I was younger, I did track and field. I did—what else? It was harder, too, as I got older, I started to work part time, and then getting home the time we get home, I didn't really get involved with sports like I wish I had, so no." Andrea similarly has a choice to make—sports or spending money: "I played basketball in high school. I played for—one year, I think I did JV one year, and then the next year I got an after school job, so I wanted money in my pocket, so I didn't go." Priscilla, a boarder from the early 1990s, says, "You know, I worked at Smith & Co. I worked at a law firm. I worked so often, like the clubs were after school and I had to go to work so I couldn't." She needed to earn money to buy herself a warmer winter jacket, among other essentials, because her mother could not afford these additional expenses.

Lack of Experience and the Costs of Concerted Cultivation

Annette Lareau (2011), in her vivid documentation of the differences in child rearing practices by social class, conceptualized the theory of "concerted cultivation" whereby middle-class parents more actively and intentionally encourage and promote their child's skills. Children of the middle and upper-middle classes experience more in the way of organized sports and other activities to promote athletic, artistic, and academic interests than do children of the working class. Parenting in Mayfair reflects the same trends that Lareau identified in her middle-class community in California. But, if Lareau's community illustrates concerted cultivation, the community of Mayfair engages in almost a professionalized parenting. Mothers have been known to cite themselves as CEOs of their families and child rearing is viewed in a sometimes competitive fashion. The community has national athletes, coaches, and franchise owners as town residents. These individuals have given clinics and seminars on sports, and at times, even coach their own children's sports teams. One step down are the numerous parents in the community who engaged in competitive collegiate sports. Not surprisingly, the children of the few professional and many former college athletes tend to be exposed at an early age to many sports in the community.

Concerted cultivation in this setting actually becomes a barrier to sports participation and, as a result, an impediment to the development of more diverse social networks and the acquisition of new forms of social capital. If sports are taken seriously, as they are here, and the ability to participate is based upon skill, then students with more experience are more likely to participate. Whether intentional or unintentional, the result is opportunity hoarding (Tilly 1999) in regard to athletic opportunities, and thus other benefits that flow from such sports engagement. This barrier is particular to the commuters and boarders, individuals not socialized from the start in Mayfair.

Alexandra, a town resident who moved to Mayfair to live in Section 8 housing midway through elementary school, talks about an early introduction into the community:

> ...We were all playing I think kickball and this one girl said, 'No, I don't want to play kickball anymore, let's play soccer' and they all stopped playing kickball, everyone, to play soccer. I didn't like soccer, I wasn't—I didn't know much about soccer, and so I was just like, you know what I'm just gonna go over to the jungle gym...

But, town residents, in general, show a clear advantage vis-à-vis the commuters and boarders, even if not all of the residents ultimately participated in high school sports. Alexandra, Jade, Hannah, Gabriella, Brianna, Flore, Faith, Veronica, and Sara all cite participating in sports at some point, even if as Veronica says, "I wasn't really terribly into sports." Similarly, Faith cites a greater interest in activities like drama and choir, but playing T-ball and softball year in and year out as a young child allowed her to play two years of softball in high school. These women, both those who grew up in Section 8 housing and those who grew up in expensive, market-rate homes owned by their parents as Faith, Veronica, and Sara did, were exposed to sports to a much greater degree than were their commuter and boarder counterparts. The lower-income residents, who would potentially have lacked exposure and opportunity had they been in subsidized housing in a less affluent community, benefit from the widespread focus on sports from an early age in their home community.

In contrast, the Reach and Aspire graduates discuss a lack of familiarity with many of the sports in town. As Yolanda says, "...I had never heard the term lacrosse...." Similarly, Sasha, another commuter, says, "The only person I knew that was on the soccer team that was black was a girl that, she lived in Mayfair. Naturally; that's what you guys do. I never played soccer, I mean except gym class. That was the only time I got a chance to play...."

Two Aspire women also talk about how their lack of experience impacted their ability to play sports in Mayfair. When asked if she felt a part of the school community, Tasha says:

> Not really. I tried to play basketball but I realized, but I realized I sucked at it. Mayfair High School is super serious about their sports. And you know,

I tried out my freshman year and it didn't work out but I was the team manager. I liked helping keep score, so I was still involved but not to the capacity I wanted to be.

She then goes on to discuss how she felt she did not fully connect with her white classmates. Tasha talks in more detail about sports in Mayfair and its impact on her: "The freshman team, they were so good. And that's awesome for them. They were in basketball their whole lives. That's great... but do you know what I mean?...I didn't make the freshman team so I definitely didn't try out for JV."

Another Aspire graduate, Kelsey, also discusses how her lack of prior sports experience impacted her time in Mayfair beyond the playing fields.

There wasn't really a way for me to start in a sport as a beginner because all these other kids had gone to camps over the summer where they could excel. Even like a junior—like a junior varsity or a junior level in the sports wasn't an option for me. Sports was a big deal for these kids because there wasn't really a whole lot to do. They, you know, they dove into extracurricular activities after school and they had made their friendships accordingly and they were based on the teams they were on. It was really hard for me as an outsider to really be part of any kind of social network being that I didn't have any sports background or any ability to really learn a sport.

At the same time, we see the role of concerted cultivation in making sports a possibility for another boarder. Marian, a boarder who had never played field hockey before coming to Mayfair, describes her mother having the capacity and willingness to send her to field hockey camp. This young woman (who clearly had some athletic aptitude) then went on to make the varsity field hockey team, and later became captain. Even as gifted an athlete as she may have been, her mother's emotional and financial support of her daughter's endeavor undoubtedly played some role in her athletic success. Her ability to gain the necessary athletic skills provided her entrée into the competitive world of sports in Mayfair, which provided her access to a whole new group of peers.

Elise, the boarding student who became the captain of the gymnastics team at Mayfair High, also discusses her experience in her home city, prior to moving to Mayfair to attend school. As a child, her single mother had put her in an after-school program which had gymnastics. She joined the team there, and was later able to leverage that experience at Mayfair High. Similarly, Sasha, when talking about her brothers' significant involvement in Mayfair football, explains that their parents had put the boys in Pop Warner football from an early age.

In contrast, Joslin, in discussing her activities prior to starting school in Mayfair, explains it this way: "I did dance here and there, but I did have a single mom, so there was a lot of times I couldn't do a lot of things."

Even within this small sample, there is significant variation in the amount of concerted cultivation and type of socialization experienced by women, based upon social class and place of residence. Relatedly, these findings speak to the role of both racial and economic residential integration in regard to the acquisition of new forms of social and cultural capital (Briggs et al. 2010; Briggs 1997, 1998; Bourdieu 1986), as some of the lower-income town residents had access to sports such as soccer and tennis. Growing up in this environment, even with significant financial limitations, still provided women with opportunities and exposure. These opportunities, in turn, provided at least a few women the ability to expand social networks via athletics, and thus access new forms of social capital, in keeping with prior research on housing integration and its connection to the diversification of social networks (Briggs 1997, 1998).

Sports as a Panacea?

None of this is to suggest that sports is some sort of a "cure all" for the sense of marginalization and liminality that many of the women experience as high school students in Mayfair. Serena, a commuter who did participate in sports to some degree, also talked about many of the barriers in place. She had this to say: "I always felt like you were never really a part, even though I was probably one of the more popular [commuting] girls because I did cheer leading, I did track, and I was like, you know, involved, I had friends, I stayed out there, it seemed really superficial to me." For her, sports and extracurricular participation do not lead to the kind of real, meaningful friendships that other women discuss.

Further, certain sports and extracurricular activities may further segregate students of color. As noted earlier, the experience of Gabriella, a resident who expanded her networks through Latin dance, may be unique. Christina also talks about starting a step team in which she was able to get a range of students involved. She says, "I was dating this guy who was white, he joined the step team and it was really cool." But, Yolanda, a commuter student, found the opposite effect in regard to her dance participation: "I think it further pushed me away from the bigger community by being involved in Fleet because it was really just the black kids, right, on the step squad." In a less extreme way, a number of women who discuss their participation in track and field explicitly talk about their contact with other students of color in the sport. These forms of sports participation strengthen relationships among students of color, and thus the bonding social capital that exists. One woman, Marian, views this ongoing homogeneity a reason to seek out other sports and meet people who are racially different from her.

But, it is important to note that for some women, participating on a team or in a club with a significant number of students of color provides an important sense of comfort at a critical stage of adolescent development (Tatum 2003). Whether the demographics of the activity are due to the ethnic-specific nature of the club, the racialization of the activity, or the points of access available, such venues can provide critical support, connection, and pride. While Marian viewed track and field as limiting because of the racial homogeneity of the team and her desire to branch out, Christina viewed it as comforting. Chantel, a commuter, talks about organizing an African American history day and having her dance group perform at it. She views this as a point of pride, and not as a form of exclusion. Similarly, Alexandra, Jade, Faith, Deana, Yolanda, Coretta, Sasha, Andrea, Christina, Tasha, Malia, and Tamara all discuss their involvement with the step team, a group started by female students of color at Mayfair High. In explaining her participation on the step team, Sasha says, "It was just—we wanted something to be our own but something that we could be proud of and be a part of." At the same time, Tasha says of her participation, "All the other minority girls, in terms of that community, I felt were a part of. But connecting with my [white] classmates...I don't know. I feel like there was something missing." There is no evidence that this type of involvement precluded other forms of involvement, however. Said differently, had these women not had the option of participating in the step team, one should not presume they would have participated in "whiter" activities. The option of the step team may have been the only way that some of these women felt they could engage in a sport or extracurricular activity.

Women discuss meeting a wider range of students through other forms of extracurricular activities, as well. May, a commuter, says about her participation in the Anti-Defamation League Club:

> It was a very diverse group of students...It was students who lived in Mayfair, I think some of the [boarding] girls did it, some of us did it, it was

very mixed into like who was interested in it and teachers who led it. We had an ADL class that met to teach us the curriculum so that we could teach it to the school.

Three residents—Faith, Veronica, and Elisabeth—discuss meeting and befriending a diverse group of students from the community as a result of their interest and participation in music and drama organizations, activities that are attractive to a wide range of students. Faith says, "I have a lot of friends who were in drama and choir that lived around town." Similarly, Karenna, a boarder, talks about her extracurricular participation in the ADL, dance groups, and musicals and says, "I did feel part of the school. I-I was very involved and I felt like that was the only way to be comfortable." But, Karenna also talks about making her first white, non-boarder friend in the community as a result of shared marginalization at a competitive dance team tryout in which she says it was clear that neither she nor the other woman (a new student from abroad) fit in. In an ironic twist, this form of marginalization leads to a form of integration.

Conclusion

Although the data suggest that sports are not an option for everyone, nor are they the only path to integration, they do appear to be one successful path in. This means of integration seems to be most successful for those with some key factors in place: an early introduction to sports, transportation, financial support, and an eye toward diversifying experiences and networks. These conditions, both structural and cultural, are lacking for many young women of color in this environment. The path should be made wider and more accessible to young women of color by making efforts to remove both the structural and cultural barriers in place, barriers which clearly mark boundaries and limit more than just sports participation. For example, maintaining a late bus, expanding less competitive, intramural sports teams, and capping sports costs are just a few policy initiatives that might remove barriers and increase participation.

The next chapter examines the way in which adults in the community build bridges and reach into this community of young women, allowing for additional paths of connection, diversity, and opportunity, and further move the school and the community from a mode of desegregation to a mode of integration.

Bibliography

Borer, M. 2008. *Faithful to Fenway*. New York: New York University Press.
Bourdieu, P. 1986. The Forms of Capital. In *Handbook of Theory and Research for the Sociology of Education*, ed. J. Richardson, 241–258. New York: Greenwood Press.
Briggs, D. 1997. Social Capital and the Cities: Advice to Change Agents. *National Civic Review* 86(2): 111–117.
———. 1998. Brown Kids in White Suburbs: Housing Mobility and the Many Faces of Social Capital. *Housing Policy Debates* 9(1): 177–221.
———. 2002. Bridging Networks, Social Capital & Racial Segregation in America. *Harvard University, John F. Kennedy School of Government Working Paper Series*, rwp02-011.
Briggs, D., S. Popkin, and J. Goering. 2010. *Moving to Opportunity*. Oxford: Oxford University Press.
Carter, P. 2015. Educational Equity Demands Empathy. *Contexts*, Fall, 76–78.
———. 2012. *Stubborn Roots*. Oxford: Oxford University Press.
Cookson, P., and C. Persell. 1985. *Preparing for Power: America's Elite Boarding Schools*. New York: Basic Books.
———. 1991. Race and Class in America's Elite Boarding Schools: African Americans as the "Outsiders Within". *The Journal of Negro Education* 60: 219–228.
Dominguez, S. 2011. *Getting Ahead: Social Mobility, Public Housing, and Immigrant Networks*. New York: New York University Press.
Eaton, S. 2001. *The Other Boston Busing Story*. New Haven: Yale University Press.
Eder, D., and S. Parker. 1987. The Cultural Production and Reproduction of Gender: The Effect of Extracurricular Activities on Peer-Group Culture. *Sociology of Education* 60: 200–213.
Granovetter, M. 1973. The Strength of Weak Ties. *American Journal of Sociology* 78(6): 1360–1380. doi:10.1086/225469.
Holland, M. 2012. Only Here for the Day: The Social Integration of Minority Students at a Majority White High School. *Sociology of Education* 85(2): 101–120.
Khan, S. 2011. *Privilege: The Making of an Adolescent Elite at St. Paul's School*. Princeton and Oxford: Princeton University Press.
Lamont, M., and M. Fournier. 1992. *Cultivating Differences: Symbolic Boundaries and the Making of Inequality*. Chicago: University of Chicago Press.
Lamont, M., and V. Molnar. 2002. The Study of Boundaries in the Social Sciences. *Annual Review of Sociology* 28: 167–195.
Lareau, A. 2011. *Unequal Childhoods*. Berkeley: University of California Press.
McFarland, D., J. Moody, D. Diehl, J. Smith, and R. Thomas. 2014. Network Ecology & Adolescent Social Structure. *American Sociological Review* 79(6): 1088–1121. doi:10.1177/0003122414554001.

Messner, M. 2002. *Taking the Field: Women, Men, and Sports.* Minneapolis: University of Minnesota Press.

———. 2007. *Out of Play: Critical Essays on Gender and Sport.* Albany, NY: State University of New York Press.

Moody, J. 2001. Race, School Integration, and Friendship Segregation in America. *American Journal of Sociology* 107(3): 679–716.

Swidler, A. 1986. Culture in Action: Symbols and Strategies. *American Sociological Review* 51(2): 273–286.

Tatum, B. 2003. *Why are all the Black Kids Sitting Together in the Cafeteria?* New York: Basic Books.

Tilly, C. 1999. *Durable inequality.* Berkeley: University of California Press.

CHAPTER 5

Bridge Builders and Cultural Guides

Isabel's Story

Isabel arrived from a city approximately 100 miles from Mayfair as a participant in the Aspire program. She came from a very low-income, West Indian immigrant family, largely raised by her single mother, who worked to make enough money to pay the bills. Even with her mother's efforts, the electricity and heat were sometimes shut off. Arriving in a community such as Mayfair, from a city and household such as the one in which she had been raised, resulted in significant challenges for Isabel. She often felt marginalized and worthless in her new community, but lacked the vocabulary and venue to express those feelings. Isabel also had limited emotional support from home. Even with these significant challenges, she was highly successful academically, graduated from a college frequently ranked in the top ten in the country, and now holds a research position at a prestigious lab, hoping to attend medical school in the future. Isabel's relationships with a variety of adults in the community, including teachers, administrators, and her host parents, played a significant role in her time in Mayfair. As she says, "I think I lucked out in the host mom department." Her host family provided her with a space where she felt wanted and loved, giving her critical emotional support. Further, these relationships provided important social leverage. Her host father found an internship for her. Her English teacher would work with her after school to help her with grammar and writing. Isabel says, "I had a lot of dedicated teachers that really understood where I was coming from...."

Adult Social Networks

In addition to developing peer friendships, both same race and cross-race, many women also discuss the development of critical relationships with adults in Mayfair. Teachers, guidance counselors, administrators, and the parents of white students in the community play important roles in helping the young women to navigate an environment which can be academically challenging, socially daunting, and racially isolating. Many of these individuals go above and beyond expectation, acting as everyday heroes in the lives of many of these young women. Adults provide critical emotional support, social leverage, and other forms of social capital beyond that which peer-to-peer relationships can offer. These relationships also help to move the community, little by little, from desegregation to integration.

Limited Networks

Much work has been conducted to better understand the experiences of people living in high-poverty areas. These are settings with limited economic opportunities, little room for educational advancement, and a dearth of social models (Wilson 1987, 1996, 2009; Massey and Denton 1993). Individuals may even live in close proximity to those with greater opportunities, knowledge, and other forms of resources, but barriers, both symbolic and physical, can limit the sharing of such critical resources (Small 2004; Bourgois 1996; Briggs 1998). As Mario Luis Small (2004) points out, communities can literally exist side by side with each other, but individuals from those communities may never cross paths.

Although Small (2004), Bourgois (1996), and Wilson (1980, 1987) have focused on those in areas of concentrated poverty, these parallel worlds can exist in less economically and racially marginalized settings, albeit with significantly fewer repercussions for those living in separate environments. Khan's (2011) study of life at St. Paul's School, one of the most elite high schools in the world, discusses the existence of both a "minority" dorm and a dorm for those who are legacies at the institution. Carter's work (2012, 2015) on race in a variety of schools in both the United States and South Africa similarly finds the existence of parallel worlds within the same environments. Groups may share many of the same physical spaces, yet remain largely separated.

As discussed in earlier chapters, the young women of color in Mayfair largely exist in their own universe, separated from the white residents of the town by a host of physical, economic, and symbolic barriers. The prior chapter explores the way in which sports and, to a lesser extent, other extracurricular activities are used to expand and diversify social networks. But, advancement through these channels is limited to those who have certain resources to begin with—experience in a particular sport, transportation, financial resources to cover the costs, and the emotional wherewithal to be the sole member of color on the team. Sadly, this translates into few young women taking this path to diversification of networks.

Further, the women who discuss diversifying their networks and developing new relationships in these venues emphasize their relationships with peers, rather than adults. Peer-to-peer relationships are certainly important, particularly in regard to emotional support for teens (Tatum 2003), but access to and relationships with adults often play a principal role in meeting certain ends as a result of the social capital that they can extend. Adults may act as critical role models, guardians of certain norms and administrators of sanctions, and sources of information (Wilson 1987; Coleman 1988; Lareau 2015). James Coleman's (1988) groundbreaking work on the role of social capital and its impact on facilitating human capital acquisition argues that children are more likely to develop human capital when they have strong relationships with their own parents, as well as when they reside in communities with higher levels of overall adult involvement.

Although few women in this study are living in the kind of concentrated poverty explored by prior scholars in the field, their networks remain largely bounded by race, class, and geographic setting. And while the young women of color who are in Mayfair as a result of one of the voluntary desegregation programs likely have significantly higher levels of social capital than their peers who remain in their home communities, their ability to further expand networks and thus gain greater social capital is somewhat stymied once in Mayfair.

Mark Granovetter's (1973) groundbreaking work on the importance of networks, and specifically the "strength of weak ties" in finding a job, argues that extended networks are critical because new information and opportunities flow through them. The broader and more diverse the social networks, the greater and more diversified the social capital. Denser networks, while particularly important for resources like emotional support, do little to provide new sources of information and are often redundant (Briggs 1997; Dominguez 2011).

The motivations behind programs such as the Gautreaux experiment in Chicago and the national Move to Opportunity (MTO) initiative largely arose from concerns around concentrated poverty as both cause and consequence of limited social networks, few middle-class role models, and a dearth of job opportunities in inner cities, trends identified in William Julius Wilson's vast body of work. Residential desegregation programs posit that individuals with fewer resources are better off when situated in racially, economically, and geographically diverse social networks (Rosenbaum 1991, 1995).

However, empirical findings are mixed in regard to the benefits of residential desegregation programs on those who move into better resourced communities (DeLuca and Dayton 2009; Briggs 1998, 2002; Briggs et al. 2010). Some contexts see higher high school graduation rates, higher rates of workforce participation, and lower levels of arrests among those who have moved, vis-à-vis comparable groups who remain in inner city communities. Other contexts see no such results. Further, participants in these moves may suffer from leaving behind critical support networks which provided emotional and logistical aid, and struggle to reconstitute similar social networks that fulfill these important roles in their new communities.

Expanding and diversifying networks can be challenging, even if one is not living and attending school in a racially or economically marginalized community. Even with geographic barriers removed, other challenges to diversification remain. Symbolic barriers (Lamont and Fournier 1992) can be difficult to overcome, and some divisions in society, particularly those around race and ethnicity, are among those most difficult to override in the expansion of networks (Briggs 1997, 1998, 2002).

Building Bridges

The formation of various types of "bridges" can play particularly critical roles in the expansion of networks and the greater dissemination of social capital, particularly to individuals who are part of more marginalized groups (Briggs 1998; Dominguez 2011). Bridges can provide important information and assistance to "get ahead" and change an individual or group's social location.

Mandated bridges come in the form of individuals working in an official capacity, such as a teacher, social worker, or low-level bureaucrat, who are explicitly employed to carry out certain duties. Embedded bridges are, in contrast, more spontaneous and informal, often coming in the form of community members who take it upon themselves to reach out. Although embedded bridges are arguably more committed and effective, growing out of their self-motivation and sense of social justice as opposed to the requirements of the job (Dominguez 2011), both forms bring diverse populations together and provide new sorts of resources to the two previously separated groups (Granovetter 1995).

According to Briggs (2002), bridge ties are most likely to develop effectively if certain conditions are met. Certainly contact is essential for the development of any sorts of bridges, but common interests, social pressure, and social conscience are also particularly important for the expansion of embedded bridges. One of the major goals of the voluntary desegregation programs of which many of these women are a part is to provide the opportunity for contact between students of color and their white counterparts. As we have seen in this study, however, this contact is generally not enough to have students develop meaningful relationships with each other. The result is that few bridges develop among peers; while bonding social capital flourishes among young women of color, bridging social capital between these girls and their white counterparts remains stymied. The prior chapter illustrates when common interests override the symbolic (and sometimes physical) boundaries, resulting in the development of bridge ties, the diversification of social networks among the students, and the growth of bridging social capital. Unfortunately, as is also discussed in the prior chapter, there are few examples of this type.

Another element allowing for and encouraging bridge building is social conscience, a particular motivation among embedded bridges (Dominguez 2011). Individuals may feel a sense of duty to provide greater access to resources to those in a community with more limited access. For example, the native-born may help immigrants to naturalize or those who tend to exist in a more middle-class milieu may reach out to provide tutoring, job assistance, or advice to those with more limited educational and economic opportunities. But, these examples of shared resources or social capital can only take place if contact between individuals and groups initially exists.

The Bridges of Mayfair

Although there is limited evidence of the diversification of peer social networks, there is ample evidence of bridge building between adults in the community and students of color, a process that leads to extended networks with new forms of social capital. These relationships often play critical roles in the lives of the young women of color, providing role models, emotional support, and social leverage via information and access (Lareau 2015; Briggs 1998; Coleman 1988). As Coleman (1988) argues, "Social capital is productive, making possible the achievement of certain ends that in its absence would not be possible" (p.98).

The bridges these women discuss are both mandated and embedded, coming respectively in the form of teachers, guidance counselors, and administrators, as well as program volunteers and parents. These adults often act as "cultural guides" (Lareau 2015), helping these young women to navigate this new and often challenging environment. Although previous research has found embedded bridges to be more effective than the paid, "official" bridges (Dominguez 2011), the findings here suggest mandated bridges provide support every bit as critical as that given by the embedded bridges. These adults often serve as crucial lifelines to the young women. Importantly, the type of bridge women experience is varied, based upon program participation and structure, as well as the symbolic boundaries and assumptions surrounding the women in their respective groups.

The Residents

The residents talk almost exclusively of the importance of mandated bridges—those who are hired in an official capacity by the school system. There is virtually no discussion of embedded bridges among the residents. This emphasis largely makes sense, as the town residents are not part of a particular program, but simply local girls going to school where they live. Throughout the resident interviews, women discuss the role and power of mandated bridges acting as sources of information (Coleman 1988; Dominguez 2011), as well as role models and "guides" throughout various processes in the school setting (Lareau 2015).

Alexandra, a resident who grew up in Section 8 housing, talks about both teachers and support staff who went out of their way to provide emotional support, access, and information to her. She says of her teachers, they "were really willing to help out." She says of one teacher in particular, "He was an awesome teacher. He just made teaching really fun...And, actually, the reason why I liked him, if anything ever happened, if, say, something big happened in school, like a confrontation with a group of kids or something like that, he would always stop whatever his lesson plan was and he'll let us talk about it." This teacher clearly provides important emotional support to his students, something that may not be explicitly mandated in his contract, but that seems to have a positive effect on them and may even influence the learning environment.

Perhaps the best example that Alexandra gives of a mandated bridge comes in the form of the school nurse. Alexandra had had frequent health problems throughout high school and spent significant amounts of time in the nurse's office. During these visits, Alexandra showed an interest in health and nursing. The nurse encouraged her to pursue this path and even wrote a letter of recommendation for her when she applied to college. Alexandra credits the nurse with helping her to get a scholarship, providing a clear illustration of social leverage. In this instance, the nurse served as an important bridge, providing emotional encouragement and critical support.

Hannah, another lower-income resident, also talks of numerous, important relationships with both teachers and guidance counselors, discussing ways in which they provided both emotional support and social leverage that allowed her to significantly alter her position. She says of her teachers, "If you have a good relationship with your teachers, they'll do anything for you." Of her guidance counselor, she says:

> My mom didn't go to college- well she went to State for I think a year, so she didn't really go to college and I don't think my dad graduated from college either so they didn't really know the process either...So, I had this completely wrong idea of what the college process was like. But then luckily, my guidance counselor—she's still there—she really helped me. She picked all the schools out for me and sent all the envelopes—sent everything out for me and helped me a lot.

Hannah went on to graduate from college, the first in her family. This is a clear illustration of a mandated bridge providing critical information to someone who does not have it through other avenues. Although Hannah's own family provides various sorts of resources, this guidance counselor serves as a critical cultural guide who helps her to navigate an unfamiliar system (Lareau 2015) by providing her with new forms of support and information that alter her position in society (Coleman 1988).

Jade, another woman who grew up in Section 8 housing in Mayfair, talks about her guidance counselor as a form of a mandated bridge. She says, "And he helped me with everything. He knew everything. He knew what I needed to do...." Again, this illustrates a mandated bridge providing women with critical information on how to achieve a particular outcome. Without this "how to" information, goals are likely to go unmet.

Gabriella recalls a different experience with her guidance counselor, unable to remember her name, but feels the teachers were always available to provide extra help and support. Brianna, a Section 8 resident, found similar academic support from teachers. She also recalls receiving emotional support from one teacher in particular. Brianna discusses this relationship: "During my junior year, I was a- I made a very good connection with my art teacher and she was amazing. And I went through a falling out with some of my friends that I had in high school, and so during free periods if I wanted to hangout in her room or work on any project that I had in there, I was always in her room." She ended up doing an intensive course in art during her senior year, as a result of the relationship.

Four town residents—Jade, Gabriella, Elisabeth, and Faith—talk about the commuter coordinator providing them with emotional support, even though they were not a part of the program. Jade discusses at various points throughout her interview her feelings of marginalization and a lack of belonging. She views the commuter coordinator as a source of emotional support:

> ...She was nice to us. She treated us like we were in [the commuter program], too, so we wouldn't feel like—cause it was different, like some kids [of color] lived in Mayfair, and then some lived in the city and she didn't want to make us feel like she couldn't be able to talk to us as much, like a counselor, just because we lived in Mayfair, so she talked to us.

Gabriella says about the commuter coordinator:

> She was great, she went above and beyond. We even had dinners at her home. She brought us home, she brought us gifts, she brought us, you know, birthday cards and she did a lot for us. I felt like she was my other grandma or aunt, you know, and she was definitely someone I could go to, and she always made sure that we felt like our ethnicities and our cultures were involved.

Elisabeth, a young woman who only moved to Mayfair from a nearby city for her senior year, also talks about the critical role of the commuter coordinator. Elisabeth felt she did not belong in this new world. The commuter coordinator provided Elisabeth with academic, as well as emotional support, and they still keep in touch more than a decade later. Faith talks about how the commuter coordinator set her up with an academic mentor, a formal part of the commuter program, even though she was a resident. She says of the English teacher with whom she was paired as a mentor, "I'm still friends with her to this day and she gives me advice and we go out to coffee and it's fun." Faith's relationship with the commuter coordinator then led her to a relationship with a teacher, who became and continues to be her mentor, providing advice and support.

These data highlight the social support provided by an individual who is a mandated bridge for the commuter students, but not for the town residents. Recall the discussion in Chap. 3 of the extensive and critical sharing of resources across the three groups of women. This administrator is exerting herself beyond her official job capacity and plays an important role to these young women of color who do not have this sort of mandated administrator in place to serve their unique needs.

It is important to note that Faith, Veronica, and Sara, women who grew up in college-educated, two-parent families and lived in market-rate homes owned by their parents, discuss the role of mandated bridges to a lesser extent than do the other town residents. When asked if they had someone from whom they could get help on homework, in the college admissions process, or for emotional support, they focused less on the role of mandated bridges, citing either a lack of need for these forms of help or their families as sources. Although Faith discusses her close relationship with the commuter coordinator and the benefits that resulted, she also cites her parents and older sister as critical sources of support and information. This distinction speaks to the role of a family's social and financial capital in social reproduction and the creation of human capital (Bourdieu 1986; Coleman 1988).

One resident, Hannah, also discusses her grandmother as an embedded bridge who played a critical role in her life and the lives of other children in her lower-income neighborhood, providing emotional support, opportunities, and other sorts of resources. Hannah talks about her grandmother organizing events and establishing relationships with various institutions in Mayfair. She says:

> We went on skiing trips. I never would have gone skiing if it wasn't for the programs that they had. We went skiing like three times. We would go to Jasper College trick or treating, and there was like a youth—there still is a youth center there, and people would come and tutor from the colleges and we would do these activities. I was forced to go to the firefighter camp.

These ties, developed by her grandmother, illustrate the types of experiences and assistance that can flow through networks. Hannah gains academic assistance, learns how to ski, accesses a college campus, and goes to summer camp as a result of the bridges built. She goes on to say that many of these programs and activities no longer exist for the children in Section 8 housing, as there is no one to organize them, further illustrating the critical role of bridges in spreading resources.

Commuters

The Reach graduates also talk about the role of teachers, guidance counselors, and administrators. Deana, who grew up in a divorced, lower-income immigrant household and now holds a graduate degree and works in the field of education, says of the teachers around her, "I was able to know what it meant to have educators around me who cared enough to see me succeed and not allow me to—not allow me to fail, so to speak, but allow me to fall on my backside, but pick myself back up with the care and support of people around me." She talks about some particular teachers:

> I mean English was where I struggled the most but where I felt most comfortable for some reason, but I think it was—it really had to do with them and their teaching style. And Mr. Smith who's a math teacher—I hated math. And he would not take, 'No, I'm done!' for an answer. And that is when I started to flourish was during junior year...

Andrea, a graduate from an earlier period who works as an accountant, echoes this sentiment, saying she always felt she had "great teachers who pushed me."

Deana also talks of her relationship with the school administrators, a relationship that started out strained, but ended up in a positive place. She says of the school principal, "Once I got in a better relationship with Ms. Jones, she was vital in me applying to school," an illustration of the social leverage provided by this mandated bridge. Like Hannah and Alexandra, this adult relationship provides information and support that helps Deana to gain access to college and alter her position in society.

May, who grew up in a two-parent immigrant household, graduated in the mid-2000s from Mayfair, and holds a degree from an elite liberal arts college, similarly discusses her relationship with teachers and administrators. She says she felt she could go to the "Vice Principal or to any of my teachers and just be like, 'This is what I'm feeling and thinking...,'" evidence of the emotional support provided through these ties. She talks about the implications of this support:

> ...I think that because they [the teachers and administrators] did believe in me or because they kept pushing me, it was just something that I started to believe. But, I think that came from the fact that the administrators really cared about me, and students in general. And our commuter coordinator always had her door open.

May feels the teachers, guidance counselor, administrators, and commuter coordinator all played important roles in her college application process and the opportunities she had. They gave advice on summer programs, looked over her college essay, and provided general guidance and support. Andrea also felt she had a guidance counselor who was "very helpful." She says, "My guidance counselor was always filling out her recommendations before I even started the application, so there was so much support that there was no reason why you couldn't do it all."

Similarly, Yolanda, a graduate from the 1990s who was raised by her mother and grandmother and went on to graduate from an elite women's college, praises her guidance counselor. She says of him, "He was amazing! He never told me, I know some students are advised, especially students of color in the city, to go to community college. I had a major university on my list. I had, you know, schools that, I had schools that were obviously reach schools, but he never made me feel like I couldn't go there." Monique, a graduate from the 1980s, recalls a similar situation, with her guidance counselor "pushing" her and "challenging her school selection." She credits the college decision that she made (and with which she is very happy) to Mayfair High, generally, and specifically, her guidance counselor.

Coretta, a young woman who grew up in a solidly middle-class, two-parent household and chose not to go to college, also talks about the support she received from teachers, guidance counselors, and administrators. She recalls her time at Mayfair High, saying, "The guidance counselors were very caring, as well. And they were always there. There was never a time where if you needed something or you needed some type of guidance or recommendations or what have you that no one- that there wasn't anyone there." There is a theme among these women of feeling both emotionally supported and academically pushed. They are experiencing certain norms and expectations that exist at both Mayfair High and in the community of Mayfair around academic performance and college attendance. The norms around achievement, coupled with emotional support and information on the steps necessary to reach particular goals, appear to play a significant role in outcomes (Coleman 1988).

Besides the more common means of supporting students academically, providing social leverage via extra academic assistance, letters of recommendation, or vetting out additional academic summer opportunities, students talk about other ways in which mandated bridges provided social leverage. Patricia discusses the important role that one administrator played in helping her figure out what she wanted to do after high school. She says, "I don't know what his position was, but there was this guy there who talked to me and me and him were talking about what I like and what I want to see myself doing and I said I like kids. And he told me about US Works...." Patricia applied and was accepted into this yearlong, paid job training program after graduating from Mayfair High.

Sasha, a graduate of the 1990s who works in human resources, talks not only about the academic quality of the teachers, "My teachers were great. I had some really, really great teachers...," but also a specific opportunity made possible by one of them. Sasha's foreign language class was taking a trip abroad and her teacher wanted her to go. Because Sasha's parents could not afford the entire cost of the trip, the teacher found a sponsor. Sasha says about her teacher, "She was so nice and so kind and she was such a good teacher. And then they did a Spanish language exchange trip and she really wanted me to go. I'm like, 'I'm not going,' and she convinced me. And so she ended up actually getting one of her friends to donate money...." This is a clear illustration of both financial capital and social capital flowing to the student through this mandated bridge. Importantly, Hannah and Gabriella, two lower-income town residents, also discuss this same foreign language trip that takes place every year, and their inability to afford to go on it. Such assistance was not extended to them.

Seven Reach students—Noel, May, Yolanda, Patricia, Coretta, Sasha, and Chantel—discuss the role of their respective Reach coordinator as a critical bridge. Although the specific coordinator referenced changed through the years, the emotional support, normative pressure, and social leverage provided by the various individuals holding the position seem to be consistent.

Noel talks about learning of a college scholarship through the Reach coordinator. She ended up at a highly selective liberal arts college. Noel views the role of the commuter coordinator as critical. She says:

> I don't think that we could have navigated through without our commuter director because she was there for us socially, to help us figure out how to talk out our feelings, and she was there for us academically. She was almost like our lawyer, there for us. She would tell us when we were right and when we were wrong.

In this statement, Noel is discussing the commuter coordinator as a bridge who provides social capital in the form of support and academic assistance, as well as a role model who exerts normative pressure to behave in particular ways.

May similarly talks about the critical role of the commuter coordinator, saying, "So she was by far the most important adult there and just really made it her job to understand us and, not only academically, but just how we were feeling and what we were going through...." Coretta says, "And if we weren't on our jobs about anything, she's just like you know, 'Come to my office.' She'd give us that talk. We'd get it together, and that's just what it would be. But she was always very supportive." This is, again, evidence of both normative pressure to meet certain academic expectations and emotional support.

Yolanda says her commuter coordinator was "fabulous" and that they went to her "for everything." She continues on, "I would say for me, all of my challenges, I would go to the commuter person. They look like me, and I felt like they at least could identify." Yolanda is touching upon the greater ease of developing bridges with those who share demographics, and implicitly citing the greater challenges associated with developing ties with those who exist across demographic "fault lines" (Briggs 1997).

The Reach program also includes a host family component, where families living in Mayfair volunteer to host a student who is part of the program at their homes on half days or for special events. These host families are assigned when a student from Urbana enters into the district.

Michelle, a commuter from the early 1990s, in talking about families in Mayfair says, "...As a kid, you get invited to everything, but when you talk to the parents...you can tell which parents really want you to come out [to Mayfair] and which parents would go totally out of their way to help you, to make it as easy as possible for you to come hang out." She talks about her sister's host family as being one of those families who would "go totally out of their way." Michelle would spend Halloween in Mayfair, and sleep over at the home of her sister's host family throughout her time in Mayfair. She describes it as a "welcoming experience."

Interestingly, Yolanda similarly discusses the relationship her mother had with her younger sister's host family, with an exchange of Christmas cards through today.

Serena, a graduate from the early 1990s who was finishing up college at the time of the interview, talks about her host family and describes a warm relationship in her elementary and middle school years. She remembers that her host family would invite her mother out to dinner, do activities together, have her over for sleepovers on a monthly basis, and help to organize her birthday party in Mayfair. Andrea says that she looked forward to her half days with her host family.

Joslin, a 1990s graduate who works as a medical technician, says of her experience with host families, "I guess I could say that if we didn't have a host family, I don't know how close I would have gotten to anyone. So, I guess in a way, it's kind of an invitation to come see our world, see what we have, and for me, that's an experience." Although her endorsement is subdued and her overall experience in Mayfair was "pretty bad," the host family does serve as a means of gaining experiences and insight into the higher echelons of society. As will be examined in the next chapter, this sort of cultural capital (Bourdieu 1986) becomes important as these women enter into the world beyond high school.

Coretta says she is still very close to the host family that she had. She describes the relationship that those parents had with her family as "awesome." This host family appears to have been less "official" and more spontaneous and embedded, however, likely explaining the strength of the relationship (Dominguez 2011).

It is important to note the more general forms of social capital that exist in the community, as well—the expectations and social norms around education that do not seem to come from any one particular bridge. Adults in the community can set important standards and reinforce expectations for children, generally, with the reinforcement of such norms acting as a form of social capital for everyone within the network (Wilson 1987; Coleman 1988).

Certainly some women felt the normative pressure around education from parents and other relatives. Lorraine, a 1980s graduate, recalls telling her mother that she was going to join the military after high school graduation. Lorraine's mother made it very clear that the only option available to her daughter was college. Noel tells of her mother earning a bachelor's degree while Noel was in elementary school. Her mother similarly made it very clear that Noel was going straight to college after high school. May remembers family conversations about college beginning when she was in fifth grade.

But, school-wide expectations also seem to play a role in the lives of multiple women, with five—Michelle, Noel, Sasha, Andrea, and Monique—explicitly discussing community standards. Noel talks about the conversations she had with adults in the community about college. Michelle talks about the expectation of college attendance. She says, "There was no, 'What are you doing?' It's just known, you go to college... that's instilled in you very early, that when you finish high school, you go to college." She regrets that her teenage son is not in a similar environment. Sasha tells a similar story about college: "I mean Mayfair kind of didn't really give you an option." She goes on to say:

> And I feel like everybody was just there, invested, and it just kind of helped push me as opposed to getting complacent because of the academic competition thing, that whole energy, the expectation for us to excel. So I feel like it's definitely kept that drive in me, too, to continue to excel. That's just probably one of my core values is, you know, doing the best you can, you know, and really putting in effort. And keeping the bar high. And I think that started then.

Monique says, "Obviously being in a community like Mayfair, which is, you know, a higher-end community, the expectation when you're going through school, you're going to college." Andrea recalls a similar feeling. She says, "The idea that because you don't have a 529 plan or your parents aren't saving money and you can't go to college- that was never an idea. My idea always was I'm going to college no matter what, and that you can go to college and that this is how you- these are the steps you take to make it there." Andrea, like residents Hannah and Alexandra, illustrates the power of the community to both set expectations and show individuals how to meet those expectations.

Boarders

The Aspire graduates similarly talk about the role of mandated bridges in their emotional and academic lives. Teachers and guidance counselors play a prominent role in the lives of these women. Christina, Tasha, Kelsey, Alana, and Malia talk about teachers providing emotional and academic support. Alana, an early graduate of the program from more than 500 miles away who holds multiple graduate degrees, explicitly says, "We had really good teachers that cared about us, that nurtured us. That was part of the extended family, if you will. We had teachers that looked out for us."

Guidance counselors are also cited as critical supports and bridges by multiple women. Alana says of her guidance counselor, "Dr. Smith, he made sure we went to college fairs, made sure we had the information, helped with any application if that was needed. He helped with identify[ing] where you really wanted to go." She talks about his commitment to "exposing us to the right people" and "calling the admissions office at different schools."

Jaqui, a graduate of the 2000s who works in education, says of her guidance counselor, "She was really good and she would usually take on all the [boarding] students and she really did a phenomenal job." Kelsey, a 1990s graduate who stays home full time to raise her children, also discusses the important role that her guidance counselor played throughout her high school experience: "I mean when it came to applying for college, my guidance counselor was really involved from the ninth grade helping me prepare for what I need to do, and start thinking about interests I would have and what areas of the country that I would want to go to school." Kelsey is experiencing the early concerted cultivation (Lareau 2011) so often seen in communities like Mayfair. She also cites the role that her English teacher played in the college application process, helping her with her college essays.

Karenna, a more recent graduate who grew up in a city about 100 miles away with her single mom, talks extensively about the importance of her teachers and guidance counselors throughout the interview. She describes her teachers as "amazing" and says, "Their doors were always wide open." Karenna discusses the academic and college assistance they provided her, "I had really great English teachers that kind of helped me fill out my applications for my summer programs, college things. Yeah, so there was always support. Always." But, beyond the important social leverage these teachers provided her, they also served as important emotional support systems. As Karenna says, "Whenever I really needed to talk with somebody, I had three teachers I knew I could go [to] and they were familiar with Aspire. They were familiar with how outrageous Mayfair could be and they were just really awesome support systems." These mandated bridges exert social leverage and act as compassionate voices.

Priscilla, a 1990s graduate who came from a very low-income, female-headed immigrant household, also discusses having important relationships with her teachers. She says, "And I never had a teacher at Mayfair who wasn't supportive and wouldn't help us." She recalls struggling with math and having a teacher who continued to work with her, never giving up. She also recalls a particularly important relationship with her English teacher who introduced her to the writings of a Latina author. She says of the experience, "He handed me Julia Alvarez's *How the Garcia Girls Lost their Accents*. That was the first book I ever read by a Latina. And I really look at that as one of the starting points of the journey of me becoming a writer, because I was like, 'Maybe I can do that.'" Priscilla went on to graduate from an Ivy League university and is now a published author. Although the teacher as a white male did not serve as a social model, he provided access to information and resources that allowed Priscilla to see what was possible. The role that he played illustrates the ability of individuals to be bridges, mentors, and partners to these women, regardless of the teacher or administrator's demographics.

Isabel, whose story opens this chapter, and who at the time of the interview was working in a lab and preparing for medical school, says this of her teachers, "I would never have been interested in medicine, interested in being a physician in the future if I didn't have teachers telling me, 'You know, you really need to do X, Y, and Z to get to the places where you can [become a doctor]." These examples given by Priscilla and Isabel are similar to those given by Alexandra and Patricia, women who learned about the professional possibilities available to them through these mandated bridges.

Isabel talks about other ways in which her teachers extended critical resources to her. She says of an English teacher:

> I took honors English and my honors English teacher, Mrs. Smith, I saw her in Tripoli Square and I almost broke down crying. She would meet with me after school and just teach me how to write a proper- how to structure a proper essay. The whole five paragraphs...You know she would meet with me about that. She would meet with me to improve my grammar, to improve my speech. I had a lot of dedicated teachers that really understood where I was coming from in terms of my middle school not preparing me...

This is a clear illustration of the role of "social capital in the creation of human capital" (Coleman 1988), with skill and knowledge flowing through teacher to student. In this instance, the teacher is extending more than just academic knowledge, but certain skills and mores essential to success in elite society. The teacher is acting as a "cultural guide" to Isabel, one who is familiar with the elite society in which Isabel finds herself (Lareau 2015).

Interestingly, numerous boarding students also discuss the role of the commuter coordinator as an important bridge and source of information and social support. Christina, a woman estranged from her parents and raised by extended family, talks about the commuter coordinator as being "one of my mentors." Karenna describes the coordinator during her time as being "like everybody's mom."

Tasha, a graduate of the 2000s who is currently enrolled in a prestigious graduate school, says of the commuter coordinator, "I was in close contact with the [commuter] coordinator at the school. You know, who all the minority students kind of personally went to." Tasha goes on to say, "She really made me feel at home at Mayfair High School. Without her, I probably would have been like [makes a face]—because it's nice to have a black face when I was in high school. She was an administrator who had a seat of power." She serves as a source of emotional support, but one who also advocates for these students, in keeping with the role of mandated bridges (Dominguez 2011).

Although many of the themes found among the boarders are similar to those found among the residents and commuters in regard to teachers and guidance counselors serving as mandated bridges, there are a few important differences. Alana talks about a teacher who she felt had been "blowing her off" becoming much more helpful after the teacher realized that she was part of the boarding program. Suddenly, Alana got significant academic assistance and emotional support, including inviting her over and taking her to the doctor when she was ill. Jaqui and Alana also talk about guidance counselors at Mayfair High who specifically were assigned the boarding students. Their enrollment in the boarding program gives these women a certain social status in the school and the community, lessening some barriers and opening up access to additional resources.

Additionally, the structure of the boarding program includes numerous built-in bridges for the young women. As with the commuter program, each boarder is assigned a host family from the community, but in the boarding program, it is a greater commitment. The host family volunteers to have the girl to their home one weekend each month, as well as to provide emotional support and assistance on a regular basis. These volunteers often serve as embedded bridges, connecting the boarder to the larger community and the resources that exist within that larger network. And, because the boarding program attracts as its volunteers some of the wealthiest and most prominent members of the community (and sometimes even larger society), the resources available are even greater.

The majority of boarders describe extremely strong and helpful relationships with their boarding families. Elise, a twenty-first-century graduate who was raised by a single, immigrant mother and has gone on to great success in corporate America, continues to feel connected to her host family, more than ten years since graduating. When asked about her experiences in Mayfair, she says, "It was hard. I got over it because I got to know the community I was living in. My host family was instrumental. I love my host family." She credits them with making the transition easier. She went on to become highly successful at Mayfair High and beyond. Tasha says of her host mother, "She was a huge part of why Mayfair was great." Jaqui echoes that sentiment. While she was in Mayfair, Jacqui's host family helped her with the college application process, even taking her to visit schools; they bought her gifts and took her on outings. She discusses her ongoing relationship with her host family, saying, "They're really good at checking in and seeing how things are going...." Tamara, a recent graduate who was still enrolled in college at the time of the interview, says of her host family, "I actually met up with them this past summer when they were in the city. When I was there, it was really welcoming. They tried to help me as much as possible."

Christina discusses a relationship marked by emotional and logistical support. Her host family helped her with the college application process and visited while she was in college (a three-hour drive from Mayfair). They continue to have a picture of her on their fridge. Besides feeling very much a part of the family over the longer term, her relationship with them helped her to develop peer relationships at the high school. She had a place to hang out with friends and was able to host a prom party, providing her with a sense of really belonging to the community.

Priscilla, a woman who graduated more than 20 years ago, is also still in touch with her host family. She stays at their house when she returns for reunions, even when they are out of town. She talks about them as providing critical emotional support for her 13-year-old self, giving her a "safe space." She goes on, "Their home to me was my escape. With them I always felt safe, you know? So, I think it's important to have a safe landing somewhere and they offered that, you know?"

Her host family also provided this future writer important intellectual opportunities: "My host dad was an English professor so they had all these books and, I would just go to his house and always read, and he would be like, 'Here have this new book' or, 'Just go ahead and see what you find.' You know? He had all these books...." Her host father even wanted her to attend the college where he taught; she declined. She credits both the social support and the social leverage as playing significant roles in her life.

Isabel, who had a hard time emotionally in Mayfair, recognizes her host family as playing an important role in her ability to stay there and graduate. She continues to be very close to her host mom:

> And Barbara and I spent so much time together. I would go grocery shopping with her. We could go and get things for the house or the dog and just go shopping and I would just tag along…It was great. I loved it. We watched movies together and Dr. Jones would come home and he would talk about his day. He runs an organ bank at Metropolitan Hospital.

The host family provided more than just emotional support, though. She learned from her host father about the field of medicine. He helped her to get an internship in the medical field and wrote a letter of recommendation for her for medical school, clear illustrations of social leverage.

Karenna similarly maintains a relationship with her host family, "I was just texting my host mom yesterday," and says she "lucked out" with them. She feels they were the only people who really welcomed her in Mayfair. Karenna discusses in more detail the various ways that this embedded bridge has helped her:

> Even in Seattle, my host mom's family accepts me and they're so nice. Yeah, they've been so instrumental in my life…For graduation, and this is not very common—they gave me their old car for graduation and that improved my life so much. I took it to the northwest with me and I'm still driving that car. And it's just, it's just so many things they've done that I'm so grateful for them and just for them taking me in as a kid.

Karenna's host family clearly provides ongoing emotional support, as well as a multitude of other resources, not least of which is a car. Although this type of gift could be viewed as an overreach on the part of the host family, Karenna makes a point of telling me that they had spoken with her mother and asked permission before they gave her the car because "she [the host mom] just didn't want to step on any toes." The host family would have

Karenna's mother stay with them when she came to visit Mayfair, and the two mothers continue to have a relationship, years after Karenna has graduated from Mayfair.

Marian, the twenty-first-century graduate and athlete highlighted in the prior chapter, says she treasures the fact that her host family treated her like one of their own children—yelling at her when she stepped out of line and questioning her about low grades, an enforcement of the community norms and expectations around academic achievement (Coleman 1988). Marian also talks about her grandmother needing a shoulder replacement back in her home city. Because her host father worked in the field, he assisted in the process and gave her mother and grandmother important information about the procedure, illustrating how social capital flows to those beyond the immediate points of contact.

The Aspire graduates also talk about other embedded networks that play critical roles in their experiences. The Aspire program is highly structured, with volunteers from the community doing everything from providing academic assistance to college and financial aid counseling, all independently of what Mayfair High offers. The community members who fill these volunteer roles are often leading professionals in the fields in which they are volunteering. For example, Christina talks glowingly of her assigned academic advisor in the program, someone who had a strong background in academia and was married to a high-ranking administrator at a prestigious university in the area. Kelsey talks about getting SAT preparation from a community member who had experience in this area. Isabel discusses her college counselor through the program, a woman who had a private and very expensive college counseling practice. Isabel and Malia also talk about a math tutor who would regularly come to the boarding house. He was a retired math professor. Tasha discusses her academic advisor helping her to apply to (and get accepted into) a mentorship and scholarship program for college. Jaqui discusses her advisor helping with college essays, taking her to visit colleges, and acting as "a sounding board for everything and anything." These are all illustrations of bridging social capital resulting from diverse social networks.

In a few instances, peer friendships become bridges to adult resources and adult bridges provide access to peer friendships. These genuine, organic relationships can be important in shaping opportunities for these young women, even with the relationships developing for non-instrumental reasons. In fact, the initial lack of instrumentality may explain the success of the bridges that develop spontaneously (Dominguez 2011). For example,

Christina talks about a friend whose father worked for the SAT and provided assistance to her and her friends. In a reverse order of contact, Karenna talks about a board member from the program, a woman of color who lived in Mayfair. Karenna says of the woman, "She knew the struggle and her door was always open." This embedded bridge led to an important peer relationship—her son became a close friend of Karenna's. She describes him as her "best friend" and someone with whom she is still in touch. Similarly, Isabel describes her host sister as her closest friend from Mayfair and someone with whom she is still in touch. She says that while they were in high school, they would get ice cream, do homework together, and just hang out. Isabel would also spend time with her host sister's friends, another means by which Isabel's networks were expanded and diversified. Kelsey and Marian also talk about developing real friendships with the children in their respective host families—other young women their age.

Bridge Failures

Although many mandated and embedded bridges exist in Mayfair, providing critical resources, including emotional support, academic assistance, and additional forms of social leverage, there are numerous instances of "bridge failures" where those located in positions to traverse boundaries fail to do so. In Mayfair, bridge failures often result from racial stereotypes, including assumptions around where girls are from, what their homes are like, and what their abilities are. These "match-ups" of larger-scale, exterior racial categories with the assumption of particular geographic, social, and academic locations within Mayfair reflect and reinforce "durable inequalities" in society (Tilly 1999). There is also evidence of bridge failures resulting from cultural insensitivities and micro-aggressions, including women being called on to represent the "black viewpoint" (Sue, Capodilupo and Holder 2008). Structural factors, including the absence of racial representation in the curriculum, may stymie bridge building. Although this latter factor is not the fault of any one individual who is positioned to be a bridge, the structural underpinnings (or the lack) make bridge building more difficult, generally.

The Geography of Race

Alexandra and Jade, both town residents, talk about teachers assuming that they were commuter students. They are experiencing a process of "othering" through this geographic misplacement and an assumption that they cannot be from Mayfair because of their skin tone. As discussed in Chap. 2, these assumptions led to feelings of isolation and liminality, but they must also be understood as behaviors that sabotaged bridge building by those explicitly there to build such connections. Alexandra says about trying to explain that she was a town resident, "It just got to the point—I just gave up and I'm like, 'Okay, they don't care.'" Alexandra says she took offense at the assumption that she was not from the community and then took advantage of it by getting out of after-school detention or staying for extra help. Had she not felt marginalized by the teachers and their assumptions, she perhaps would have been willing to access the resources held by these potential bridges.

Jade found the teachers to be "very ignorant." She, too, took advantage of their assumptions, but this likely translated into her academic disadvantage. She needed extra help, but was not required to stay after school because the teachers were concerned that she would miss the bus back into the city.

Veronica, another town resident, similarly experienced the assumption of otherness and geographic misplacement from teachers, students, and parents. Unlike Alexandra and Jade, though, Veronica was assumed to be a boarding student because of her strong academics. She says the assumptions "made it a little kind of awkward at times." The frequent geographic misplacement that she experienced eventually led her to move out of Mayfair after she and her white husband, who was also from Mayfair, had graduated from college. She said she just grew tired of being asked if she was their child's nanny.

The Assumption of Poverty

In addition to young women, particularly residents, experiencing assumptions about where they were (or were not) from, multiple women discuss assumptions about what their homes and neighborhoods looked like. These women are assumed to be from poverty-stricken households and violent, dystopic communities. This stereotype seems to most often arise from embedded bridges, parents who volunteer as host families for the two programs in the community. As discussed previously, bridges are sometimes built with the goal of social justice and a desire to spread opportunities to those with fewer resources. The residents of Mayfair who volunteer in the programs, be it as part of the commuter program or as part of the boarding program, may be motivated by that sense of social justice. Unfortunately, the commitment to social justice, or perhaps the execution of it, sometimes falls short and women describe feeling like "charity cases," growing out of the residents' assumptions that the women come from homes of dire poverty.

This feeling of being a "charity case" is described by both commuters and boarders, although to differing degrees. Six of 15 commuters—Deana, Sasha, Noel, Serena, Joslin, and Chantel—discuss feeling this way. Serena, a commuter, says of her host family, "You just started to feel more like that was their good deed, you know what I mean, like they helped the poor black kid get through elementary and middle school and now they're kind of done with you type thing." Joslin says, "I felt like a lot of times, they're doing their part by letting you come to school there, and that was enough."

Although the volunteers in the boarding program generally seem to be more effective bridges than the volunteers in the commuter program, boarding women talk with even more feeling around this issue than do commuters and at a higher rate. This is likely because of the greater involvement of the host families and other community volunteers in the boarding program. Greater engagement translates into both more good and more bad. It is also likely the result of boarding students being more dependent upon the community, as a whole, than were the commuter students who had parents and homes to which they returned each night. Six of 12 women—Christina, Isabel, Karenna, Marian, Tamara, and Alana—talk about these feelings, some at great lengths.

One boarder, Isabel, says she constantly felt like a "charity case." She said she lived in constant fear of being "the poor, black girl." Christina says there were times when she just wanted to go to school like everyone else: "I don't want to feel like charity. Why are we going to a fundraiser, and people taking pictures of us? And all this other stuff." Marian says it was "almost like we were a charity case." Karenna, the child of a nurse, says, "I had people, adults, friend's parents be like, 'Oh, yeah, I know about the Aspire program, do you need money?'" She goes on to say:

> I think the battle of the charity case was a thing that was hard for me because we do have a very supportive board of people at Mayfair. We have a supportive system but I think there were a lot of times where we felt like, I don't know. I don't really know how to put words into it but I never really wanted to- I think there were just moments when I felt bad for being there.

Alana says, "I think they thought we were so dirt poor." She continues, "One thing I kept hearing a lot of was, 'Underprivileged, underprivileged, underprivileged.' I think that's the wrong talk. Like I told you, we may not have had as much as wealthy or middle-class white people, but in our community we were middle-class." She felt like she was a "little black doll" or plaything that the family grew tired of. Tamara makes a similar comment. She says, "I guess the one thing I would change is- a lot of times being black in Mayfair means people perceive you as automatically being some type of charity case." She says that she and her counterparts in the boarding program "were always reminded that we were being helped out." Such assumptions chill relationships between these young women and adults in the community, even those adults who have positioned themselves to theoretically serve as bridges.

Viviana Zelizer (1989) discusses the different meanings of money in society. Instead of these women being made to feel or feeling like they were entitled to this support, they often felt that the support they received came in the form of gifts upon which they were dependent. These "gifts" were at the discretion of the town residents and board members, placing women in a subservient position. Tasha says of her host family, "It was kind of- I love my host family, but my host mom at some points didn't understand where I was coming from." She goes on to say that she thinks it was a combination of both racial and economic differences.

Academic Expectations

Residents and commuters also talk about the stereotypes related to academic abilities and how it impacted their relationships with adults who should have been bridges into the community. Elisabeth, who moved to Mayfair as a senior in high school, said the teachers and administrators assumed she would be academically behind, given her background. Elisabeth recalls:

> I was told by the Vice Principal that I wouldn't graduate, that I would probably be left back and would have to repeat the twelfth grade because she didn't think that I had the proper education coming from an inner city school compared to being in a suburban school. I didn't really like that because it was like she never really gave me a chance.

During her senior year at Mayfair High, she was able to make a diverse group of friends and ended up excelling academically, but felt those in power stereotyped and underestimated her. She says that she never felt that she fit in because of these assumptions.

Monique, a commuter who had positive experiences with many of her teachers, had this to say: "I'm still friends with my English teacher from high school, and even talking to him, you know, just about the commuter program and things of that nature, he was just saying that I guess there was a thought about, 'Oh, you know, it's the poor black kids and we just have to, you know, kind of treat them a little bit differently.'"

Women also discuss how these generalized stereotypes and assumptions of lower academic abilities have real-world implications. Deana, a commuter who came to be a leader among her racial counterparts and the community as a whole, had to fight to be put into an AP U.S. History class. Chantel, another commuter, says:

> I took honors English. And that was unusual for commuter students to do. And so from day one, I felt like I needed to prove that I was supposed to be there. And my freshman year English teacher was difficult- often pushed back in the first place, about me being in the class, with my mom. He was condescending to her when she tried to be a support system for me, and then I think with those things combined, I just felt like I needed to be on my A game in English class. So I went in already feeling like I needed to be a certain type of person, and kind of like everyone around me was my competition. And I think the culture of Mayfair High School is very competitive in general. And so being the enigma in the room and being a token and feeling like everyone is looking at you like you are a charity case on a regular basis, which in this particular class, you're especially exceptional, that was hard. That was really hard....

Serena, also a commuter student, says:

> The other thing I didn't tell you is that they discouraged us from ever being- like we never had the chance to be in the honors classes. They would tell us that it's too much pressure on us, so we never really had a fair chance at being at the top of the class. They wouldn't allow us to. So from my frustration with that too, because I took- I was in Spanish, I got straight A's in Spanish, the teacher wanted to put me in honors Spanish. And they wouldn't allow it. So at that point, I was just kind of like 'Whatever.' You know, you just kind of feel like you're not worth it, so why try type of thing. They said that it's too much pressure getting up early in the morning to deal with the pressure of being in an honors class.

Alexandra talks about how the lower-level classes she took were comprised primarily of minority students, a trend of lower expectations identified in prior research on African American adults (Fleming et al. 2012). These lower expectations on the part of teachers and guidance counselors arise in other interviews, as well, particularly around college applications. May recalls the experience of an older friend in the commuter program who ended up going to a prestigious college in the Northeast, but, "Her guidance counselor told her she should only apply to state schools…And it really made her angry." Sasha, who describes feeling a general expectation of attending college, still felt a differentiation. She says, "It wasn't necessarily the expectation that we got into the best colleges, it was just the expectation that we went to college. And so it was a different rat race [from the white residents]." These young women seem to be evaluated through a different lens (Asad and Bell 2014). Although a less common occurrence among Aspire students, Karenna had a similar experience with a college guidance counselor telling her not to apply to the school to which she had always aimed. She says, "I remember them telling me, 'No, you don't need to apply. You're not going to get in.' And, I'm like, 'Why are you telling me these things? This is the reason that I came to Mayfair.'" Karenna applied, was accepted, and graduated four years later.

On a larger level, the interactions between teachers and residents, and students of color, respectively, help to perpetuate the inequality and labeling in place in Mayfair and reaffirm larger racial divisions in society (Tilly 1999; Omi and Winant 1994). These types of assumptions around both geographic belonging and academic ability stand as barriers to bridge building and reflect Tilly's (1999) argument around the maintenance of societal inequality through categorically differentiated responses to and opportunities for groups.

These differential placements and expectations also reflect Tilly's (1999) theoretical argument around differences in rewards by category—what level of class one is placed in, what colleges one should apply to. They also suggest a form of opportunity hoarding (Tilly 1999), whether intentional or unintentional. These sorts of experiences further illustrate Du Bois' (1903/1994) theory of double consciousness. The women both know what they are capable of—excelling in a course or getting accepted into an elite university—and realize how they are perceived by at least some members of white society. Their time in a town and school like Mayfair has likely honed their double consciousness to a degree experienced by few, as these women live as Americans of color, but in the most elite corners of American society.

On the flip side, boarding students experienced different sorts of stereotypes and expectations. Six students—Malia, Christina, Priscilla, Karenna, Isabel, and Marian—discuss higher expectations, often feeling as if they were under a "microscope," again in keeping with prior research (Fleming et al. 2012). Malia says that the board members did not have the same high expectations for their own children that they had for the boarding girls. She says, "I feel like they didn't treat us as fairly as they should have because they'd be expecting so much more of us compared to what they would [their children], because we went to a high school with their children, as well. We knew their kids, and it was like they wouldn't be asking their kids for most of the things that were expected of us...." Marian similarly feels differences existed in expectation and this affected her relationship with them: "I feel like it was hard to listen to someone tell you, 'You can't do this.' But yet their child is doing the same thing." This was true both academically—Marian was sanctioned for receiving a "C" on her report card in her freshman year and was required to do extra study hours—and socially. Isabel says, "I think it was really hard because we were expected to perform well academically, we were expected to fit into this community, we were expected to be involved in school...." The boarding girls were expected by the adults who ran the program to be better academically, more involved, and better behaved than their own children.

In these varied examples, the embedded members of the community are enforcing the social norms, through awards and sanctions, around academic achievement (Coleman 1988), but they are doing so at a cost to their relationships with the young women. It is as if the girls in the boarding program are viewed as the "talented tenth" (Du Bois 1903/1994), those individuals of color best suited to lead their community. It is unclear whether this results from bias on the part of board members, their sense of responsibility for serving in loco parentis, or perhaps an understanding that as women of color of more moderate means, these girls needed to be better than their wealthy, white peers. Regardless of the motivation, the feeling on the part of these women is one of categorically distinct responses to similar behaviors (Tilly 1999).

Representing a Whole Population

Bridges also fail to be built for another reason—the cultural insensitivity and micro-aggressions that women experience. Women recall being asked to represent the viewpoint of people of color on topics such as slavery, racism, and affirmative action. There are illustrations of this behavior, and its effect on bridge building, from women across the three residential groupings. Veronica, a resident, says:

> One of my strongest memories of an uncomfortable moment with one of the history teachers there was, you know, we would ultimately have to talk about slavery, and there would be maybe 3, 4 of us at max, you know, people of color in the class, and he would point out, 'Well, you know, if it was during these times, you and you and you would all be slaves.' And I'm like, 'Well, that's an obvious thing.' Why does that need to be mentioned? But it was something that happened from time to time.

Tasha, a boarder, similarly felt she was often called upon to provide the "black" point of view. Lorraine recalls being the only student of color in her history class when they were learning about slavery. She says, "We divided the class up. And me being the only black student in the class, of course the teacher assigned me to be the slave and my mom was pissed off. I remember my mother coming up to the school to address the issue." These experiences understandably chill the relationship between the student and the mandated bridge, making it less likely she will access the resources she needs. Yolanda, who graduated nearly two decades after Lorraine, tells a similar story of reading *Uncle Tom's Cabin* in English class. She says, "Anytime he [the teacher] talked about Kizzy the slave, he would look at us and identify us and say that we knew what it was like." Yolanda goes on to say, "I don't know what it's like to run barefoot for Massachusetts- I mean from, wherever the hell she was, North Carolina all the way to Boston." She finishes by adding, "He always said our names wrong," suggesting another way in which she felt marginalized by the teacher.

Noel recalls a discussion on race and affirmative action. She says, "And I remember talking [about affirmative action], and someone told me in my class not to pull the race card. And I was like, 'This isn't a race card, I live this life every day. It's not something I put in my back pocket.' And I remember thinking that teacher left me there. Didn't say anything, left me on my own, by myself." This was an opportunity missed by the teacher to establish a sense of trust and, from there, build a bridge to Noel.

No Place in the Curriculum

There are also structural barriers that keep bridges from being built, particularly around what is taught in the classrooms. Although these structural failings cannot be attributed to any one individual and speak to the institutionalized racial inequality in larger American society, they serve to create a foundation upon which bridges become harder to build. Priscilla, in talking about the curriculum, says, "You know, we need to see ourselves in literature that you share." She feels that the absence of history and literature about and by people of color makes students of color "feel like we don't matter." She finishes by asking, "What do you read? Mostly dead white men."

Deana similarly takes issue with what is taught. Noel, while not having a personal issue with the curriculum, recalls friends wanting to take AP U.S. History: "That was the only class that had a supplement black curriculum and I remember that was a big deal." This sense of being left out of the curriculum, of not having a place at the table, influences how connected these young women feel. Isabel says, "There wasn't anything positive about being a person of color at the high school. I mean we didn't ever have- we didn't do anything for- for Black history month."

Although these are structural barriers that need to be addressed at the higher, administrative level, there are instances of bridge building that go on between teachers and students, despite and sometimes explicitly because of these lapses. Priscilla talks about her English teacher introducing her to Latino literature. Deana talks about the support she received from her AP U.S. History teacher after she fought the administration to get into the class. Certainly having more adults who "look like me," as Yolanda says, would likely help the building of bridges between these young women and adults in the community. It would help these students to feel that they are not quite so alone in a world that often feels foreign and marginalizing. But examples exist that suggest that bridges can be built even by those who are demographically opposite—older, white men who see it as their responsibility to reach out to these young women of color.

Conclusion

There are many illustrations of effective bridge building, with teachers, administrators, and volunteers reaching across borders at critical times to provide invaluable assistance to these young women. Adults, who appear motivated by both a deep concern for these individual students and a larger concern with structural inequality in society, often make the difference in the lives of these high schoolers.

Even with the many examples illustrated in this chapter, there are formal, structural steps that could be taken to minimize some of the bridge failures that do take place. For example, the programs and school could require cultural sensitivity training on the part of both mandated bridges and embedded volunteer bridges. Guidance counselors should be given explicit training on advising students, including training that helps them to become aware of their (unintentional) biases. Curriculum could be diversified to create a more inclusive atmosphere and allow everyone in the system, regardless of race, to have a better sense of the contributions of various racial and ethnic groups in society. All of these formal, structural changes could go a long way in altering the culture in classrooms, guidance offices, and in volunteer homes, which would increase the likelihood of bridge building.

Although the bridge failures are significant, so too are the effective bridges that are built. Both the mandated and embedded bridges go a long way in providing social and emotional support, as well as social leverage (Briggs 1997; Dominguez 2011). These connections across groups that lead to bridging social capital are critical in helping these young women to change their positions in society and "get ahead." Chapter 6, "The Acquisition of Cultural Capital," examines the ways in which the social capital flowing across successful bridges translates into cultural capital wholly owned by the young women.

It is also critical to remember that bridges connect two previously unconnected groups and just as social capital can and does flow from adults in the community to the young women of color, these young women also share critical information and resources with their elder counterparts on the other side of the bridge. Chapter 7, "Race, Place, and the Power of Interactions," explores the ways in which these women, as young students, held up their end of the bridge, providing social capital in the form of information, insight, and exposure often lacking on the part of the dominant group. These women also act as important bridges to their families and home communities. As bridges within and across communities, these women effect social change on both sides of the divide.

Bibliography

Asad, A., and M. Bell. 2014. Winning to Learn, Learning to Win: Evaluative Frames and Practices in Urban Debate. *Qualitative Sociology* 37: 1–26.

Bourgois, P. 1996. *In Search of Respect*. Cambridge: Cambridge University Press.

Bourdieu, P. 1986. The Forms of Capital. In *Handbook of Theory and Research for the Sociology of Education*, ed. J. Richardson, 241–258. New York: Greenwood Press.

Briggs, D. 1997. Social Capital and the Cities: Advice to Change Agents. *National Civic Review* 86(2): 111–117.

———. 1998. Brown Kids in White Suburbs: Housing Mobility and the Many Faces of Social Capital. *Housing Policy Debates* 9(1): 177–221.

———. 2002. Bridging Networks, Social Capital & Racial Segregation in America. *Harvard University, John F. Kennedy School of Government Working Paper Series*, rwp02-011.

Briggs, D., S. Popkin, and J. Goering. 2010. *Moving to Opportunity*. Oxford: Oxford University Press.

Carter, P. 2015. Educational Equity Demands Empathy. *Contexts, Fall* 2015: 76–78.

———. 2012. *Stubborn Roots*. Oxford: Oxford University Press.

Coleman, J. 1988. Social Capital in the Creation of Human Capital. *The American Journal of Sociology* 94: S95–S120.

DeLuca, S., and E. Dayton. 2009. Switching Social Contexts: The Effects of Housing Mobility and School Choice Programs on Youth Outcomes. *The Annual Review of Sociology* 35: 457–491.

Dominguez, S. 2011. *Getting Ahead: Social Mobility, Public Housing, and Immigrant Networks*. New York: New York University Press.

Du Bois, W. 1903/1994. *The Souls of Black Folks*. New York: Dover Publications.

Fleming, C., M. Lamont, and J. Welburn. 2012. African Americans Respond to Stigmatization: The Meanings and Salience of Confronting, Deflecting Conflict, Educating the Ignorant and 'Managing the Self'. *Ethnic and Racial Studies* 35(3): 400–418.

Granovetter, M. 1973. The Strength of Weak Ties. *American Journal of Sociology* 78(6): 1360–1380. doi:10.1086/225469.

———. 1995. *Getting a Job*. Chicago: University of Chicago Press.

Khan, S. 2011. *Privilege: The Making of an Adolescent Elite at St. Paul's School*. Princeton and Oxford: Princeton University Press.

Lamont, M., and M. Fournier. 1992. *Cultivating Differences: Symbolic Boundaries and the Making of Inequality*. Chicago: University of Chicago Press.

Lareau, A. 2011. *Unequal Childhoods*. Berkeley: University of California Press.

———. 2015. Cultural Knowledge and Social Inequality. *The American Sociological Review* 80(1): 1–27.

Massey, D., and N. Denton. 1993. *American Apartheid: Segregation & the Making of the Underclass*. Cambridge: Harvard University Press.

Omi, M., and H. Winant. 1994. *Racial Formation in the United States: From the 1960s to the 1990s*. New York: Routledge.

Rosenbaum, J. 1995. Changing the Geography of Opportunity by Expanding Residential Choice: Lessons from the Gatreaux Program. *Housing Policy Debate* 6(1): 231–269.

———. 1991. Employment and Earnings of Low-Income Blacks who Move to White Suburbs. In *The Urban Underclass*, ed. Christopher Jencks and Paul Peterson. The Brookings Institute: Washington, DC.
Small, M. 2004. *Villa Victoria: The Transformation of Social Capital in a Boston Barrio*. Chicago: University Of Chicago Press.
Sue, D., C. Capodilupo, and A. Holder. 2008. Racial Micro Aggressions in the Life Experience of Black Americans. *Professional Psychology: Research and Practice* 39: 329–336.
Tatum, B. 2003. *Why are all the Black Kids Sitting Together in the Cafeteria?* New York: Basic Books.
Tilly, C. 1999. *Durable Inequality*. Berkeley: University of California Press.
Wilson, W. 1980. *The Declining Significance of Race*. Chicago: University of Chicago Press.
———. 1987. *The Truly Disadvantaged*. Chicago: University of Chicago Press.
———. 1996. *When Work Disappears: The World of the New Urban Poor*. New York: Random House.
———. 2009. *More than Just Race: Being Black & Poor in the Inner City*. New York: W.W. Norton.
Zelizer, Viviana. 1989. The Social Meaning of Money: 'Special monies'. *American Journal of Sociology* 95(2): 342–377.

CHAPTER 6

The Acquisition of Cultural Capital

Gabriella's Story

Gabriella, a resident of the town, graduated from Mayfair in the mid-2000s. She grew up in a single-mother, working-class household with her brother. She talks about what she gained from having attended school in Mayfair—first and foremost her education. Gabriella also talks about other benefits of growing up and attending school in town, including her exposure to different cultures. She celebrated Chinese New Year, learned Spanish, and attended Bat Mitzvahs. Gabriella also talks about the way she learned to speak: "Because we were raised in this white snobby town." She notes that her clothes were different, relative to her friends and cousins in the city. Gabriella was raised in an upper-middle-class white milieu and incorporated many of those practices, even as a lower-income Latina woman. She also talks about having Mayfair High on her resume and a Mayfair address on her driver's license, factors which helped her in a variety of settings. These illustrations speak to the various forms of cultural capital that Gabriella and other young women gained from living or attending school in Mayfair, benefits that existed beyond the classroom and which have stayed with them over time.

CULTURAL CAPITAL

French sociologist Pierre Bourdieu (1986) began his exploration of the concept of cultural capital when examining the varying educational trajectories of French schoolchildren. In identifying the consistently poorer academic outcomes among children of lower socioeconomic status, vis-à-vis their wealthier counterparts, he began to consider the social and economic advantages conferred at home on this latter group, and how they might benefit in the schoolroom and beyond.

Bourdieu's (1984, 1986) related theories of habitus and cultural capital help to make sense of the distinct social advantages directly and indirectly resulting from economics, and heavily predictive of future successes in both academic and workplace settings. Our habitus is our set of expectations and beliefs that develop unconsciously, guiding our behavior and providing us with a framework in which to make sense of the social world. Through our habitus, we become primed for future social encounters—what those encounters look like, how we interpret them, and what we take away from them. Cultural capital is comprised of the non-economic resources, such as insider knowledge, that grant us access to a particular segment of society. Bourdieu argues that habitus and cultural capital acquisition are intimately connected. Our initial habitus primes us to acquire and utilize future forms of cultural capital to which we may be exposed (Bourdieu 1984). It is not simply education that allows us to "understand" a work of art, but our initial disposition or habitus that places us in that setting and determines our ability to acquire specific skills of art appreciation, a form of cultural capital.

Two forms of cultural capital that Bourdieu identifies—the embodied and the institutionalized—particularly speak to ways in which individuals can possess non-economic resources that are used in societies as symbols or markers of who should be included and who should be excluded in particular settings (Lamont and Fournier 1992).[1]

Embodied cultural capital is the form that is most often associated with the general term, coming in the form of exposure, knowledge, accents, mores, and the "long lasting dispositions of the mind" (Bourdieu 1986). Both our habitus and much of our embodied cultural capital often develop unconsciously through early socialization in the household, as well as through daily interactions embedded within the larger, stratified institutions that comprise society.

Institutionalized cultural capital is that which comes in the form of socially recognized statuses around us, be it a literal title such as "Senator" or a degree from an elite institution. Such capital is accompanied by widespread honor and deference, accorded in proportion to the exclusivity of the title. As with embodied cultural capital, it is held by an individual and cannot be passed down, but in contrast to embodied cultural capital which often results from subconscious socialization, the institutionalized can, at times, be acquired through active acquisition.

The educational realm, perhaps more than any other, reflects and reinforces the stratification that exists in larger society (Bourdieu and Passeron 2000). The distinct orientations, practices, and skills emanating from middle- and upper-middle-class white households serve as critical cultural capital in the school setting, rewarded by educational gatekeepers (Coleman 1988; Bourdieu 1986, 1991; Lareau 2011, 2015; Calarco 2014). Conversely, orientations and practices from lower-income households may be penalized. For example, Hannah, a town resident, recalls a teacher writing on her younger brother's report card that "He spoke Ebonics." The teacher viewed his dialect as unacceptable in this elite educational environment. In contrast, Yolanda, a woman who graduated from the Reach program, talks about her mother's emphasis on the "2 Es": education and experience. She says, "Even before I started at Mayfair, my mom would take us out to fancy restaurants and teach us how to eat, exposing us to different things." While she may not have been a part of elite society, Yolanda's mother had the insight and ability to provide her with the cultural capital she would need to succeed in such an environment. One of the significant benefits found for young people of color attending elite, white schools is the significant amounts of elite cultural capital gained (Zweigenhaft and Domhoff 1991, 2003; Eaton 2001; Anson 1988; Cookson and Persell 1991).

If social capital is only possible through the existence of social relationships and the ability to marshal resources that exist within one's network, the acquisition of cultural capital is less obviously dependent on relationships. This is *not* to say that social relationships are irrelevant in the acquisition of cultural capital. In fact, relationships of the earliest and most intimate variety unconsciously socialize children into certain ways of "being," playing a critical role in the development of their habitus. Later relationships, such as the ones discussed in detail in the previous chapter, also illustrate the role of social relationships in the acquisition of cultural capital. Recall the access to books that Priscilla was provided by her host father, an English professor, or Sasha's ability to travel to a foreign country as a result of her relationship with her foreign language teacher. These women were embedded in resource-rich social networks that provided certain forms of social capital—knowledge, intellectual exposure, financial support. But, the knowledge, experiences, and exposure, originally resulting from these important and deeply personal relationships, become incorporated into an individual's way of being, regardless of whether the initial relationship remains.

Embodied cultural capital can also be acquired through daily, mundane interactions with acquaintances and even strangers (Garschick Kleit 2001; Wilson 1987). This form of capital may result from how we see people interact with one another when they meet on the street. Do they make eye contact and shake hands? Cultural capital may result from what we watch on television—knowledge about art and antiques from a PBS program. In short, the acquisition of cultural capital, although certainly related to social networks, social capital, and economic capital, is an independent resource.

Cultural Capital in Mayfair

Mayfair is a community comprised of individuals who are resource rich. The various forms of capital in the town, from the economic to the human to the social to the cultural, all reinforce each other and perpetuate the status positions of families within the community. Parents with degrees from elite universities and graduate schools hold high-powered and well-compensated positions in law, medicine, academia, and finance. Their economic and human capital is passed down to their children in the form of expectations, opportunities, and exposure to exclusive aspects of society— the initial formation of the next generation's habitus and the transmission of embodied cultural capital. As legacies at some of the most elite colleges and universities in the world, their children are, at birth, provided with a significant advantage of entry 18 years hence, thus paving the way for the acquisition of institutionalized cultural capital.

The community is also a setting in which parents engage in concerted cultivation (Lareau 2011). Dozens of elementary schoolchildren each year participate in weekly social etiquette classes. The public elementary schools take the children to a world-class art museum in the city from which the commuter students come. Preparation for admission to top colleges begins early, with children taking after-school math classes, engaging in formal SAT preparation, and meeting with college counselors for assistance in preparing for interviews and applying to college. Travel, including international travel, is commonplace. At one elementary school during the course of data collection, four families were separately going to the same European country for a summer vacation and actually met up in a foreign capital. This is not to suggest that everyone in Mayfair has the economic wherewithal to take such vacations or afford private college counseling. What it is to suggest is that such behaviors are far from aberrant and the community "feel" is one of wealth, privilege, and high degrees of elite cultural capital among its residents.

Parents and other adults in the community also share their considerable resources by giving lectures at Mayfair High, holding talks at the local public library, and volunteering in one of the many non-profit organizations in town. But, can these young women of color acquire cultural capital from within the community, even while being largely left out of the social networks that provide new forms of social capital? Are they able to acquire cultural capital in a community so rich in it, or, alternatively, do the high levels of cultural capital in Mayfair leave women feeling marginalized and isolated? Further, are there variations in the types and amounts of cultural capital acquired by point of entry?

Various forms of embodied cultural capital appear throughout the interviews, most commonly around general exposure to and comfort in elite white society, learning how to navigate dominant systems, acquiring knowledge about and exposure to specific aspects of elite society both inside and outside of the school setting, and gaining speech and self-presentation skills. These acquisitions are often interconnected with one another. Although these themes exist in all three groups, there is variation based upon point of entry. The acquisition of institutionalized cultural capital is also discussed, but exclusively by residents and commuters, with a notable absence of such discussion among boarders.

Residents

Among the residents, six of the ten women speak explicitly about acquiring embodied cultural capital in various forms. Town residents Alexandra, Jade, Hannah, and Gabriella discuss broad exposure as a result of Mayfair. Alexandra, a resident of Section 8 housing, says, "I was able to experience lifestyles of different kinds and just the fact of being able to grow up in Mayfair." Jade makes a similar comment: "I had friends from all different walks of life, and it's just good to blend and get to know each other and do different things." Gabriella connects her exposure in Mayfair to a certain level of confidence and comfort in this exclusive club: "I mean I can converse with so many different kinds of people because of Mayfair, whether you're the elite or the poor or the middle-class or the working-class—I can relate in every way, in some kind of way. I definitely got that from Mayfair."

Hannah and Gabriella discuss elite knowledge gained within the confines of school. Hannah says, "I spoke German in high school and in college, so I think I was probably part of the German club, which we would eat food and watch a movie in German." Gabriella also talks about exposure to diverse cultures and wide-ranging opportunities: "We even did it for Chinese New Year. There was a whole segment on that. I can do calligraphy now because of that. I can, you know, I know the difference between Japanese, Korean, Vietnamese, Asia—I know the whole dynasties." She discusses having read *Fahrenheit 451* and George Orwell's *1984*. Gabriella goes on to say:

> I'm blessed that I got to experience how to play all these cool instruments. They brought us stuff from Africa, China, the drinking gourds from slavery. I mean we had a planetarium, you know, that thing's like 100 grand just to freaking light up and blow up…I know the stars just because of that. And this is information that I'll probably never use, but just to be an educated intellectual is amazing…

She recognizes that some of this knowledge may have limited applicability in the "real" world, but that her possession of it is important symbolically (Bourdieu 1984; Lamont and Fournier 1992).

Five residents—Alexandra, Jade, Hannah, Gabriella, and Faith—discuss how formal programs at Mayfair High helped them to acquire embodied cultural capital that serves them beyond high school, such as how to create a resume or engage in a job interview. Gabriella says many of these skills were "just integrated into our curriculum." She talks in more detail about those skills:

> I always knew how to write a research paper, I always knew how to write my resume, I always knew how to write an essay…It was because Mayfair taught me at such a young age. It was never a, 'Oh, come learn how to do a resume so you can get a job.' No, it was, 'This is what you need to know for life.' You know, that's just always stuck with me.

The required coursework around resume building, essay writing, and interview preparation clearly has implications for Gabriella long after she has left Mayfair. Gabriella says as a result of her preparation in Mayfair, "College was a breeze." This is a trend among all ten residents interviewed, all of whom attended college for at least some period of time and all stated that they were "prepared" or "very prepared" for college.

Hannah discusses in more detail her transition to college and speaks of the role of cultural capital in easing that transition. She discusses knowing how to write an outline for an essay as something she had learned when she was young and of going to meet with professors when she was struggling. This latter skill speaks to her confidence in approaching those in positons of authority and knowing how to navigate systems, a critical skill often gained in elite settings (Khan 2011). Hannah says, "It was exactly how high school was, so for me I could see the connection." In contrast, Hannah discusses the social and academic struggles of a college teammate, another lower-income woman of color, but one from an urban, poorly financed public high school. That woman did not graduate. These findings closely reflect Jack's (2016) work on the "privileged poor" versus the "doubly disadvantaged," with the former showing more successful social and academic outcomes in college as a result of the elite forms of cultural capital they possess.

When I asked Faith if everyone had to participate in college preparation classes, even if one was not interested in attending college, the response was, "They definitely did. But I don't remember any kids who ended up going down that path [of not attending college]. Because I know if kids wanted to join the army or something like that, they still would take the class." This comment speaks to the high academic expectations within the school and larger community and the organizational habitus of Mayfair High. A mandated course such as this is one way of formalizing the acquisition of embodied cultural capital and, in some small way, leveling the playing field.

Gabriella also speaks to specific aspects of elite society to which she was exposed outside of the school setting—ballroom dancing, knowing how to set a formal table, and being able to eat in a five-star restaurant. Jade, without being prompted, talks about particular illustrations of elite exposure. She says, "I was exposed to skiing. I would never—I would never do that with my family or anything, and I would go with my friends to go skiing and all types of places." Hannah, who grew up in both Section 8 housing and later a rental apartment in Mayfair, also talks about this type of experience. She says, "We went on skiing trips. I never would have gone skiing if it wasn't for the programs that they had. We went skiing like three times." These women are learning the "scripts" and gaining the "cultural toolkit" expected of individuals living in a particular segment of society (Swidler 1986; Tilly 1999). But, as one will see later, this type of knowledge and cultural capital does not make one immune to the sting of economic marginalization. These women may be able to emulate the behaviors of white, dominant society, but it does not fully make up for the limited financial resources; inequality remains (Tilly 1999).

Three of the women speak explicitly about speech and accents. Flore, the daughter of immigrants who grew up in Section 8 housing in Mayfair and was on the Speech and Debate Team, says people say about her, "I speak like a white girl. But I just see it as you just speak proper English. That's it. Period." Flore is troubled by both the racialization of her speech and the credit accorded to Mayfair for it. Gabriella says, "I would always get teased with my cousins because we were raised in this white snobby town and we didn't speak the same way or we didn't know the terms or the lingo." As a lower-income Latina woman with relatives living outside of Mayfair, Gabriella exists in a liminal space (Turner 1969), with cultural capital acquired in one setting failing to translate in other settings (Carter 2003, 2006). Faith, a young woman who grew up with her two college-educated parents in a market-rate home that they owned, says that through a program she did at school she learned "how to express yourself and how to express yourself the right way so that people receive it well."

Residents cite numerous instances of institutionalized cultural capital, capital held by individuals simply by virtue of having grown up in Mayfair and having graduated from the high school. This is the result of the community's reputation both across the state and even beyond state borders. Three women talk about the role of the town in terms of academic and professional opportunities. Brianna, a young woman who grew up in Section 8 housing and was still in college at the time of the interview, says about growing up and attending school in Mayfair:

> I liked it because I had always been told as a child that growing up here and getting the education from the Mayfair Public Schools would benefit me later on in life when I went to get a job, or college interviews, and knowing that Mayfair is a very hard school, educationally, that it would look better for things like that.

Alexandra, another woman who grew up in Section 8 housing, discusses the benefits of the name:

> A lot of times they see that I went to Mayfair High School, a lot of people are like, 'Oh, you went to Mayfair, that's a really good school.' Cause actually, the years that I went there, we were number one in the public schools

in the state. We've always been number one. I think the majority of the time I was a part of the school it was always number one and Rumfield was number two, right behind us. But, yeah definitely education-wise and it's always good to be known that I'm from Mayfair.

Jade, another former resident of Section 8 housing, provides more evidence of the weight held by being affiliated with Mayfair. She says, "I mean it's on my resume. I don't know if someone looks at it and says, 'Oh, she graduated from Mayfair, let's hire her.' Well that did happen with one job because one of the managers actually graduated from there."

Besides just having Mayfair High on their resume, three residents—Alexandra, Gabriella, and Flore—also talk about the institutionalized cultural capital they possess by having Mayfair on their driver's licenses. Alexandra says simply, "I can tell you this much, too, with it on my license, if I ever get pulled over, I usually get off."

Gabriella tells two stories of having had run-ins with the legal system and her Mayfair address coming in handy. She says:

> …So I was sad when I had to change my license from my Mayfair address… So I went to school [out of state], right? I had a Mayfair license. Long story short, I guess I was hanging with people I shouldn't have been hanging with, but I borrowed a car from one of these people and the car was, I don't know, red marked, it was stolen or something. I ended up getting pulled over, and I'm [out of state] and I show a license with a Mayfair address…and he's like, 'Hey, do you know you're driving this?' and I was like, 'Officer, I go to the school down the street and I borrowed this car' or whatever, I showed him my license. Because of my Mayfair [address], he saw the Mayfair [address] and he was like, 'What are you doing all the way out here?' and I was like, 'I'm going to school.' He knew Mayfair. And the fact that I had this license…his first response was, 'What are you doing here?' It wasn't, 'Is this your car?' or, 'Are you part of this?'

Gabriella tells another story of getting caught shoplifting in another town with her half-sister. She says, "I, well—by then you had to fill out a form, and so I wrote 'Student, Mayfair High,' and then my address… He was an alumni, graduated from Mayfair High. His family used to live in Mayfair, they moved. I was like, 'Are you kidding me right now?' I got away from that too."

Flore also discusses the status and benefits of having Mayfair on her driver's license:

...You know I had friends in Oldton through sports or just we became friends...We'd go to parties, you know, be a little wasted here and there. And you get pulled over and you pull that license, and they look at the town—it says Smith Road on it—they don't know what Smith Road is. But they see Mayfair and I guess I speak well, whatever that means. You know, pulled over by Coldline Police, pulled over by Oldton Police, all in one night and I should have been probably arrested but, 'Oh, do you think, can we take you home?'...I mean you learn that Mayfair has power. Just different things that, you know, yeah. You can get away, you know, you can get away with certain things and I didn't realize that until, 'Oh, so you're from Mayfair.' Yeah. So, you know, got away, just I mean there are different stories but that's one that I'll always remember because it's like, 'How did I get away?' Or, I was very [pauses], or I would say, 'Why are you pulling me over?' you know, kind of like with authority. I shouldn't—I should just be very calm and probably not say anything, but I would ask, 'Why are you pulling me over?' and easily they could have just said, 'Get out of the car' and, you know, 'We smell alcohol, your eyes are bloodshot blah blah blah' and, 'Let's search' and nothing. Like, 'Can we take you home?' things like that. They were probably thinking, you know well we don't want a lawsuit...

In addition to her driver's license providing a sort of institutionalized cultural capital, Flore also drove a used Mercedes that her parents had bought her. The car seemed to fit with her address. Additionally, she insisted on a certain amount of respect from the officer. He accords Flore a privileged status, which she attributes to her home address, her attitude, and his fear of crossing those in power. She finishes the interview by saying, "I mean you can definitely get away with a lot of things just being from there."

Commuters

Graduates of Mayfair through the Reach program discuss a variety of ways in which their worldviews and expectations were altered and elite forms of both embodied and institutionalized cultural capital acquired as a result of their time in town. Like residents, they discuss embodied cultural capital in their ability to socialize with diverse populations, their exposure to specific forms of high-level culture, and their acquisition of speech and self-presentation skills. Women in the Reach program also discuss institutionalized cultural capital in the form of a high school diploma from Mayfair.

Unlike the residents, many of whom spent the totality of their young lives in Mayfair and acquired certain forms of embodied cultural capital unconsciously, the commuters held dual reference frames resulting from attending school outside of their home communities. Because of this clear point of comparison, commuters discuss to a greater degree their initial exposure to elite society, altering their habitus, and their active acquisition of various forms of embodied cultural capital. For example, Andrea, a commuter who graduated at the turn of the twenty-first century, has a degree from a major university, and works as an accountant, talks generally about how Mayfair influenced her. She says, "Mayfair opened my eyes to a world of possibilities—not only a list of things that you could have but just things that you could achieve...." Yolanda, a woman from the 1990s whose mother made sure she was exposed early to elite society, still likens her experience in Mayfair to waking up in the basement of a house. She says about entering into Mayfair, "You're in the basement of this grand house that you don't even know you're in the basement [of] until one door opens and you realize, 'Oh, there are other parts to this house.'" Yolanda goes on to say how that affected her: "And I was like 'Wow!' It gave me this drive. I'm gonna succeed. I, I'm gonna, I should be living in a house like this." It should be noted that her mother's concerted efforts likely provided Yolanda with a baseline of expectations and transferable skills, a habitus that primed her to acquire additional forms of elite cultural capital in the new setting.

Eleven of 15 women talk about their feelings of confidence and adaptability across worlds, critical forms of embodied cultural capital. Shamus Khan (2011) argues that in twenty-first-century America, the elite need to be comfortable and well versed in a range of settings, not simply at the opera house and the country club. Although these women are generally the reverse of Khan's subjects at an elite boarding school, where they were socialized at the top and are being taught to engage with people lower down on the social and economic spectrum, the critical concept of comfort across a range of settings and adaptability is well taken. The key difference is that while Khan's students might be even more successful than they would be by gaining an ability to navigate down the socioeconomic ladder, these students *must* learn to navigate up it to succeed.

Lorraine says, "I'm very easily adaptable, I can—I can fit in pretty much anywhere and have a conversation with anyone." Michelle almost exactly echoes this sentiment when asked what she gained from Mayfair: "I think just being able to interact with people I probably wouldn't have interacted with if I had stayed in the city...." Serena talks about her adaptability: "The experience definitely has—I think it has given me an outlook that most people don't have and I'm able to fit in everywhere." Sasha says, "Mayfair has made me more flexible, more adaptable, a sense of 'I can be in any environment.'"

Both Monique, a graduate of the late 1980s who works as a travel agent, and Yolanda, a 1990s graduate, talk about how exposure to elite society has helped them as adults. Monique says:

> So I think it was just a good, you know, a good overall preparation, if you will, for the world at hand, and being able to kind of function in that environment, and it's interesting in comparison to some of my friends that went through city public schools and went through the black colleges, when they graduated, they kind of struggled a little bit, you know, becoming emerged in the world as we live it, because the world isn't all black.

Yolanda says, "So I think my education and also just my ability to socialize with different people" comes from Mayfair. She explicitly ties this to her exposure in town: "I knew what a Bat Mitzvah was, I knew about different sports. I was exposed to things that I may not have been exposed to had I went to school in my neighborhood." She goes on to talk about how that has impacted her life today:

> Like sometimes, my city accent may come out a little strong in a meeting, but that's the grit I have, that's what makes me a great leader. Sometimes I may say very big, large words in a very soft, corporate way, but I'm not going to call it talking white. But that's who I am. I'm all of those things—I can go from the boardroom to somebody's basement playing spades in the hood that you might hear gun shots outside of. And that's one of the things my husband says about me—he does like that. I think some of my friends—the circle that have gone to Reach—we—you can put us just about anywhere. And I knew that was the beauty of the experience. We can go anywhere and know how to navigate. That doesn't make you want to be there, but we can navigate it. We can be the only black person in a conference of 150 people and still sit proud and do our thing because of that experience.

These women possess the inside knowledge and symbolic markers that allow them to operate comfortably in two distinct worlds. These insights into what elite society looks like and the confidence gained from being a part of it is in keeping with prior research on the experiences of students of color in exclusive boarding schools. Students are not only exposed to an exclusive world but are encouraged to make it their own (Zweigenhaft and

Domhoff 1991, 2003; Khan 2011). Further, the confidence that many of these women express in regard to their ability to survive and thrive in multiple worlds suggests a level of cultural flexibility, a critical factor for success (Carter 2012). As children and young adults, straddling two worlds may have been a treacherous balancing act, but for some, it has clearly paid off beyond the academic benefits of attending a highly ranked high school (Carter 2003, 2006). Interestingly, this is not a trend found among residents who had only one world in which to live.

Women also discuss acquiring confidence in their academic skills as a result of their time in Mayfair. Noel says by the time she got to college, she felt, "I deserve to be here" and attributes that confidence to the support she received from teachers and administrators at Mayfair High and through the program. Andrea says, "I have always felt that it's made me believe that I can do anything." May, a graduate from an elite college, discusses the evolution of her world outlook. She says, "I think because they [the teachers and administrators] did believe in me or because they kept pushing me, it was just something I started to believe." Deana cites the confidence she gained.

The feelings of confidence in the academic realm may result, in part, from learning the systems and approaches necessary to be successful. Women explicitly discuss the acquisition of effective "strategies of action," sometimes through formalized programming, to meet their academic and professional goals (Swidler 1986). Six women—Joslin, Deana, Noel, May, Michelle, and Patricia—talk about general skills that translate into success. Joslin says, "You learn a pattern on how to learn." Noel says, "I mean I used the systems that any kid would use in school. So we had the writing center, I went during my prep period. You go and see a teacher after school. I wasn't a kid that was scared of using—going to see a teacher. I understood—I knew how to do school really well." This comment of going to see teachers echoes Hannah's statements about transitioning to college. Michelle says, "I always feel like, well, I know enough to get to the next step to do that. And I think a lot of that is from going to Mayfair." Deana references the "structures and routines you have to learn when you move into adulthood." Patricia says, "With going to Mayfair, I've learned more things about myself to have known exactly what I like and how to get to it and I just have to work my way to find it." This ability of learning how to learn and knowing how to reach a goal, critical information for success, has been found in prior research (Jack 2016; Khan 2011) and again speaks to Swidler's (1986) theory of learning effective "strategies of action."

The acquisition of artistic and literary knowledge, often used as markers of belonging and a clear illustration of elite cultural capital (Lamont and Fournier 1992; DiMaggio in Lamont & Fournier, 1992), is discussed by four commuters—Michelle, Noel, Yolanda, and Sasha. Michelle talks about her extensive literary exposure in high school. By the time she got to college, she said, "I read this, I read this, I read this." Noel, now a teacher, discusses her exposure to theater and how she found her passion for the arts while at Mayfair. She says:

> I did drama all the way through high school and even took honors acting in high school—that was a passion. I remember I was in the City Children's Theater and I started in middle school because of my classes I took. I think—what did I take? I think I did a *Mid-Summer Night's Dream* in middle school. So I remember being exposed and having a lot of choices. We had to do chorus and music class, but I remember that that's where I was first introduced to *Porgy and Bess*—that music. Just knowing that I know my students now as middle schoolers—students don't get those things. And that it's sad that I have to go to almost a literally all-white community to get that enrichment in my life.

Sasha says, "I was reading authors that, you know, really advanced—to this day I'm like, 'How did I understand Song of Solomon?' I mean that's a heavy book." She discusses writing a required thesis paper on a major artist. She says, "It was a challenge, but to me, because it was just the expectation, you met it." These data illustrate critical aspects around the concept of habitus and cultural capital. Sasha's comment, "Because it was just the expectation...," speaks to the organizational habitus of the school and community, expectations that she came to possess. Monique and Serena also discuss the high expectations within the school; Serena says she wishes her son had been exposed to an atmosphere that had such standards. Faith, a resident, had also referenced the high expectations.

Few experiences change an individual's worldview like travel does and four commuters—Noel, Yolanda, Sasha, and May—discuss their travel experiences. This travel is either the direct result of Mayfair High, or facilitated through the system. Noel went to South Africa during her junior year for free (she likely had to do fundraising), May recalls taking Italian and Roman History and then traveling to Italy with her class during her junior year, Sasha with the financial assistance of her teacher went on a three-week trip to Europe as part of Mayfair's foreign language program, and Yolanda went to Washington, DC. This is in contrast to the lack of travel among residents. Town resident Sara discusses trips to visit family in North Africa and Europe, but this is the only mention of travel abroad and was family initiated.

Commuters discuss other ways in which specific forms of exposure outside of school transformed outlooks and expectations and became forms of embodied cultural capital. Lorraine and Noel talk about being exposed to the homes of Mayfair. Although this could be viewed as an unimportant or irrelevant experience, these women tie this exposure to the development of their taste. Lorraine, a graduate of the mid-1980s, says, "In hindsight, it developed my love of looking at pretty houses." She feels that this early exposure helped her to develop particular ideas about what she wanted in life—marriage and a house in the suburbs. She also goes on to attribute this early exposure to her decision to become a real estate broker. Noel, a graduate from the mid-2000s, says, "And I mean I think that's where I acquired my taste for certain styles of homes. I've been to so many homes before."

These comments speak to the connection between exposure, habitus, and cultural capital acquisition. Whether it was women, as young girls, seeing large homes, learning about theater, reading major literary works, or researching artists, these examples all illustrate ways in which exposure leads to new views about the world and expectations for themselves. Further, these exposures often provide individuals with new forms of embodied cultural capital—being knowledgeable about a style of architecture or an artist, for example. And the cycle continues from there, with new forms of cultural capital providing individuals with the interest and confidence to seek out still more experiences, as Noel did with the theater.

Seven women discuss self-presentation and language skills, including explicit discussions about learning to "talk white." Multiple women think their elite cultural capital in this area helps them to mitigate racial stereotypes they encounter in white society. Edith, a graduate from the mid-1980s, says, "I know how to talk white." She goes on to say, "We're [people of color] looked at as, in a certain way. You know if you act a certain way, then it'll be okay. But you have to know that. You learn that by being around them [white people] and watching them." Serena, an accountant who graduated in the early 1990s, says:

> ...The way I speak was because of where I went to school and a lot of times, other black people, especially down here in the south, they hear me speak, and it's automatically, 'Oh, you're trying to be a white girl, you're trying

to be this.' But because of the education and the experience that I had in Mayfair and—I'm able to now go on an interview and a lot of times people don't know that I'm black over the phone, you know, and that's kind of stereotypical, but that's just what it is…

Serena is able to manipulate the location of the "veil" (Du Bois 1903/1994) when she is on the phone, temporarily moving to the other side. Coretta, a more recent graduate and another accountant, also views language and presentation as a means of overcoming harmful stereotypes. She says in response to a question about the longer-term impact of Mayfair that it helped her to "become a more well-rounded, polished adult. It's just not, you know, I don't want to be labeled as, you know, that stereotypical ghetto black girl." The women, through their use of double consciousness (Du Bois 1903/1994) and elite cultural capital acquisition, overcome significant racial barriers. These additional forms of capital are used as a means of "whitening" and gaining mobility.

Relatedly, three women—May, Deana, and Noel—discuss learning how to effectively advocate for themselves. Noel, in talking about a friend of hers, says, "And I think she learned from that experience that she can vocalize herself and that someone is going to listen if you do it in the right way." She discusses her friend as having "vision." May says:

> And learning how to advocate for yourself. So in and out of the classroom. All things that I don't know that I would have been able to do anywhere else. I don't know that I wouldn't have, obviously because I never had that experience, but for a lot of reasons I would argue other [college] peers I had who didn't feel like they had that high school experience and things like that—just things I knew before even getting to college.

Deana says about Mayfair, "I found my voice" while there. She explains that she learned to speak in a way that she could be heard by teachers and administrators.

As with residents, commuters Edith, Michelle, Joslin, Noel, and Coretta discuss institutionalized cultural capital of the elite variety. Edith, a woman from the 1980s who recently completed college, says, "The most valuable thing that I gained is, as of today, 2014, is being able to write that on my resume and being able to put that down on my applications. 'Where did you go to high school?' It carries a lot of weight, the name itself. So for that in itself, I'm glad that I went to Mayfair." She goes on to say, "When

I write down Mayfair on applications, not only am I putting that down, I also can back it up with different—you know, how I speak...my education background." Edith is highlighting both the embodied and institutionalized cultural capital she has gained from Mayfair. Michelle makes a similar comment, saying, "I think it's like a credential for other people, when they find out, 'Oh, you went to Mayfair?'... So I think there's a certain status to it."

Coretta, a woman who did not attend college, says, "It's impacted my life a lot. I think just letting people know that I went to school there." She goes on to say, "And they're like, 'Oh wow, you know, she went to school in Mayfair.' The education is stellar, so you know, it's just I think that's where people are like, 'Oh, yeah, you know, good for you.'" Again, the embodied meets the institutionalized in this exchange. Joslin, a medical technician who did not complete college, says, "I didn't finish college, but people look at my high school before they look at what college I went to." She attributes it to helping her to get a job "easily." On the other side of the educational spectrum, Noel, a commuter with undergraduate and graduate degrees from two of the world's most elite institutions, thinks her ability to access top post-secondary schools grew out, in part, from Mayfair's name. In this case, the human and cultural capital acquired in one setting help her to advance to the next level.

Boarders

The Aspire graduates discuss the various ways that Mayfair altered their worldviews and expectations via exposure to an elite environment, a similar trend seen among the Reach graduates. Jaqui, an Aspire graduate who went on to an elite university and now teaches, says entering Mayfair made her realize, "There's this whole different world and realm outside of this world, and that was inspiring to me to just do better and be better," echoing the sentiments of commuting students Andrea and Yolanda.

As with commuters, the boarding students discuss the growth of their confidence in elite environments, a critical form of cultural capital, and a trend noted in prior research (Khan 2011). Five women—Christina, Alana, Tamara, Marian, and Karenna—discuss the issue of confidence, comfort, and adaptability that grows out of general exposure and expectations in Mayfair. Christina talks about being "in this predominantly white culture so you sort of get used to it." She discusses becoming much more adaptable and being able to converse with people all along the socioeconomic spectrum. Alana similarly says, "I learned how to be around White America. I lived in Duluth, Minnesota for ten years." Karenna feels that she got to see "the larger picture of the world. I think I'm well prepared for that." Tamara also talks about having to adapt: "The most valuable thing was the fact that I learned how to adapt to that environment."

As with some of the residents and commuters, the boarders also cite their ability to navigate college and the workplace as a result of the lessons they learned in Mayfair. Marian explains it this way: "…It was literally every specific thing there was a different person for. So I think what it taught me to do was just reach out and ask for help." She said she did not feel intimidated by this. Once in college, her professors would say to her, "'You seem so comfortable.' Yeah, because I had to do this," she tells me. Her comfort in meeting with professors speaks to her expectations and confidence, and is similar to what Hannah, a resident, and Noel, a commuter, describe.

The women in Aspire also discuss confidence that grows explicitly from their program and the unique challenges that they faced as 14-year-olds moving away from home. Jaqui discusses how she learned to do things outside of her comfort zone and that she would be okay. Priscilla learned from her participation in the program that "I could pick up and build a new life somewhere else. I could do it and thrive." Isabel, a young woman who was highly successful academically, but experienced significant emotional trauma, says her participation in the program "helped me to realize that despite what I thought of myself, I was pretty tough." Kelsey says, "If I can do anything as hard as that, then everything else is kind of a breeze." Tasha feels she gained a sense of independence. After Marian graduated from Mayfair, she spent her first college semester abroad as part of the school's freshman program. She credits Mayfair as giving her the ability to "take the next step." The challenge of leaving home to move to a vastly different, often lonely and even hostile, environment can translate into confidence and strength.

Women in the boarding program also discuss learning how to network, echoing findings from previous research (Zweigenhaft and Domhoff 1991; Zweigenhaft and Domhoff 2003). Elise talks about having to socialize at "a pretty high level and knowing how to network…." She discusses learning the value of "small talk." Jaqui echoes the development of this skill set. She says, "I also just learned how to network and how to talk to people. That was a field that I learned there." Marian talks about "the dozens of white women" (the volunteers) she had to interact with on a regular basis for what she needed. Tamara says, "I loved interacting with the adults to get the most out of my experience."

Although residents and Reach graduates discuss their ability to socialize with people all along the social and economic spectrum, the explicit notion of networking is largely absent. Women like Elise and Jaqui recognize the use of these contacts and informal channels to gain access to a world of possibilities, such as hard-to-access internships. The explicit discussion of this skill is virtually absent among women in the other two groups. In fact when it is raised among women in the other groups, it is in terms of its absence. As Yolanda, a commuter says, "Even to this day, I think my mom, like I remember in college, when it was happening to me, when I was looking for internships, I'm like, 'Mom, use your connections.' She didn't understand that piece of it." Although residents, such as Alexandra and Jade, talk of the importance in the prior chapter of developing and maintaining diverse social networks for the purposes of getting ahead, they seem less able to capitalize on these informal connections and tend to rely on formal programs and channels. At the same time, the resource-rich networks in which the boarding students are embedded, as discussed in the prior chapter, illustrate to the young women the power of networks and the value of networking skills.

As with the residents and commuters, boarders Christina, Elise, Isabel, Tasha, and Alana discuss explicit forms of elite exposure both inside and outside of school. Tasha talks about going to the opera with her host family, a particularly elite experience (DiMaggio in Lamont and Fournier 1992). Christina says, "I remember we had a poem night in the library and the principal reciting a poem that was very meaningful to her, and it's just like, if I stayed here I wouldn't have had those experiences. I wouldn't have been as cultured." She explicitly links exposure and elite cultural capital. Isabel talks about her love of literature, particularly Jane Austen. She wrote her sophomore thesis paper on the author. Alana talks about being part of the German club, going to see musical theater, and playing the clarinet in high school. Elise talks about the "great" foreign language programs at Mayfair High. This is where she started French and ended up majoring in it in college, suggesting the role of school and community on her academics, as well as her expanded vision and expectations.

Travel, again, appears as a critical form of cultural capital, but to a greater extent than seen among the other two groups. Virtually everyone of the 12 boarders interviewed traveled either domestically or internationally as a result of the program or the high school. Elise talks about traveling to Europe over a summer, as well as going to Africa. She says, "I went to Africa for the first time at 17 and climbed Mount Kilimanjaro. I don't know too many people who do those things...Ever!" Kelsey traveled to Asia, participating in a three-week program during her junior year of high school. Marian went to Europe through Mayfair High. Priscilla talks about spending a summer on an Ivy League campus. Isabel did a variety of summer science programs on various college campuses. Other women engaged in outdoor adventure and girls' leadership programs during their summer vacations.

As with the residents and commuters, numerous boarders—Jaqui, Isabel, Christina, Alana, and Elise—discuss gaining speech and presentation skills as a result of Mayfair. Sometimes these skills are acquired unconsciously, sometimes consciously. Jaqui, a teacher in a major city, talks about improving her vocabulary. When asked what she gained from Mayfair, Isabel says:

> I think also Mayfair High School helped me improve my speech, how I present myself and I mean I'm always told that I, I do a pretty good interview because of how I present myself and I try not to do the fidgeting or the looking down. Just learning how to be professional, more-more professional. I think Mayfair taught me that. Learning how to speak well. Learning how to write well. Just being able to engage in academic conversations.

Christina says, "I think I really learned how to be personable and approachable—which is so big in daily life." She goes on to say, "It's more than just doing well in school. It's the day to day with jobs and interviews. This is something I excel at because I know how to speak for myself, and I know how to, you know, show the best. I guess, I'm not sure how to say it but it's something I feel confident in." Alana says, "So I think I gained the social skills that were necessary for the workplace environment...." Women learn the value of "soft" skills that often play a critical role in life.

Interestingly, the trend around institutionalized cultural capital that clearly exists among the residents and Reach students is virtually absent among the Aspire women. Malia is the only woman to make any reference to Mayfair as granting that sort of capital. She feels that the high school name helped her when she was applying to college. Even when Malia references Mayfair as this sort of institutionalized cultural capital, it is solely to leverage the name in pursuit of the next level of elite educational acquisition.

Variation across Groups

Although women in all three groups were clearly exposed to high levels of society and acquired significant amounts of elite cultural capital as a result of living or attending school in Mayfair, point of access seems to significantly mediate the experience. Those who gained access to Mayfair through one of the engineered pathways entered into a structured system explicitly intended to advance elite cultural capital, as well as human capital. Further, as students in the Mayfair system, but not of Mayfair, they possessed dual reference frames which allowed them to see the distinct nature of Mayfair, something largely lost on the residents.

In particular, the Aspire program's expectations, structure, and opportunities are explicitly suited to instilling significant amounts of elite cultural capital in the young women. Although many young women may have arrived in Mayfair with mothers who held high expectations and emphasized opportunities, the boarding program goes a long way in filling in the gaps left by households and communities that lacked elite knowledge and/or economic resources. Beyond the exposure to elite white society and the acquisition of speech and presentation skills which are discussed by many of the boarders, these women also acquire the most elite forms of cultural capital—foreign travel, exclusive internships, networking skills, and a growing ease with privilege (Khan 2011).

In contrast, town residents, especially the young women who grew up in lower-income housing, may have lived in Mayfair much of their lives, but this does not translate into the same opportunities, expectations, and support provided to those who accessed the school district via one of the programs, most notably the boarding program. There are no programs or structures targeting these residents. Although women in all three groups discuss exposure to elite white society, what that means really varies. For residents, it may be learning how to ski or how to ballroom dance, potentially useful skills that suggest a familiarity with exclusive worlds. These young women are not, however, traveling to Asia, Africa, or Europe, meeting with senators and Pulitzer Prize winning authors as Aspire students did, or, perhaps more importantly, accessing world-class internships or gaining networking skills, cultural capital that may have longer-term implications.

The Reach students exist between residents and boarders. They are participating in a structured program, as opposed to just being a local kid going to her local high school. At the same time, the commuter program is not nearly as structured or all-inclusive as the boarding program. Commuters discuss gaining general exposure to elite society, learning how systems work, acquiring high-level intellectual capital, gaining speech and presentation skills, as well as a smaller number discussing the opportunity to travel. Although the cultural capital gained among the commuters may not rise to the level of that acquired by the boarders, it appears to significantly overshadow that which residents gain.

What the students in the two different programs clearly share is a dual-reference frame, a comparison of their home communities with the community of Mayfair. This distinction is important in that it allows these young women to see a contrast and an expansion of worldviews and possibilities. For residents, Mayfair is the only world that they know; they are fish swimming in water. As such, they are privy to the existence of such an exclusive place, but they are not fully a part of it. Further, these young women of color who exist on the lowest economic and social rungs of Mayfair have no place from which to derive a sense of confidence and place. Their outlooks and expectations grow from this relatively deprived position. In contrast to the residents, commuters and boarders see the differences that exist in the multiple worlds that they occupy and their relative privilege at home. Both boarders and commuters, to varying degrees, have been selected into Mayfair, with boarders most clearly the "chosen ones." Unsurprisingly, institutionalized cultural capital in the form of addresses and high school diplomas is most relevant for residents and commuters, and largely irrelevant for boarders who view Mayfair as a means to an end, rather than an end in and of itself.

The Limitations of Cultural Capital and the Ongoing Influence of Financial Capital

Although cultural capital is a form of currency distinct from financial or social capital, these various forms of exchange are all interconnected. Boarding students who find themselves in the most resource-rich networks are often able to convert this social capital into cultural capital. For example, Isabel's relationship with her teacher translated into lessons in vocabulary and speech. These lessons were only possible because of the social relationship she had developed with someone who could serve as a cultural guide. But, these lessons become a part of who Isabel is, her knowledge base and self-presentation. They result from social capital but they become cultural capital.

Similarly, cultural capital is intimately connected with economic capital. Money is what makes many experiences possible—be it a trip to the opera or a trip abroad. Although women provide multiple examples of overcoming economic limitations, via their social networks, to acquire cultural capital (consider Sasha's trip abroad as a result of her relationship with her teacher), the economic basis of many forms of cultural capital acts as a barrier and a means of marginalization. Five women talk about how their limited economic circumstances limit social and cultural experiences, particularly in regard to travel.

Gabriella, a former town resident of more modest economic means, says, "I can't take family trips to Europe and, you know, Santa Monica every other week, you know, every school vacation. You know, when we came back from vacation, we talked about what we did. I went to Philadelphia or Baltimore, and they went to Maui...." Yolanda, a commuter, also talks about vacations in Mayfair and compares her experiences to those of her classmates who went to Europe, saying, "Whereas for me, my vacations were either at home or we would go down south in a car. My grandmother once made me get on the Grey Hound. That was the last time, all the way to Atlanta. I thought I was gonna die." Isabel, a boarder, also talks about how she spent her vacations versus how her classmates in Mayfair did. She says they were "Talking about trips they had gone on. You know, for me it was going home. Maybe going out to dinner one of the days we were on vacation." The seemingly requisite family vacation to Europe is a common occurrence in Mayfair and an isolating experience for those who cannot afford it.

Hannah and Gabriella, residents who graduated years apart, both talk about the annual foreign language trip with Mayfair High in which they would have liked to participate, but could not because of financial limitations. For some, this relatively lower-cost trip for which many students do fundraising could be a replacement for the family vacation to Europe. It is a formal school opportunity to provide experiences for students, increase international exposure, and create cultural capital. However, even with the lower price tag than a full-fledged family vacation to Europe, it is still out of reach for many. Gabriella says, "I really wanted to go abroad so bad with—like a lot of my friends went abroad and had the exchange students come and that was like close to $15,000 and my mom just doesn't have that hanging around, you know, I couldn't do that. So that bummed me out...." The trip did not cost nearly $15,000, but Gabriella's estimate suggests how far it was from being a possibility for her. It is important to note that while these town residents were not provided with financial assistance to go on a trip abroad, one of the graduates of the commuter program received financial support from her teacher, suggesting how different points of access into the district may mediate access to social capital and thus cultural capital.

Marian, a boarder, talks about how her prior travel experiences made the transition to Mayfair a little bit easier, but views the situation as challenging for many. She says:

> That's overwhelming to go into Mayfair or any extreme predicament, because for me it was a culture shock to go on the train [and go to Mayfair] and I've actually been well traveled. I did all these different activities growing up. My mom worked so hard to give me the best in life, but even still going to Mayfair was like, 'Whoa!' for me. I can't even imagine it for someone to who didn't have access to those privileges. It wasn't too overwhelming [for me]. I think in most cases those are the ones who struggled more than I have, because I've had windows into different things, not in that extreme, but because I had little similarities, when we talked it wasn't like, 'Oh, I've never been to those countries.' It was like I was able to connect on that level.

Marian recognizes that she has the habitus and initial cultural capital to connect at least partially with her classmates, but those without such experiences may undergo a profound shock upon arrival in Mayfair.

Because so much cultural capital abounds, even young women who have had opportunities beyond the norm in American society continue to feel at a loss. There is a form of "runaway" cultural capital in the community with which these young women cannot catch up. Just as women expressed feelings of deficiency in regard to the cars they drove relative to their wealthier counterparts and their athletic abilities on the sports field, so, too, do they feel that they cannot catch up on the cultural capital front.

Conclusion

The implications of these findings are significant, showing that access to an elite system has meaningful effects on individuals, outside of the classroom. Women across all three groups discuss gaining various types of cultural capital from their access to Mayfair. Having said that, the types and amounts of cultural capital discussed vary somewhat by residential group. For the high-achieving boarding students, Mayfair is a step along the way.

Here they will acquire a solid high school education that will prepare them for top colleges. In addition, they will become more comfortable in elite white society, gain insight into the trappings of those at the top, and acquire experiences and mannerisms that provide them with the necessary skills to take their place in that world. These women also acquire some of the most elite forms of cultural capital in the form of travel, networking skills, and internships.

For many residents and some commuters, Mayfair may be the pinnacle of their academic life. They, too, gain broad exposure and greater comfort and confidence in being in a white-dominated world, as well as gain critical skills for college and the workplace. They, too, learn how to navigate systems and present themselves. The overall level to which they are exposed tends not to be quite so extreme as it is for the boarders, however. Further, much of the cultural capital gained by residents and commuters is accessed through formal programs, rather than informal networks, as well as coming in the form of institutionalized cultural capital—the address on the driver's license or the name on the high school diploma.

It should also be noted that the cultural capital identified by participants is understood as a form of inequality in society (Eaton 2001). Just as Edith, a commuter from the late 1980s, talks about the benefits of having Mayfair on her resume, she also states, "So, for that in itself, I'm glad that I went to [Mayfair], but it's sad on the flip-side...that I have to rely on a school not in the area of where I grew up in order to be recognized." Alana notes that her young host sister, still in elementary school, was learning mathematics not covered in her urban home district in the Midwest until high school. Noel, a graduate of Aspire who teaches in an urban district, is troubled that her students will not receive the same intellectual experiences and exposure to which she was privy in Mayfair. And in a difference in flavor, but not kind, when Gabriella had an encounter with the Mayfair police, but was no longer living in Mayfair, she saw the downside of such favoritism, with the officer siding with the resident still living in town.

Further, the significant amount of cultural capital which some women bring with them from their homes and communities is not identified as such within the borders of Mayfair. This lack of recognition of different types of cultural capital is often damaging to these young students. Research (Carter 2003, 2006) shows the tremendous importance of understanding non-dominant forms of cultural capital as highly important in its own right, and as a means by which students possess the confidence to reach out across borders and acquire new, dominant sorts of resources and become culturally flexible (Carter 2012).

At the same time, the changed habitus of these women and the new forms of embodied cultural capital often place them in a liminal status. They are not fully part of Mayfair, but new outlooks and patterns of behavior may make these young women subject to rejection or ridicule in their home communities—be that community 15 or 150 miles away (Cook and Ludwig 1998; Eaton 2001; Tyson 2011). Although the data here suggest that many women are eventually able to capitalize on possessing both non-dominant and elite forms of cultural capital to survive and even thrive, the road is highly challenging and often psychologically traumatic. Acquiring elite forms of cultural capital may allow one to cross symbolic and geographic boundaries, but it may also create new barriers to overcome.

Note

1. The third form of cultural capital discussed by Bourdieu (1986) is the objectified, the physical manifestation of one's knowledge, sophistication, and status. Objectified cultural capital may come in the form of a musical instrument, a piece of art, or a library. Although these are all physical items which can be purchased, given enough money, objectified cultural capital is thought to be much more. The physical item exists as a symbolic representation of one's skill in, knowledge about, or appreciation of some aspect of elite society. Within the context of this project, the forms of cultural capital most consistently acquired are the embodied and institutionalized, with virtually no reference to the objectified.

Bibliography

Anson, R. 1988. *Best Intentions*. New York: First Vintage Books.
Bourdieu, P. 1986. The Forms of Capital. In *Handbook of Theory and Research for the Sociology of Education*, ed. J. Richardson, 241–258. New York: Greenwood Press.
———. 1984. *Distinction: A Social Critique of the Judgement of Taste*. London: Routledge.
———. 1991. *Language & Symbolic Power*. Cambridge: Harvard University Press.

Bourdieu, P., and J. Passeron. 2000. *Reproduction in Education, Society and Culture*. London: Sage.
Calarco, J. 2014. Coached for the Classroom: Parents' Cultural Transmission and Children's Reproduction of Educational Inequalities. *American Sociological Review* 79(5): 1015–1037.
Carter, P. 2012. *Stubborn Roots*. Oxford: Oxford University Press.
———. 2003. "Black" Cultural Capital, Status Positioning, and Schooling Conflicts for Low-Income African American Youth. *Social Problems* 50(1): 136–155.
———. 2006. Straddling Boundaries: Identity, Culture, and School. *Sociology of Education* 79(4): 304–328.
Coleman, J. 1988. Social Capital in the Creation of Human Capital. *The American Journal of Sociology* 94: S95–S120.
Cook, P., and J. Ludwig. 1998. The Burden of 'Acting White': Do Black Adolescents Disparage Academic Achievements? In *The Black-White Test Score Gap*, ed. C. Jencks and M. Phillips, 375–400. Washington, DC: Brookings Institution Press.
Cookson, P., and C. Persell. 1991. Race and Class in America's Elite Boarding Schools: African Americans as the 'Outsiders Within'. *The Journal of Negro Education* 60: 219–228.
DiMaggio, P. 1992. Cultural Boundaries and Structural Change: The Extension of the High Culture Model to Theater, Opera, and the Dance, 1900–1940. In *Cultivating Differences: Symbolic Boundaries and the Making of Inequality*, ed. M. Lamont and M. Fournier, 21–57. Chicago: University of Chicago Press.
Du Bois, W. 1903/1994. *The Souls of Black Folks*. New York: Dover Publications.
Eaton, S. 2001. *The Other Boston Busing Story*. New Haven: Yale University Press.
Garschick Kleit, R. 2001. Neighborhood Relations in Scattered-Site & Clustered Public Housing. *Journal of Urban Affairs* 23(4–5): 409–430.
Jack, A. 2016. (No)Harm in Asking: Class, Acquired Cultural Capital, and Academic Engagement at an Elite University. *Sociology of Education* 89(1): 1–19.
Khan, S. 2011. *Privilege: The Making of an Adolescent Elite at St. Paul's School*. Princeton and Oxford: Princeton University Press.
Lamont, M., and M. Fournier. 1992. *Cultivating Differences: Symbolic Boundaries and the Making of Inequality*. Chicago: University of Chicago Press.
Lareau, A. 2011. *Unequal Childhoods*. Berkeley: University of California Press.
———. 2015. Cultural Knowledge and Social Inequality. *The American Sociological Review* 80(1): 1–27.
Swidler, A. 1986. Culture in Action: Symbols and Strategies. *American Sociological Review* 51(2): 273–286.
Tilly, C. 1999. *Durable Inequality*. Berkeley: University of California Press.
Turner, V. 1969. *The Ritual Process*. New York: Transaction Publishers.

Tyson, K. 2011. *Integration Interrupted*. Oxford: Oxford University Press.
Wilson, W. 1987. *The Truly Disadvantaged*. Chicago: University of Chicago Press.
Zweigenhaft, R., and G. Domhoff. 1991. *Blacks in the White Establishment: A Study of Race and Class in America*. New Haven: Yale University Press.
———. 2003. *Blacks in the White Elite: Will the Progress Continue?* Lanham, MD: Rowman & Littlefield.

CHAPTER 7

Race, Place, and the Power of Interactions

The previous chapters have explored the extent to which women of color in Mayfair have been able to reach across boundaries at the intersection of race, gender, and class, forming connections with the dominant white community, acquiring new forms of social capital, and attaining cultural capital. Although there is significant evidence of women gaining new forms of capital through a variety of channels, barriers clearly remain. Many of these women describe an existence in large part outside of that world, unable to bridge significant chasms resulting from physical distance, economic differentials, cultural differences, racial insensitivities, and even hostilities. Their experiences in late-twentieth and early twenty-first-century America recall experiences similar to those of Du Bois, who lived and wrote 100 years prior. Women across all three groups recall interactions reflective of Du Bois' (1903/1994) interconnected theories of racial awakening and, with it, the recognition of the veil and a sense of double consciousness. Although there are certainly variations across the three groups, suggesting that the meaning of race can vary by context, there are also patterns that emerge that are indicative of race in twenty-first-century America.

Through interactions with white Mayfair residents, these women encounter general assumptions about people of color. Relatedly, the women, both as individuals and as members of these separate subgroups in Mayfair, make distinct and important contributions. The varied contributions are often tied to the way in which being a woman of color is interpreted by white students, parents, teachers, and administrators in the school and the community, and, more importantly, the ways in which these individual women transmute those interpretations and overturn stereotypes, slowly working against the institutionalized racial projects and durable inequalities that exist in American society (Omi and Winant 1994; Tilly 1999). These women are powerful beings and important agents of social change.

THE MEANING OF RACE

"You Can't Be From Here"

Two residents of the community, both of whom are of middle- to upper-middle-class backgrounds, describe an "Ah ha!" moment of racial awakening—an instance when they realized they were different from others in their community because of their race and that that difference had negative implications (Du Bois 1903/1994). As Du Bois says of his own "Ah ha!" moment, "Then it dawned upon me that I was different from the others..." (Du Bois 1903/1994, p.2). Faith and Sara, who were born and raised in Mayfair, both recall such experiences. Faith describes playing house with her young friends and being told that she could not be a part of the family because of her skin color. Sara, the child of a successful North African immigrant, recalls bringing in a hajib to school from a recent trip to visit family in North Africa and being asked if her father was a terrorist.

Mayfair residents of color also experience the assumption of otherness in additional ways, as well. Faith tells of being put on a bus to return to Urbana, the city from which the commuter students come, because she was assumed to be from beyond the borders. A boarding student tells the story of a male friend of hers, a town resident, put on the commuter bus as a child and sent "back" to the city. Numerous other such school bus incidents were cited to me in informal conversations with people in the community. Alexandra, Jade, Hannah, and Veronica all retell assumptions by teachers and parents that they are from elsewhere. Veronica, as a high-performing woman of color, is assumed by a teacher to be part of the Aspire boarding program. Alexandra and Jade are assumed to be part of Reach. They are told through words and deeds that they are different, that they do not fit in this place. This is not home.

Commuters and boarders also experience this sense of otherness, and sometimes in extreme ways. Priscilla, a Latina woman who graduated from the boarding program in the early 1990s, recalls a young man from a passing car screaming a racial epitaph at her and telling her to return home as she walked down the street with other girls from her program. Although Priscilla is not from the community and is thus not being disowned in the way that the residents are, the assumption of otherness and the fierceness of this young man's demand are every bit as shocking and painful.

"Ghetto" Assumptions

The racial stereotypes held by the white residents, teachers, and administrators in Mayfair speak to intertwined assumptions about race, class, and geography. Being a person of color is heavily tied up with expectations about the urban underclass (Wilson 1987, 1996). It is not simply that some segments of white Mayfair see a person of color and assume that they do not belong in this community; it is beyond that. Peers, parents, teachers, and administrators seem to have an image of what these women's lives look like—images of poverty-stricken ghettos.

Yolanda, a commuter student, talks of being asked if she lived in the projects and knew drug dealers. Sasha, another commuter student, remembers, "Someone said to me in the middle of—like in front of everybody in class, 'Oh, my gosh—you live in Dexter? I'd be so scared to live where you live that as soon as I walk out of my house I'd get shot.'" Karenna, a boarding student and child of a nurse, recalls people offering her money, assuming that she was from a poor household. She says, "I had people, adults, like friend's parents be like, 'Oh, yeah, I know about the boarding program, do you need money?' You know, things like that—that were very like, 'Okay, yes, I'm here but I choose to be here.'" Elisabeth, a resident who moved to Mayfair late in her high school career, was assumed to have an inferior educational background because she had grown up in an urban area and was told as much by administrators.

Although some of the women of color, both town residents and those who accessed the district through one of the programs, were actually lower income, assumptions were automatically made about them. Isabel, a boarder, from a very low-income family, recalls being asked by a wealthy white Mayfair peer how she was paying for the expensive private college counselor that both were seeing for advice. The assumption was that Isabel could not possibly afford the services. Flore, a town resident who grew up in Section 8 housing, says, "We did have a bad rep, a very, very bad rep." There are both assumptions that these women of color do live in poverty and, further, assumptions about what it must mean to live in poverty.

The Role of Racialized Interactions

Du Bois (1903/1994) and later Mead (1934) and Goffman (1955) all explore the ways in which social interactions shape our sense of self. As Du Bois discusses at the turn of the twentieth century, individual interactions between blacks and whites within the larger racialized social context in the United States provide black Americans with a sense of two-ness, a double consciousness, a second sight. But, Du Bois also argues that while these interactions provide black Americans with unique insights as both blacks and Americans, it causes black Americans to see themselves through the eyes of another and, in this case, a more powerful other who controls the institutions and rules of the game. Mead (1934) and Goffman (1955) follow in Du Bois' footsteps decades later, both arguing that everyone's sense of self and view of the world is shaped through interactions with others, for better or worse. They fail, however, to consider the role that an individual's demographic characteristics, such as race, play in the interactional creation of a sense of self.

The racialized interactions that the women have with members of white Mayfair, based upon the varying assumptions and stereotypes discussed above, are often highly painful. These interactions, at times, appear to reinforce feelings of inferiority and only further cause Americans of color to see themselves through the eyes of white society, as Du Bois (1903/1994) argues. Sasha, recalling the assumption that she lived in a scary, dangerous place, says, "It kind of made you feel shameful." A small number of women with whom I spoke still cite unhealed scars, ongoing therapy, and a refusal to let their children participate in such programs. Such painful interactions and experiences inevitably raise the question of whether the benefits of attending school in Mayfair are worth the price of admission.

What is easier to see is that the presence of these women and their day-to-day interactions with the larger community make significant contributions to both the school and the town. Not only do the better educational opportunities, more diverse networks, and increased social and cultural capital come at a price, as discussed above, but they are also repaid time and again by the young women. The benefits of and acquisitions made in Mayfair do not exist as part of a one-way street, and the bridges that allow these benefits to flow to the girls also allow information to be passed the other way. And these women have much to pass along. They are neither passive beings, nor empty vessels to be filled up. The girls who come here for a better education often become unintentional educators, with all of the emotional costs associated with this role.

The women talk of requiring their white peers to encounter another version of young black women and reconsider stereotypes, including stereotypes around where people of color "must" live or that all people of color must be poor. These women often view it as their responsibility to educate their peers, faculty, administrators, and the larger community in a number of ways. They talk of altering policies and introducing new programs. Women also discuss, explicitly and implicitly, ways in which their experiences in Mayfair influence their families and home communities. These women, as outsiders living between social structures (Turner 1969), as those who hold double consciousness (Du Bois 1903/1994), push the boundaries on all sides. They see and do what those more firmly embedded in their respective structures are unable or unwilling to take on.

The Many Contributions

Does Mayfair Have Anything to Learn?

When I ask women what they view as their biggest contribution to the town, school, or program, a few are quite stunned, thinking they did not contribute anything. One woman tells me she has never been asked that before, nor has she ever thought about it. Joslin, a commuter student, says:

> I don't know if I contributed. I don't feel that Mayfair learned anything from—or, I don't—the feedback that I have gotten from a few Mayfair people that I know of was they don't see the point of us being there. Or didn't see the point—I work with a doctor and I graduated with his daughter and he told me, like, 'I don't even know why commuter kids are there, they don't participate in anything. I don't get it. Why is there [the commuter program]?' And I've heard that growing up through high school.

Sadly, Joslin does not feel she contributed anything to the school or town, and some in the town do not feel her presence added anything.

The white, elite residents of Mayfair, rich in social, cultural, human, and financial capital, are in many ways highly sophisticated and worldly. As discussed in prior chapters, elite degrees and international travel are fairly commonplace. Household incomes and housing prices are approximately triple that of the state-wide averages. Individuals exhibit high levels of efficacy, professionally, personally, and politically. In many ways, the residents of Mayfair know few bounds. Ironically, this can translate into a sort of closed-minded provincialism, a sense that there is nothing to learn from those who live literally or metaphorically beyond the boundaries established and policed by elite society. Isabel, a boarder, says, "I had the feeling that Mayfair was comfortable being white and wealthy and not really interested hearing otherwise." Serena, a commuter student, explains her experience:

> I invited Mayfair friends to come home. You know, I've been to where you live, I've seen your environment, I want you to get to know me and my environment up here, you know, which a lot of times, parents would not allow at all…To me, diversity isn't a one way street. We come to be in your environment and you don't ever experience mine, you know.

Interestingly, two residents, Alexandra and Faith, identify these shortcomings of their fellow Mayfairians and cite the need for patience on their part in order to educate those around them. Alexandra talks about what she gained from growing up in the community:

> Like from teachers, students, from strangers in the town, I definitely was able to build my patience and understand the fact that people are ignorant and they're not—they're not used to certain things, they don't realize certain things, and it's not their fault but, at the same time it's like when you live in a bubble, you don't know anything out there.

Faith continues this theme. She says:

> Because there are a lot of good hearted people who don't know how to ask certain questions or word certain questions and are just curious about your race and your history and they want to know. And if you're very hostile and you're up tight, then you'll never be able to explain and educate people. So patience is definitely needed to be able to explain and say this and not that to someone so that they understand where you're coming from.

Faith and Alexandra both cite patience as the greatest benefit of living and going to school in Mayfair, but it most certainly could be viewed as their greatest contribution. They view this trait as essential to not only survive in the town but also to educate their fellow classmates and neighbors. Education as a response to racial marginalization and stigmatization has been documented before among African American adults (Fleming et al. 2012).

In this setting, these young women are able to maintain their dignity and retain a sense of self through educating their classmates, neighbors, teachers, and administrators. Without these women's presence and patience, white Mayfair has little interaction with people of color and largely falls back on racial stereotypes.

Disconnecting Race and Place through Exposure

Many women feel they make substantial contributions to the school and community through their individual relationships with peers, teachers, and administrators, often talking about how they represent another model of a woman of color. Women are essentially working to disconnect the stereotypes and societal expectations from the individual, and thus in their own small way, chip away at the durable inequality that exists (Tilly 1999). Women talk about seeing the world through their own eyes, but also through the eyes of white America (Du Bois 1903/1994). But, these women move a step *beyond* double consciousness. They seek to alter the view reflected back at them through the eyes of their white contacts, forcing peers, parents, teachers, and administrators to see them as individuals, rather than as the generalized, racialized other. They force white Mayfair to reconsider stereotypes about where people of color live, dislodging the tie between race and place, and how people of color live, disconnecting poverty and color. These women respond to marginalization and stigma by educating the school and community on racial issues and working to overturn stereotypes (Fleming et al. 2012).

The residents who are frequently assumed to be from elsewhere work to change this assumption by teaching their white counterparts that although they may have different skin tones, they can share a zip code. Hannah, a star athlete and active member of the community, discusses her biggest contribution. She says, "So I think having to see someone who is like them, but just a different color, probably, without even trying, clicked in their head that we're the same. I am just brown, that's all." As a highly successful athlete who developed friendships with her teammates, her ability to bridge out to the white, elite community benefits both her and those on the other side of the network. She talks about dating a white boy from the town, someone whom she feels would never have considered dating a woman of color before he met her. She goes on later to talk about the connection between race and place, "I think a lot of the time people think that I'm just a random girl…but they don't realize that I live here. I grew up here."

Faith, another town resident, makes similar statements, when asked about her contributions:

> I hope some positive diversity, a different outlook...Before people always thought, 'Oh, you—you have brown skin, you come from the city,' or, 'You can't be from here.' And I feel like I was an example of someone who can be your neighbor because I'm not different from you. It's just skin color. And I hope people just were able to change their perspective on life by having me in their class and living down the street from them.

Faith is explicitly talking about breaking the link between race and geography. Elisabeth, a resident who moved to Mayfair late in high school after spending most of her life in the city, also seeks to disconnect stereotypes about geography and expectations. She illustrates that although she originally came from an urban school district, she can excel academically.

Women from the commuter program also talk implicitly and explicitly about geography. Just as the residents attempt to teach their white counterparts that although they look differently, they can be neighbors, the commuters attempt to teach their white peers that although they are not neighbors, they are not that different. They discuss trying to highlight similarities over differences and teach their peers about life where they live. Yolanda, a commuter from the late 1990s, says:

> I think I challenged the school and the students to think differently about life in the inner city and that we were just like them. And so I think that that was, for me, like we're all kind of just going through the motions of, you know, being young adults and I want the same thing you want, like I want to get an education, I want to go to college, I want to have a family one day, I want respect, I want to be friends with people that I can trust. Like all the values and the ideals were more the same than they were different.

Andrea, another commuter student, talks about the assumptions the white Mayfair community has about children of color from the city. She says, "I've seen kids who come to the program and who didn't want to be there, who didn't try, who got in trouble, and I think that can happen no matter what the race, but the tendency might be that this kid—she's going to be a problem kid or he's going to be a problem kid just because of where they're from." Monique, a commuter from the late 1980s who was active in both "white" sports and community service, says the following about her role in and contribution to the school:

Well in the 80s, 70s or 80s, the city was still racially charged to some extent, and so I think people have, you know, certain conceptions or misconceptions of people that they're not familiar with, because obviously, Mayfair—I think the black population at the time may have been like 2% of people that live there. And so it's just, you know, I think for me and people that interact with me who are friends, I think at the end of the day, it's just people are people, you know, and they may come from different places and have different backgrounds and experiences, but people are people. And, you know, I would think that even my white friends now would just say that—it's just Monique. It's not necessarily black Monique, it's just Monique. And I think that was one of the things, too, that I walked away with is, you know, people are people. You have good people and you have bad people. It's not necessarily going toward race and economic background, that's just a visual. And so I think that was, you know, one of my contributions is to be who I was, you know, to be seen in a positive light, not that I'm representing the whole black culture, but just one microcosm in that greater scheme. And to just have good rapport with the people around me.

Commuters Michelle and Sasha, both from the 1990s, explicitly discuss the issue of urban stereotypes, even citing the media they need to counteract. Michelle says she provided an example different from "whatever you see on TV or whatever you think you know about city—people who live in the city, you know kids from the city...." Fellow commuter Sasha also feels she challenged stereotypes about urban black youth. Sasha says, "And I'm not a stereotype, I'm not what you see on TV, so just being my authentic self, I think, just to show them that it's not like one definition of somebody—and it's not even black/white, it's city/suburban. It's different."

Noel, a more recent commuter student, talks implicitly about counteracting both racial and geographic stereotypes. She recalls hosting a sleepover during her time in Mayfair:

> I invited the girls to my house and I know a lot of them came—or their parents made sure they came out of curiosity. And they were very shocked—because I remember Sally Jones, her mom stayed and had a long conversation—she just could not believe that my mom owned a triple decker in the city with a wonderful rose garden. And I just remember a lot of it was just curiosity of what the situation was.

Elise, a boarding student, also discusses working to break down stereotypes, including those connected to place. She says her contribution was "just being a bold advocate for diversity and inclusion, that was one thing

I was really, really passionate for me. And not just thinking that everyone who is black or Latino or Asian or whatever comes from one type of area."

All of these women feel that through their presence and engagement, they are able to highlight the commonalities that exist across people and reduce assumptions and stereotypes. The residents try to get across to their peers that they are, in fact, neighbors and that having a darker skin tone does not mean one is from beyond town borders. The commuters and boarders try to illustrate to their peers what it does and does not mean to be from an urban area and that although they may look differently from one another and may even live in different settings, they actually share many commonalities.

Counteracting Urban Stereotypes through Achievement

A number of women also discuss their specific achievements as a means of breaking down stereotypes about urban black youth. Elisabeth, the resident who moved to Mayfair late in high school from the city and did extremely well academically, says, "I think I actually brought a sense of diversity. A student can come from any type of school and still make it." Noel, a commuter student, says, "Like I racked up—I got awards—I always had academic excellence. I did my part. The whole point was if we're going to take an empty seat, we're going to make sure we're doing it right...." Andrea, another commuter student who excelled academically, says, "I did what I was supposed to do. I worked hard."

Women also show the community what they are capable of through the leadership roles that they seek and sometimes gain. Mayfair resident Flore ran for class president, with the slogan "the first black president." Chantel, a commuter student, was class president in her freshman year in high school. She says, "So that was great. I was—my freshman year, I was class president. And I was the first African American class president at Mayfair High." Elise, a boarding student, also ran for president in her senior year. These women are also soccer players, volleyball players, and gymnasts. They are team captains and founders of clubs and organizations.

Social scripts tell us how to behave in generalized social situations, based upon who is participating and in what setting; they "provide models for participation in particular classes of social relations" (Tilly 1999, p. 53). These societal scripts, while useful for the functioning of society (Swidler 1986), can also be highly detrimental as they reinforce many stereotypes that we hold. It is through small-scale interactions, and the changing of local knowledge, that we may be able to change harmful societal scripts and it is the hope of many of these women that they have been able to play a piece in changing the conversation.

Counteracting the "Charity Case" Stereotype

Many of the boarding and commuter students recall feeling like "charity cases." Marian discusses how her relationships with people in the community through her athletics and social life altered their view. She says:

> I think it actually changed their view, too. Instead of just seeing a flyer [about the program] or just seeing them [the boarding girls] like charity, almost like we were a charity case. But when you actually get to know the person it's different because they don't even think of the boarding program anymore they think, 'Oh, the boarding program! Marian!'

Karenna, a woman from a middle-class family, also discusses being made to feel like a charity case and her and her mother's efforts to make it clear that she was not that. In repeating her mother, she says, "Yes, you are educating my daughter but you are not my daughter's parent." Elise's mother similarly made it clear that she was an active participant in her daughter's life and was not to be replaced. Tamara, a woman from the boarding program who is still in college, says, "A lot of times being black in Mayfair means people perceive you as automatically being some type of charity case, like that was your reason for being there." These women counteract these presumptions in various ways.

Noel, a commuter student, says, "...So my mom used to be the president of the Mayfair Commuter PTO so I mean—I would almost say we were a model family for the program, like we were involved—my mom was involved." Her mother makes it clear to both parents and teachers that she is fully capable of taking care of her daughter. This includes bringing snacks for the sports teams on the weekends when it is Noel's turn and keeping in close contact with the teachers and guidance counselor. Deana, another commuter, talks about her single, disabled mother who made it very clear what her parental responsibilities were. She says her mother was not "trying to burden anyone and did not want to feel like 'I'm not capable of doing this for my own child.'"

Educating the Community

Women also talk about explicitly educating their peers, teachers, and administrators through a variety of channels. Hannah, a resident, and Malia, a boarder, both develop diverse friendship networks while in Mayfair and they reach out to their white friends to educate them. Hannah, a graduate from the mid-2000s, talks about hearing her white friends use the "n" word and telling them it is not okay. She felt that her friendship not only made it possible for her to correct them, but imperative. Malia was also able to educate her white peers as a result of the diverse friendships that she developed. She says, "You know, they would sometimes say things that weren't really true about, I don't want to say about black people, but they would just say some things that just weren't true. Being able to correct people just because they didn't know. Just out of ignorance." Malia is engaging in education in response to racial marginalization, as Faith, Alexandra, Marian, and others did, as well.

Elisabeth, the town resident who moved to Mayfair late in her high school career, talks about the initial encounter she had with the administration. The Vice Principal told Elisabeth that it was unlikely she would graduate on time, given her "inferior" education to date. Elisabeth's academic performance, including graduating in the top 10% of her highly competitive Mayfair senior class, provided a clear lesson to the administration. Elisabeth retells the story of graduation: "You know I graduated in the top ten percent of my class. And, she [the Vice Principal] spoke about me at our graduation, how we shouldn't judge somebody about where they come from, or the color of their skin." Although Elisabeth is a town resident, she is working to break the stereotypes around what it means to be a person of color from an urban area.

Women also start formal programming to educate the community. May, a Latina commuter, says, "I think a lot of us were really passionate about seeing change in Mayfair and having people understand diversity more and how it wasn't playing out well in the school and how people felt different. And I think that I was a very big part of pushing those conversations." She helped to start and run a branch of a national equality group at Mayfair High. Chantel, a commuter student, started an African American Heritage Day at the school. She says, "And it was a day for the entire community to come to Mayfair High School and learn from students and from other people from other communities about topics that they wanted to discuss. We served food and we had vendors come and sell African jewelry and things of that sort." Karenna, a boarding student, also instituted new programming. She says:

> I was just as vocal as can be. I advocated for—like I started a couple programs. Just really trying to push the agenda that the world is bigger than you, it's bigger than Mayfair and you need to open up. And you need to open up to others. So I would like to think that I assisted in opening up the minds of some of the Mayfair kids.

An Outsider's Perspective

As women who are in many ways outsiders, they are able to see and willing to say things that others cannot or will not. This is often the insight of those who exist in a liminal space (Turner 1969). Teachers and administrators often begin by bristling at the concerns of these women, but frequently come around over time. Yolanda, a commuter, sought to push the conversation around marginalization. She talks about one particular event while she was at Mayfair High:

> I will say one memory—when Columbine happened, that was our senior year. And they brought in a psychologist to talk to the class. And the question was asked from the psychologist, 'Do you guys think that this would happen here? Could Columbine happen here?' So of course, nobody raised their hand. But I did, and I had this monologue. And I used the platform to talk about—like basically my message of, 'Yes, this could happen here, here's why.' And I said, 'If you look at the cafeteria, the nerds sit here, the Jews sit here, the blacks sit here.' And I kind of broke it down.

Yolanda says the principal quickly took the microphone away from her, but over time she and the principal developed a relationship. Yolanda has even been invited back to Mayfair High as a speaker.

Deana talks about her early interactions with the administration and how she came to be a resource for them, even discussing curricular and disciplinary choices. She says:

> I felt like—after I stopped raising hell, and I found my voice, the administrators listened and I think that I uncovered—or we helped them discover things that they needed to help their staff with. And kind of being able to understand and see what we were experiencing through our eyes as much as they possibly could. We had so many meetings with the Principal... And

there were just so many discussions with her about curriculum. Some of this culturally insensitive curriculum, like *To Kill a Mockingbird*, I can remember was on our list of things that we just took issue with. Down to how we're called by the intercom when the bus is here, down to how segregated the cafeteria was. How punishment was given and consequences were given out—a level that we felt was unfair, and I mean at that point, we had started the program with seven boys—how many had gotten expelled by that point—four? We graduated with three. That was significant to us. And we needed, we needed to connect those dots ourselves, but also for the administrators to come take a look and be a bit reflective about how things got so bad.

Deana continues to serve as a resource for her former teachers and administrators at Mayfair High, returning to speak on multiple occasions. Other women report these ongoing relationships, with faculty and administration turning to these women for insight when they realize they do not have the background or knowledge themselves. In this way, these women act as cultural brokers (Flores 2009), educating their white teachers and administrators about what is problematic in the system.

Chantel, a commuter, talks about her relationship with the Principal. She says:

…I went to his office quite often to vent and to, for some reason I felt like it was okay for me to tell him what to do, so that—especially in my freshman year, when I had struggles with honors English, and convincing my teacher that I deserved to be there, he was the first person that I would talk to about that. And by my junior year, he was asking me what I was going to do, and so that felt great. So yeah, those things were awesome.

Priscilla, a boarding student, recalls being asked by a teacher, "What do you need?" She told him what she felt both she and other women of color needed—"We need to see ourselves in literature that you share. You know, as a person of color we need to see that our stories now, especially now [pause], because we feel like we don't matter because the truth is that the educational system—what do you read? Mostly dead white men." She goes on, "So I think that's how I contributed, like, 'What do these students need?' We need to know that we matter, and the way for you to show us that we matter is to show us our history."

These conversations, at times, lead to structural and curricular changes. Jade, a resident, recalls her role in changing policy. She says, "Me and my friends, we met with our guidance counselor and we made them change it. At least have two black people, at least in the same classroom, just so we can feel more comfortable when it comes to like making those discussions [around race]. So that helped a lot." Deana's critique of the end-of-day commuter announcements led to a change in the way those students were referred to and the practice continues through today.

Du Bois (1903/1994) argues that people of color can respond to the dominant structures in one of three ways: rage, assimilation, or self-realization. Many of these women talk of tremendous anger and frustration during their time in Mayfair. But, some appear to travel through a period of rage, and onto self-realization. Women such as Deana and Yolanda talk of being the "angry black woman," but also of finding their "voice." As a result, they move the entire community forward bit by bit.

Contributions beyond the Borders

The women make significant contributions beyond the borders of Mayfair, utilizing their education, social networks, and social and cultural capital to help relatives and those in their home communities. Isabel, a boarding student, talks about helping her mother with writing as her mother worked to get through community college. Alana, another boarding student, talks about helping those in her home district hundreds of miles away. She says:

> I took all of the stuff I learned from Mayfair, academic—all that. I took it to the school [back home] and come to find out there were people who benefited from that...because there's no way Louis would have been in Bane College. He told me that, he never thought about it. He hadn't heard of the school.

Another student from Alana's home district also ended up at Bane College, a highly selective liberal arts college in the Northeast, and yet another went to a different college that Alana had considered and told them about. It is unlikely these students would have attended the colleges that they did without the spread of information. These instances are reminiscent of the sorts of social remittances that immigrants may send back to their place of origin (Levitt 2001), although sadly, these women are required to do it within the context of their own country.

Women also serve as social models (Dominguez 2011) to relatives, neighbors, and friends. Gabriella, a former town resident, talks about helping her younger cousin get the resources she needs to become a doctor. She says:

...Her mom used to live in the projects, so you know I'm trying to give as much resources to them. I got her into [a college prep program], which is a good thing, so I'm so happy. And I try to get her into gymnastics or I find little programs in the city, but it's so hard. And then there's not really a way to find it, like I have these resources because again I got the care and all of this because of the Reach coordinator because she wanted the commuter kids and the boarding kids to not only know what's going on in the city, but in Mayfair, too. Like that's why I have everything that I can help a city kid...

Although Gabriella talks about not having taken advantage of all of the possible resources available to her, they were far from wasted as she is passing on her knowledge and skills to her cousin.

Alexandra, a former town resident, also talks about her ability to help relatives because of what she gained from living and attending school in Mayfair. She tells her younger brother, who recently graduated, and her younger cousins, to take advantage of all of the opportunities in Mayfair. She also encourages them to continue on with sports, something that she did not do, but feels can provide significant opportunities and expanded networks to those who participate. Alexandra is passing on the value of social networking, even if she did not benefit from those lessons.

The contributions women make ripple out even beyond their families and neighborhoods. Of the 30 women interviewed who are not full-time students, 11 of them are in professions that *directly* impact marginalized communities. These women are teachers in urban districts, guidance counselors, social workers, and program assistants at non-profit organizations. Yolanda, for example, leads efforts to engage women in business at an international non-profit. Chantel, a teacher in an urban district, talks about helping immigrant students of color to realize the existence of an achievement gap, overcome it, and prepare them for the significant challenges they face in predominantly white colleges. May works at an organization that matches up urban youth with internship opportunities.

Further, the women who either return to their home communities or move to urban communities from Mayfair may alter these environments, little by little, in other ways. Economists Chetty et al. (2014), in examining the increasing income inequality in American society, identify five characteristics of more economically equal environments: a significant presence of two-parent households, less residential segregation, better primary schools, substantial amounts of social capital, and a larger middle-class. Although some of these women may have originally left their communities because of poor primary schools, likely connected to high levels of residential segregation, their attendance at Mayfair High and then their return or resettlement in various urban areas may help contribute to some of these stabilizing characteristics. More than half of the women interviewed grew up in single-mother households. Seven women talk about how they had never considered the idea of getting married before coming to Mayfair, as it was just not a model that they had seen. Marian, a boarder, said:

> At Mayfair I saw all these married couples. Successful or not successful I feel like the point was they were married, so even learning that—because I think, I didn't realize how much that shaped me. But I just remember when we were writing our letters at the beginning of senior year, and I remember the biggest thing I kept saying was I just want to have my kids. I don't really care who the father is, just because I admired and I wanted to mimic my mom so much and I just didn't realize how much it affected me. Going to Mayfair just made me feel like, you know, you can live your own life. I know it sounds so stupid and so silly, but then on I was like 'I'd like to get married.' But before that was never even in my thought process.

Other women make similar remarks. Although this small handful of women will not change family structures across a city, their individual experiences may translate into changed views about family formation and family structure. Lorraine, an early commuter, said that attending Mayfair was what made her want to get married and live in the suburbs, goals she has met. This is not a moral plea for more married households, but a recognition that single-parent households are associated with lower rates of high school completion and higher rates of poverty.

The Chetty et al. (2014) research also highlights the importance of middle-class households and the presence of social capital in the formation of economically healthier communities. Again, higher earnings and greater amounts of social capital are characteristics that these individual women are more likely to possess, as a result of their Mayfair educations. Virtually all of the women interviewed have acquired some post-secondary education, with 23 holding at least a bachelor's degree and seven more still in college at the time of the interviews. And, although their development of social capital was somewhat mixed while in Mayfair, as discussed in Chapter 5, they likely possess more, and more diverse forms, than they would have had they not lived or attended school in Mayfair.

At What Cost?

Living and attending school in Mayfair is not easy for women of color and it takes a serious psychological toll. Multiple women cried during the interviews in recalling their time in the community. They discuss having needed to take mental health days, of being emotionally exhausted, of feeling like they had no safe place to go. These social and emotional challenges likely impacted academic performance while in Mayfair, and some women still bear the emotional scars.

Part of this emotional pressure comes from women understanding the importance of individual interactions, which, little by little, may work to change the societal script. They also understand the ongoing prevalence of racial stereotypes and fear that their individual behaviors will only reinforce these ideas among the white community.

Alexandra, in retelling a story about a physical fight in which she was embroiled, appears most upset about how it reflects on the black community. She says:

> Because it's bad enough that we're black living in Mayfair. They already look at us a certain way, probably think we're completely getting handouts to live here. They already look down at us and think of us a certain way and then you bring this type of behavior into our school and it—it's just not good to really represent us this way. Cause it's [pause]—nothing like this ever happens any other time. But then it comes in and it happens and it has to be a group of women of color that's having this fight and it's bad cause they even insulted a couple of teachers on top of it so it's like—it just makes it look so much worse.

Alexandra fears living up to what she thinks the white community expects of her. Coretta, a commuter, says, "I don't want to be labeled as like, you know, that stereotypical ghetto black girl." Michelle and Sasha both talk of "not being a stereotype." Isabel similarly fears being "the scary black woman." These women appear to feel pressure to be better than the low expectations and stereotypes they think are held by their classmates, neighbors, and teachers, a pressure that is not felt by white students.

Women also experience pressure not to be other sorts of stereotypes. Yolanda and Deana both talk of being the "angry black woman." Yolanda says, "And I think maybe one of the things that was misunderstood from the administration and maybe some classmates was that they confused my passion for justice and equality for anger, like angry black girl. And that wasn't the case. It was just what I was really passionate about—just making sure we were doing the right thing." As women of color, individual behaviors are understood within a larger racial context, something not experienced by members of white society who have the privilege of being seen as individuals (McIntosh 1988). Further, these young women of color are failing to "do gender" properly (West and Zimmerman 1987), only further marginalizing them (Ispa-Landa 2013).

Women of color on the high side of the academic spectrum—the "model" students who receive high marks and awards and participate in extracurricular activities—feel different kinds of pressure. Noel talks of being the "model commuter family" and needing to prove that she was "worth the seat." Andrea talks about showing that there were "good kids" that came from her community. These women are individually working to remove the stereotypes that collapse race, location, and expectations. Although white students at Mayfair likely feel significant academic pressure resulting from the outsized expectations and concerted cultivation arising from an elite community (Lareau 2011), Andrea and Noel likely feel great pressure arising from the need to represent an entire race. As Yolanda says, "It's very stressful, if you think about it. Like the mental health of a black woman—I wonder what our brains look like because it's like you can't catch a break."

The Bigger Picture

These women contribute significant amounts to the school, community, and the world beyond. They refute stereotypes around who is a resident of Mayfair and who is not, what it means to be from an urban area, and what it means to be a smart girl of color. Through their presence, their participation, and their insistence, they expose a wealthy and sophisticated, but often insular community, to a larger world. Although the extreme wealth of Mayfair makes the chasm even bigger for many young women of color to overcome, Mayfair is precisely the sort of community that needs to better understand the racial challenges that we face as a society, given that this is the type of community from which leaders in business, academia, and the government come.

Unfortunately, the contributions these young women make go unnoticed by many members of the school and community. These lessons need to be better understood and highlighted. Further, these significant contributions come at a significant psychological cost to the individuals. Women feel pressure within Mayfair to represent an entire community. They also feel marginalized in multiple worlds, existing in a liminal state (Turner 1969), even while those who participate in the marginalization may come to benefit over time from these women's experiences and contributions.

The goal behind virtually all racial desegregation programs is to improve educational opportunity for all, with the belief that education is the means by which we can, as a society, level the playing field. Greater educational equity across districts is one means of improving educational opportunities for all, but this alone will neither level the playing field completely nor increase the much-needed cross-racial contact for both white students and students of color. Decreasing isolation is critical to end, or at least limit stereotyping, prejudices, and discrimination on the part of white students, teachers, and administrators. It is also critical to prepare students of color as they enter colleges and workplaces still largely dominated by white America. Our daily interactions also provide us with social networks and cross-cultural knowledge essential for success in American society.

At another level, these individual interactions are essential to knit society together as we find ourselves in a country that is increasingly polarized and frayed. Consider the conversation between Christina, a boarder, and her host father, a white, upper-middle-class man, about the Obama presidency. Christina describes how amazing it was to learn, "how he felt and being able to share these ideas with someone who's totally different. I mean I'm a twenty year old black female and he's a forty year old white male." She has a similarly close relationship with her host brother, who reached out to her to get together when he was visiting her home city for a college lacrosse game. The increasing rate of assortive settlement by race and class, as well as political leanings and social beliefs, suggests an even greater need to have these types of diverse interactions.

This is in no way to dismiss the tremendous challenges and hardships experienced by the women of color who live their lives in a predominantly white environment. Much more must be done to provide emotional support and crucial tools for those who stand on the front lines and work to dismantle centuries of racial segregation. Besides providing support, white society also needs to provide reinforcements. These young women must not be alone on the front lines. Efforts at greater integration in both housing and school settings are critical for communities on both sides of the equation and must be understood as such. In that same vein, the symbolic and physical barriers that maintain distinctions among racial groups and advantage one over another must be recognized as disadvantageous for all of society. This must not remain a fight by Americans of color, with white Americans standing by as passive viewers or even as allies; this must be a battle that all Americans take on as their own.

Deana recalls fighting to enroll in an AP U.S. History class during her junior year. As one of the first people of color to ever take the course, she fondly recalls her teacher referring to her as a "black pioneer." Like pioneers exploring new lands, these women bear the brunt of the pain and hardships, but they may also experience new worlds that the rest of us never see. James Baldwin, a black man and one of the most important American authors of the twentieth century, discussed his journey in an interview a few years before his death: "I don't feel bitter about the journey, and that may be indicative of something. I don't feel bitter and I don't feel betrayed. I was a maverick, a maverick in the sense that I depended on neither the white world nor the black world. That was the only way I could've played it. I would've been broken otherwise. I had to say, 'A curse on both your houses'" (Lester 1984). It is imperative that we all come to feel broken by *not* journeying out onto the frontlines, for until we do, there will be a curse on all of our houses.

Bibliography

Chetty, R., N. Hendren, P. Kline, and E. Saez. 2014. Where is the Land of Opportunity? The Geography of Intergenerational Mobility in the United States. *Quarterly Journal of Economics* 129(4): 1553–1623.

Dominguez, S. 2011. *Getting Ahead: Social Mobility, Public Housing, and Immigrant Networks*. New York: New York University Press.

Du Bois, W. 1903/1994. *The Souls of Black Folks*. New York: Dover Publications.

Fleming, C., M. Lamont, and J. Welburn. 2012. African Americans Respond to Stigmatization: The Meanings and Salience of Confronting, Deflecting Conflict, Educating the Ignorant and 'Managing the Self'. *Ethnic and Racial Studies* 35(3): 400–418.

Flores, J. 2009. *The Diaspora Strikes Back*. New York: Routledge.

Goffman, Erving. 1955. *Interaction Ritual*. Garden City, NY: Anchor Books.

Ispa-Landa, S. 2013. Gender, Race, and Justifications for Group Exclusion: Urban Black Students Bussed to Affluent Suburban Schools. *Sociology of Education* 86(3): 218–233.

Lareau, A. 2011. *Unequal Childhoods*. Berkeley: University of California Press.

Lester, J. 1984. James Baldwin-Reflections of a Maverick. *New York Times*, May 27.

Levitt, P. 2001. *Transnational Villagers*. Berkeley: University of California Press.

McIntosh, P. 1988. *White Privilege and Male Privilege: A Personal Account of Coming to See Correspondences through Work in Women's Studies.* Wellesley: Wellesley Centers for Women.

Mead, G. 1934. *Mind, Self, and Society.* Ed. C.W. Morris. Chicago: University of Chicago Press.

Omi, M., and H. Winant. 1994. *Racial Formation in the United States: From the 1960s to the 1990s.* New York: Routledge.

Swidler, A. 1986. Culture in Action: Symbols and Strategies. *American Sociological Review* 51(2): 273–286.

Tilly, C. 1999. *Durable Inequality.* Berkeley: University of California Press.

Turner, V. 1969. *The Ritual Process.* New York: Transaction Publishers.

West, C., and D. Zimmerman. 1987. Doing Gender. *Gender & Society* 1(2): 125–151.

Wilson, W. 1987. *The Truly Disadvantaged.* Chicago: University of Chicago Press.

———. 1996. *When Work Disappears: The World of the New Urban Poor.* New York: Random House.

Appendix A: Interview Protocol for Residents of Mayfair

I would like to start by asking about your general experience growing up.

1) Can you begin by telling me a little bit about how long you lived or have lived in Mayfair? Were you born here? Did you move here? If so, at what age? When did you start school here?
2) Whom did you live with in Mayfair? Parents? Siblings? Extended family?
3) How would you describe your overall experience living in Mayfair? What did you like about it? What did you dislike about it?
4) What was the most valuable thing you gained from living here?
5) Did you feel a part of the larger community of Mayfair while you were growing up?
6) Did you participate in any community groups? Church groups? Boy or Girl Scouts, etc.?

I would now like to ask you about your school experience in Mayfair.

7) How would you describe your overall school experience? What did you like about it? What did you dislike about it?
8) What was the most valuable thing you gained from going to school here?
9) Did you feel a part of the school community? For example, did you participate in any school clubs or sports?

10) When you needed help with your schoolwork, did you have someone you could go to? Who was that person?
11) When you had social struggles in school or problems with friends, did you have someone you could go to? Who was that person?
12) Did anyone help you with things like getting a job while you were in school, working on a resume, or applying to college?
13) What was the biggest challenge of attending school in Mayfair?
14) What was the most valuable thing you gained from going to school in Mayfair?
15) What was the most valuable contribution you made to the school?

I would now like to ask you about the relationship between your home and your school.

16) Do you remember if your family ever participated in any school activities? Volunteered in PTO or attended back to school nights?
17) Did you have friends from school? Were those friends similar to you, racially, ethnically, or economically?
18) Did you bring friends over to your house who did not live in your immediate neighborhood? What was that experience like?
19) Did you go to friends' houses who did not live in your immediate neighborhood? What was that experience like?
20) Overall, how do you think attending school in Mayfair has impacted your life today?
21) If you have children, have you chosen to raise them in a town like Mayfair? Would you want to if you could?

Appendix B: Interview Protocol for Reach Students in Mayfair

I would like to start by asking about your general experience growing up.

22) Can you begin by telling me a little bit about where you grew up?
23) Who did you live with in Urbana? Parents? Siblings? Extended family?
24) How would you describe your overall experience living in Urbana? What did you like about it? What did you dislike about it?
25) What was the most valuable thing you gained from living there?
26) Did you feel a part of the larger community of Urbana while you were growing up?
27) Did you participate in any community groups? Church groups? Boy or Girl Scouts, etc.?

I would now like to ask you about your school experience in Mayfair.

28) When did you start attending school in Mayfair?
29) Did you have any say in participating in this school program and going to school in Mayfair? How was part of that decision?
30) How would you describe your overall school experience? What did you like about it? What did you dislike about it?
31) What was the biggest challenge of participating in this school program?
32) What was the most valuable thing you gained from going to school in Mayfair?

33) Did you feel a part of the school community? For example, did you participate in sports or any clubs?
34) When you needed help with your schoolwork, did you have someone you could go to? Who was that person? What kind of help did you receive?
35) Did anyone help you with things like getting a job while you were in school, working on a resume, or applying to college?
36) When you had social struggles in school or problems with friends, did you have someone you could go to? Who was that person?
37) What was the biggest challenge of participating in this program?
38) What was the most valuable thing you gained from going to school in Mayfair?
39) What was the most valuable contribution you made to the school? The program?
40) If there was one thing you could change about your school experience, what would it be?

I would now like to ask you about the relationship between your home and your school.

41) Do you remember if your family ever participated in any school activities? Volunteered in PTO or attended back to school nights?
42) Would you have liked your family to be more involved? Less involved?
43) What was your relationship like with your host family? Did they have a relationship with your family in Urbana? Was it a helpful relationship?
44) Did you have friends who grew up in Mayfair? Were they similar to you or different from you, racially, ethnically, economically?
45) Did you bring friends from Mayfair over to your house? What was that experience like?
46) Did you go to friends' houses in Mayfair? What was that experience like?
47) Overall, how do you think attending school in Mayfair has impacted your life today?
48) Would you have your children participate in Reach or a program like it? Would you want them to attend school in Mayfair or a town like it?

Appendix C: Interview Protocol for Aspire Participants in Mayfair

I would like to start by asking about your general experience growing up.

49) Can you begin by telling me a little bit about where you grew up?
50) Who did you live with? Parents? Siblings? Extended family?
51) How would you describe your overall experience living in _____? What did you like about it? What did you dislike about it?
52) What was the most valuable thing you gained from living there?
53) Did you feel a part of the larger community of _____ while you were growing up?
54) Did you participate in any community groups? Church groups? Boy or Girl Scouts, etc.?

I would now like to ask you about your school experience in Mayfair.

55) When did you start attending school in Mayfair?
56) Did you have any say in participating in this program and going to live and go to school in Mayfair? Who was part of that decision?
57) How would you describe your overall school experience? What did you like about it? What did you dislike about it?
58) Did you feel a part of the school community? For example, did you participate in any school clubs or sports?
59) When you needed help with your schoolwork, did you have someone you could go to? Who was that person? What kind of help did you receive?

60) Did anyone help you with things like getting a job while you were in school, working on a resume, or applying to college?
61) When you had social struggles in school or problems with friends, did you have someone you could go to? Who was that person?
62) What was the biggest challenge of participating in this program?
63) What was the most valuable thing you gained from going to school in Mayfair?
64) What was the most valuable contribution you made to the school? The program?
65) If there was one thing you could change about your school experience, what would it be?

I would now like to ask you about the relationship between where you lived and your school.

66) Can you tell me a little bit about what it was like to be a boarding student in Mayfair?
67) What was the hardest part about being away from your family?
68) Were there any benefits to being away from your family?
69) Because you boarded in Mayfair, do you know if anyone attended things like back to school night or had parent-teacher conferences on your behalf?
70) Would you have liked your family to be more involved? Less involved?
71) What was your relationship like with your host family? Was it a helpful relationship? Did they have a relationship with your family in _____?
72) Did you have friends, outside of this program, who grew up in Mayfair? Were they similar to you or different from you, racially, ethnically, economically?
73) Could you bring friends from Mayfair over to the boarder house? What was that experience like?
74) Did you go to friends' houses in Mayfair? What was that experience like?
75) Overall, how do you think attending school in Mayfair has impacted your life today?
76) Would you have your children participate in Aspire or a program like it? Would you want them to attend school in Mayfair or in another town like it?

Appendix D: Survey

1. In what year did you graduate from high school? _____
2. What were your grades like in high school, overall?
   As   As & Bs   Bs   Bs & Cs   Cs   Cs & Ds   Ds & Fs
3. Were you ever on honor roll or dean's list? Yes No
4. On a scale of 1 to 5, with "1" being the worst and "5" being the best, how would you rate your overall Mayfair High School experience? 1 2 3 4 5
5. What would have made your time in Mayfair easier? Please choose <u>all</u> that apply.

   a. More academic assistance
   b. More transportation to get around the community
   c. More financial support
   d. More students of color
   e. More culturally sensitive students at Mayfair High School
   f. More culturally sensitive host families and volunteers **(Reach/Aspire only)**
   g. More culturally sensitive teachers
   h. My transition was easy—I did not need anything done differently
   i. Other (please specify:_____)

6. Did you or do you currently attend college?

   a. Yes (College:_____)
   b. No

7. If you did attend college, on a scale of 1 to 5 with "1" being unprepared and "5" being completely prepared, how academically prepared did you feel? 1 2 3 4 5 NA

8. If you did attend college, did you graduate?

   a. Yes (College:_____)
   b. No
   c. Still in college
   d. Never attended college

9. Did you or do attend graduate school?

   a. Yes (Institution and program_____)
   b. No

10. What is your occupation? _____
11. To what extent do you think attending school in Mayfair helped you to achieve your goals?

    a. A tremendous amount
    b. To some extent
    c. Not at all

12. **Reach/Aspire Only.** In what ways do you think your experience with the program impacted your overall life experience? Please choose all that apply.

    a. Provided better academic opportunities
    b. Provided cultural opportunities
    c. Provided networks and connections
    d. Provided friendships with a more diverse group of people
    e. Led me to have serious challenges with my family and/or friends from home

f. Led me to have a really difficult high school experience
   g. The experience did not impact my life, overall
   h. Other (please specify:_____)

13. How do you identify racially or ethnically? (Please choose <u>all</u> that apply)

   a. Black/African American
   b. Caribbean
   c. White
   d. Latino/Hispanic
   e. Asian
   f. Native American
   g. Other:_____

Index

A
academic outcomes, 7, 9, 13, 49
achievement gap, 5, 7, 12, 192
adults. *See also* host families; parents and parenting; teachers
  adult social networks, 116–19
  and boarders, 129–36
  bridge building, 118–36
  bridge failures, 136–44
  commuter coordinators, 78, 84, 86, 122–3, 125–7, 132, 192
  and commuters, 124–9
  as cultural guides, 120, 121, 132, 170
  and cultural insensitivities, 142–3
  grandparents, 21, 89, 106, 123–4, 135, 171
  guidance counselors, 116, 120–2, 124, 125, 129–30, 132, 141, 145, 187, 192
  and residents, 120–4
  school administrators, 3, 19, 42, 57, 79, 84, 115, 116, 120, 123–6, 131, 132, 135, 139, 179, 181, 183, 188–90, 196
  school nurses, 121
  and stereotypes, 136, 137, 139–42
"apartheid" schools, 6
Asad, Asad L., 141
athletics
  barriers to participation, 91–3
  and boarders, 97–9
  and commuters, 95–7, 104–6, 108, 110–11
  commuting as a barrier to, 102, 104, 107–8
  costs of concerted cultivation, 107–10
  costs of participating, 105–6
  and gender, 101–3
  implications of not participating, 99–101
  and economics, 105–10
  in Mayfair, 103–10
  opportunity costs, 106–7
  as panacea, 110–12
  and residents, 93–5
  role of diversified social networks, 90–1
  sports in society, 91–3

B

barriers, 4
  to athletic participation, 91–3, 102, 104, 107–8, 110, 112
  to bridge building, 116–18, 132, 141, 143, 144
  cafeteria as, 55–7
  commute and school bus as, 53–5, 104
  cultural barriers, 91, 92, 105, 107–8, 112, 177
  to cultural capital, 171
  economic barriers, 57–61, 107–10
  legal, 7
  and liminality, 32, 36, 39, 45, 53–61
  physical barriers, 8, 33, 53–7, 62, 92, 99–103
  and race, 14, 60–1, 90, 177, 178, 196
  structural barriers, 32, 91, 93, 104, 105, 112, 143–4
  symbolic barriers, 33, 39, 53–5, 62, 85, 92, 96, 100, 116–18, 154
beauty, 48–52
Bell, Monica C., 141
benefits, 4
  academic benefits, 8, 161
  and athletics, 96, 98, 107
  of bonding, 80–5
  and bridge building, 123
  and community, 67, 80–5
  and cultural capital, 149–51, 156–7, 173
  of desegregation, 7, 8
  of integration, 7–8
  and liminality, 41, 42, 59, 60
  non-academic benefits, 8
  and race, 180, 182, 183, 192, 196
Better Chance, A, 8

boarders. *See* school boarding program
bonds and bonding, 4
  and athletics, 90, 91, 98, 111
  benefits of, 80–5
  and community, 71, 72, 75–9
  and commuter office, 78–9
  and money, 4, 79–80
  and school bus, 75–7
  and shared house, 77–8
  and social capital, 90, 119
Bourdieu, Pierre, 25, 110, 123, 128, 149–51, 154, 174n1
Bourgois, Philippe, 116
bridges and bridge building, 4
  and athletics, 91, 98, 135
  and boarders, 129–6
  and community, 65–7
  and commuters, 124–9
  embedded, 118–20, 123, 128, 133–7, 145
  failures, 136–44
  mandated, 118, 120–4, 126, 129–32, 136, 143, 145
  of Mayfair, 119–36
  and money, 4, 129, 138–9
  and race, 177, 180
  and residents, 120–4
  and social consciousness, 119
  and social leverage, 120, 121
Briggs, Xavier de Souza, 80–1, 85, 90, 116–18
Brown v. Board of Education, 6
bus. *See* school bus

C

Carter, Prudence L., 7, 8, 90, 91, 116
Chetty, Raj, 192, 193
civic engagement, 2
civic organizations, 2
Civil Rights Project, 6

Coleman, James, 6, 8, 13, 80, 117, 120, 121, 123, 126, 128, 131, 135, 142
community
　benefits of bonding, 80–5
　and boarders, 70–2
　bridge building, 65–7
　and commuter office, 78–9
　and commuters, 67–70
　cross-group relationships, 74–5
　emotional support, 81–4
　economics as source of, 79–80
　and housing, 77–8, 86
　and residents, 72–4
　role of place in, 75–9
　and school bus, 75–7
　social leverage, 81, 84–5
commuter program. *See* school commuter program
concerted cultivation theory, 107–10, 152, 195
contributions to the community, 177, 180–95
Crenshaw, Kimberlé, 18, 67
cultural brokers, 190
cultural capital
　and boarders, 165–8, 173
　and commuters, 158–65
　defined, 149–52
　and economic capital, 170–2
　embodied, 150–5, 158–9, 163, 165, 174, 174n1
　forms of, 150
　institutionalized, 150–3, 156–8, 164–5, 168, 170, 173, 174n1
　limitations of, 170–2
　in Mayfair, 152–70
　objectified, 174n1
　and residents, 153–8
cultural guides, 120, 121, 132, 170
culture shock, 89, 172

D

degree attainment, 5
desegregation. *See also* school boarding program; school commuter program
　and integration, 14, 24, 26, 62, 90, 91, 112, 116
　prior research, 6–8, 12
"deserving" girls of color, 35, 38, 45
de Tocqueville, Alexis, 2
Domhoff, G. William, 8, 9, 161, 166
Dominguez, Silvia, 118, 119, 128, 132, 135, 145, 191
double consciousness, 34, 38, 39, 66, 141, 164, 177, 180, 181, 183
Du Bois, W.E.B., 24–5
　and color line, 31
　and community, 66, 67, 85
　Damnation of Women, 46
　double consciousness, 34, 38, 39, 66, 141, 164, 177, 180, 181, 183
　and liminality, 32–4
　and racial awakening, 43–4, 177, 178, 191
　and second sight, 60
　Souls of Black Folk, The, 43–4, 66
　and talented tenth, 38, 142
　and the veil, 32, 34, 37, 41, 44, 56, 67, 164, 177
durable inequality, 5, 7, 178, 183. *See also* inequality

E

Eaton, Susan, 8, 53, 90, 173, 174
educational attainment, 13, 24. *See also* academic outcomes; achievement gap
　cultural argument of, 9

Elementary and Secondary Education Act (1965), 5
extracurricular activities, 14, 58, 92, 110, 117, 195. *See also* athletics

F
Fleming, Crystal M., 182, 183
friendship
   and athletics, 89–103, 109, 110, 112, 183
   and bridges, 135–6, 138
   and community, 65, 67–76, 85, 91
   and cultural capital, 149, 153
   friendship networks, 85, 92, 188
   and liminality, 36, 39, 41, 53–4, 57–62
   and race, 36, 39, 41, 53–4, 57–62, 183, 188

G
Garrity, Arthur, 6
Gautreaux Project (Chicago), 118
gender
   and athletics, 91, 187
   categories, 5, 18, 32, 67, 136
   construction, 36
   "doing" gender, 198
   and liminality, 33, 34, 36, 46–52
   theory, 18
Goffman, Erving, 180
graduation rates, 7, 13
Granovetter, Mark, 117

H
Hendren, Nathaniel
hierarchy, 46, 66, 69
homophily, 85
host families, 12, 19, 82, 115, 127, 128, 132–9, 167

housing. *See also* school boarding program
   access to, 90
   and community, 94, 99, 108
   integrated, 196
   Mayfair Housing Authority, 13, 20
   prices, 2, 181
   rental apartments, 21, 94, 155
   Section 8 (subsidized housing), 17, 19, 20, 31, 60, 61, 73, 79, 80, 93, 94, 99, 108, 120–2, 124, 153, 155–7, 179
   segregated, 5, 6, 8, 56, 190, 192, 193

I
income gap, 5, 169
inequality, 34, 72, 141, 143, 156, 173, 178, 183, 192
   durable inequality, 5–7, 32, 136, 183
immigration and immigrants, 37, 40, 44, 50, 115, 177, 178
   Asian immigrants, 9–10
   North African immigrants, 44, 178
   West Indian immigrants, 115
in-betweeness, 34, 67, 163
integration, 7–8, 103, 154, 196–7
   in athletics, 52, 79, 92–3, 102–3, 110, 135
   and cultural capital, 110
   and desegregation, 24, 26, 34, 35, 46, 68, 86, 91, 112, 116
   and romantic relationships, 46, 47
inter-racial dating, 48, 50
interview process, 4, 16–26
isolation, 3, 7, 137, 196
   and athletics, 91, 100
   and boarders, 15–16, 45–6, 58–9
   and bridge failures, 136

and community, 42, 44, 62, 68, 82, 86
and commuters, 35, 38
and cultural capital, 128, 171
and liminality, 24–5, 35, 37, 43, 47
"noblesse oblige," 58
and race, 11, 79, 137, 196
and residents, 35
and romantic marginalization, 46

J
job information, 84–6, 90

K
Khan, Shamus Rahman, 159
Kline, Patrick, 197

L
Lamont, Michèle, 162
language and language skills
  advocacy, 9, 126
  and barriers, 36
  and cultural capital, 163, 164, 167, 171
  and double consciousness, 164
  foreign language education, 151, 162, 167, 171
  gaps, 5
  and liminality, 36, 53
Lareau, Annette, 9, 13, 25, 92, 107, 117, 120, 121, 130, 132, 151, 152, 195
leadership, 168, 186
liminality, 4, 8, 24, 31–3
  and boarders, 35–8, 45, 46, 49–50, 58–9
  cafeteria as a physical barrier, 55–7
  and community, 65–8, 75, 77
  commute as a physical barrier, 53–5
  and commuters, 38–41, 46–8, 59–60
  and economic barriers, 57–61
  and physical barriers, 53–7
  and residents, 42–6, 50, 60–1
  and romantic marginalization, 51–2
  and two-ness, 31–3, 66, 85, 180
local knowledge, 26, 187

M
marginalization, 4, 9, 25. *See also* liminality
  and athletics, 91, 99–100, 110, 112, 122, 135
  and bridges, 115, 116, 118, 122, 137, 143, 144, 177
  and community, 66, 67, 72, 74, 76, 79, 81
  and cultural capital, 156, 171
  and gender, 51–2
  and liminality, 34–46, 49–53, 59, 60, 62, 66–8, 75, 77
  and race, 182, 183, 188, 195
Mayfair, 1–4. *See also* resident students of color; school boarding program; school commuter program
  demographics, 7–8
  history of integration programs, 8–14
  methodology and interviews, 14–26
Mayfair Housing Authority, 13, 20
Mead, George Herbert, 180
methodology and interviews, 14–26. *See also* school boarding program; school commuter program
  instruments, 15
  interview process, 16–17
  sample, 17–24
  selectivity of subjects, 24–6
Move to Opportunity (MTO) initiative, 118

N

networks. *See also* community
  adult social networks, 116–19
  and athletics, 90–8, 100–3, 107, 109, 110, 112
  commuter networks, 84–5
  and cultural capital, 151–3, 166, 167, 170, 171, 173
  diversified social networks, 89, 102, 117, 136, 145
  friendship networks, 85, 92, 188
  and liminality, 38
  and marginalization, 4, 72
  and methodology, 14
  and race, 180, 183, 188, 191, 195, 196
  social network sites, 19
No Child Left Behind Act (2002), 5

O

oppositional culture theory, 9
opportunity hoarding, 107, 141
Orfield, Gary, 6
otherness, 31–3, 43–4, 55, 62, 85, 137, 178–9

P

parents and parenting, 9–10. *See also* host families
  adult cultural guides, 115–17, 120, 170
  and athletics, 103, 107, 109, 135
  and community, 107
  concerted cultivation theory, 107–10, 130, 152, 195
  and cultural argument of educational outcomes, 9
  and cultural capital, 152–3, 156
  household statistics, 8–9
  and liminality, 42–3, 77
  organizations and associations, 2
  and resources, 7, 103
poverty, 11, 66, 67, 79, 116–18, 137–9, 183, 193
privilege, 14, 60, 139, 153, 170
Putnam, Robert, 2, 13, 80

R

race, 177–97. *See also* stereotypes
  and achievement, 186–7
  and athletics, 89–91, 95, 103
  and barriers, 90, 103, 164, 177, 196
  and benefits, 180, 182–3, 191, 192, 196
  and bridge building, 116–18, 136–7, 141, 143, 145
  and class, 57, 59–61
  and community, 65, 72–3, 79, 81, 85
  and cultural capital, 177, 180, 191
  and exposure, 183–6
  and friendship, 62, 65, 67, 73, 85, 101, 116
  and gender, 32, 34, 46, 51, 57
  "ghetto" assumptions, 179
  inter-racial dating, 48, 50
  and isolation, 3, 7, 43, 196
  and liminality, 32–4, 43–7, 51, 57, 60–2
  and marginalization, 182, 183, 188–9
  meaning of, race, 178–9
  and networks, 180, 183, 188, 191, 192
  racial awakening ("ah ha" moment), 43–4, 178
  racialization, 34, 96, 98, 100, 105, 111, 156, 180, 183
  racism, 36, 37, 142

role of racialized interactions, 180–1
and social capital, 177, 192–3
Reardon, Sean, 6
research
   on unequal resources across schools
      and neighborhoods, 5–7
   on unequal resources within home
      and communities, 8–10
   on voluntary school desegregation,
      7–8
resident students of color, 3, 6–8, 17
   and athletics, 93–5
   and bridge building, 120–4
   and community, 72–4
   and cultural capital, 153–8
   and liminality and marginalization,
      42–6, 50, 60–1
   and race, 178–9, 181–4, 186–8,
      190–3, 195
rites de passage, 33
Robinson, Jackie, 92
romantic marginalization, 46–52
   and boarders, 49–50
   and commuters, 46–8
   gendered nature of, 51–2
   and residents, 50

S
Saez, Emmanuel, 197
school bus
   as barrier, 53–5
   and community, 75–7
school boarding program, 3, 7, 8, 12,
   17, 18
   and athletics, 97–100, 102, 106–9
   and bridge building, 129–36
   and community, 70–2
   and cultural capital, 165–8
   and liminality and marginalization,
      34–8, 49–50, 58–9

and race, 178, 179, 182, 185–93,
   196
school commuter program, 2, 12, 19,
   21
   and adult bridges, 124–9
   and athletics, 95–7, 104–5
   busing, 53–5, 75–7
   and community, 67–71, 78–9
   commute and school bus as barriers,
      53–7
   commuter office, 78–9
   commuter coordinators, 78, 84, 86,
      122, 123, 125–7, 132
   and cross-group relationships,
      74–5
   and cultural capital, 158–62, 173
   and liminality and marginalization,
      38–41, 46–8, 59–60
   and money, 59–60
   and race, 178, 179, 184, 189–95
   and romantic marginalization,
      46–8
separate but equal doctrine, 6
sexlessness, 46–52
Small, Mario Luis, 116
social capital, 17, 24
   and athletics, 90, 100, 107, 110
   bonding social capital, 81, 84–6, 90,
      111, 119
   and bridges, 116–20, 126–8, 131,
      135, 145
   and community, 80, 81, 83–6
   and cultural capital, 151–3, 170,
      172
   and race, 177, 192–3
social etiquette classes, 2, 152
social leverage, 25, 81, 84–5, 115,
   116, 120, 121, 124, 126, 130,
   134, 136, 145
social networks. *See* networks
sports. *See* athletics

stereotypes, 26, 33, 38, 45, 62, 90
  counteracting through achievement, 186–7
  and bridge failures, 136–44
  "charity case", 38, 58, 138–40, 187
  "deserving" minorities, 38
  and language skills, 163
  urban, 34, 38, 48, 178–9, 186–7
St. Paul's School, 116
Supreme Court, U.S., 6

T
talented tenth, 38, 142
Tatum, Beverly, 55, 69, 72, 91, 111, 117
teachers
  and athletics, 94–5
  and bridge building, 118–19, 121–6, 129–32, 136, 137, 140, 141, 143, 144, 180
  and community, 61
  and cultural capital, 151, 161, 162, 164, 170–2, 178, 179
  and cultural insensitivities, 142–3
  and liminality, 31, 38, 42, 44–5, 54, 56, 61
  and race, 178, 179, 182, 183, 187–90, 192, 194, 196, 197
test score gap, 5, 9, 11, 13
Tilly, Charles, 5, 7, 32, 33, 107, 136, 141, 142, 155, 156, 178, 183, 186
travel, 89, 151, 152, 160, 162, 167–73, 181
Turner, Victor, 24–5, 33–5, 46, 66, 69, 77, 81, 85, 156, 181, 189, 196
two-ness, 31–3, 66, 85, 180

V
veil, concept of the, 32, 34, 37, 41, 44, 56, 66, 67, 164, 177

W
Welburn, Jessica S., 146, 197
whiteness, 9, 41, 142
Wilson, William Julius, 9, 57, 116, 118, 152

Z
Zelizer, Viviana, 139
Zweigenhaft, Richard L., 8, 9, 11, 151, 160, 166

The manufacturer's authorised representative in the EU is Springer Nature Customer Service Centre GmbH, Europaplatz 3, 69115 Heidelberg, Germany. If you have any concerns regarding our products, please contact ProductSafety@springernature.com

Printed and bound by CPI Group (UK) Ltd, Croydon, CR0 4YY

24/03/2026

02077370-0001